AS IT WAS

D0540302

*For
the grand-daughters,
who ask questions*

NAOMI MITCHISON

AS IT WAS

SMALL TALK . . .
ALL CHANGE HERE

RICHARD DREW PUBLISHING
Glasgow

SMALL TALK . . . first published 1973 by
The Bodley Head Ltd

ALL CHANGE HERE first published 1975 by
The Bodley Head Ltd

This edition AS IT WAS first published 1988 by
RICHARD DREW PUBLISHING LIMITED
6 Clairmont Gardens, Glasgow G3 7LW
Scotland

The publisher acknowledges the financial assistance of
the Scottish Arts Council in the publication of this book.

British Library Cataloguing in Publication Data

Mitchison, Naomi, *1897* —
  As it was.
  1. Fiction in English. Mitchison, Naomi,
  1897— Biographies
  I. Title
  823'.912

ISBN 0-86267-208-2

Printed and bound in Great Britain by
Cox & Wyman Ltd., Reading

Small Talk . . .

Memories of an Edwardian Childhood

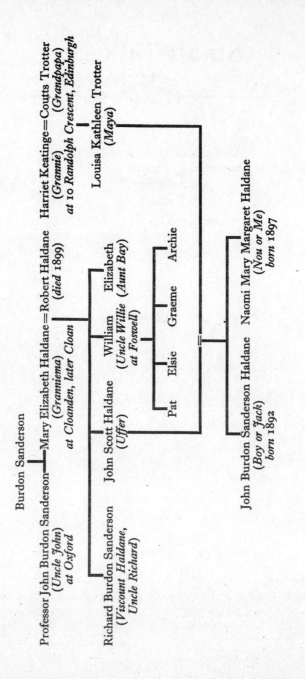

CONTENTS

I

Becoming Oneself

It was bright and bobbing. Out of my dark cave I reached for it. My hands wavered up to it. It came nearer. Did I catch it? The importance was the attempt. My brother's long fair hair was cut before he was six years old, which means that I, under the hood of my pram, was under a year old. But me.

Then I had a mail-cart made of brown cane instead of a pram. I sat in it. Nobody made me lie down. True, there was a strap but it had a grown-up type buckle. No shawls or blankets but instead horrid gaiters with buttons which always pinched my legs. Sometimes (or perhaps once) grown-ups, speaking of me in my mail-cart, called it a pram. I became terribly indignant. My new status had been denigrated: how could I bear it? Certainly I couldn't explain. I think I screamed. Status—essential for all gregarious animals, essential in the farmyard. Now I knew it and would always know it.

Everyone went to Studland, a suitable place for a young and not highly pecunious upper-middle-class family from Oxford. I have no idea where we stayed but there was a large object up on a cliff round which I ran in a somewhat ritual manner because I was frightened of it. Why? Well, I was frightened of a lot of things and today it is not clear how these things were related. I did not speak of them except on the very rare occasions when terror drove me into hysterical screaming. It was quite clear to me at the time that if I told anyone 'They' would make it a lot worse for me. 'They' who appeared in dreams and in triangular shapes which I recognised with alarm in Gabon metal work many years later and in obvious reds and purples. 'They.' Are other people's 'They' like mine?

> *'They' said if you choose*
> *To boil eggs in your shoes . . .*

And, oh, that was what I always did! Tell me, do your 'They'
allow you to do offbeat things? Or on the contrary, do 'They'
insist that you do them?

But apart from that we went down to the beach by what was
either a tunnel or an overgrown green lane. I think there were
bathing boxes or tents. My mother floated in a long white cotton
gown; she never could swim but float she did in very shallow water
and I perambulated her fluttering wet edges.

The dresses which my mother wore on dry land would have
been extremely fashionable today. There was a splendid silvery
brocade with mauve and green thistles, no doubt worn for best
Oxford dinner parties, cut low; there was much lace and an infra-
structure of whale-boned stays built by her *corsetière*, and longish
white bloomers. Never to my knowledge did I see her wearing less,
though she did, I understand, suckle me for nine months. She wore
opaque black cotton stockings; the best of them had silk clocks.
Her mother, on the other hand, had white ones of finer cotton or
even silk. My two grandmothers dressed differently. Grannie, my
mother's mother, *née* Keatinge, was, I suspect, rather expensively
dressed with foamings and flouncings of lace, black or white, and
really beautiful and romantic caps of lace and broad satin ribbons.
For all this a lady's maid was essential. But Granniema, my Haldane
grandmother, would not exactly have had a lady's maid. Indeed,
this might have savoured of Tory episcopalianism. Probably the
upper housemaid washed her smalls, sewed and mended, though
perhaps Baba, who had been nurse to my father's generation, did a
bit of that after her charges grew up, she having accurately foretold
their future careers. Baba lived in a special little room in the older
and prettier part of Cloan and sometimes asked us children to tea
there. We had to behave. But the one I remember at Cloan, who
was always called a maid-companion and did not wear uniform,
was Irving, always referred to by her surname and not to be mis-
taken for a servant. One had therefore to be very much aware of the

social boundaries and not to make mistakes. Granniema wore stiff black; her caps tended to have violets and small fountains of jet and she had a shining black stick. As children, we were rather frightened of her, but she became more and more of a friend.

I doubt if either grandmother would have gone to Studland; did they go away for holidays except to other people's houses? If so, I guess it would have been to a reputable resort, perhaps in Germany or France, a place where one might take the waters and go to an occasional good concert of serious music. One awkward thing about Studland was that there were trippers. What they were like has vanished, but, dreadfully, I did once find myself in some form of social contact. What? No, that has vanished, but I remember my mother speaking to me very seriously about my *faux pas*. Guilt was duly aroused, though I never knew quite what I had done. This, however, was the beginning of class-consciousness.

That curious word 'tripper', probably right out of the current vocabulary! It dates from the time when most people could only afford a few days' holiday but when they did they came irritatingly into the very same places which those who could afford longer holidays had claims on and when they got there they made uncouth noises and wore unsuitable townee clothes. Perhaps one notices a touch of the same feeling among the conservation-minded today. The word disappears; the feelings remain.

Meanwhile, I was being taught to read by my mother at home. It was a phonetic system and at four I had no bother with cat, mat and sat but suddenly I was confronted with four-letter words. A feeling overwhelmed me that I would never be able to understand, never. I have had that feeling since: about economics, about physics and, oddly, about lawn tennis. These were all things I wanted to be competent at, but felt deep down I couldn't do. Other subjects I was either good at or didn't particularly want to understand or else felt that I could if I took trouble—and sometimes did. But this dead-end feeling is unmistakable. On this first occasion it was clearly infuriating to my maternal teacher. She spanked me hard and I was put into my cot, the nursery curtains were drawn and I was left to think it over as soon as I had stopped howling. It hadn't really hurt. The offence was to my human dignity. I did not forgive it. But it made me understand how other people feel about affronted human dignity. This has been useful. It was also useful because suddenly I was able to read not only words of four letters but all words. Unhappily I never got a sufficient jolt over economics or physics.

As far as I remember my main punishment as a child was not being smacked but being told that I was 'hurting Mother'. If one was disobedient—and this was rubbed in from early readings of Kipling's *Jungle Book* which put a great emphasis on obedience as did, I think, Montefiore's *Bible for Home Reading*—or told lies or was in any way treacherous, it hurt Those who Loved One Most. Let me add that this was not a God-centred household; we were brought up as highly moral agnostics. It never occurred to me that it was treachery to conceal my fears and secret propitiations of 'Them' which sometimes involved things like knocking my head against the bars of my cot for a specified number of times.

But I do remember the first time I got away with a lie. There was a large tea-party with my favourite goodies: those little cakes with marshmallow inside and chocolate on top. I was tempted. A plate was discovered with one missing. I denied it passionately and with tears; at last I was believed or possibly it was thought better that I should appear to be believed. In general I wasn't much of a liar. In fact, I was a fairly good little girl and I was allowed to do a reasonable amount of physically dangerous things like climbing trees and rocks, running along the garden wall and of course, when the time came and I was five years old, going to school across Banbury Road, a thing which no parent would allow a child to do in today's Oxford. But then the main traffic was still the horse trams which one could race, always catching up at the stops.

I got away with a lie later on when I suppose I was seventeen or eighteen and my father inadvertently opened an indiscreet love letter addressed to my brother whose initials were the same as his own—something every family should avoid. My father became very much upset and I took a deep breath and jumped right in, explaining that I knew the lady in question and she was all that could be desired and so on. I had no idea who she was but knew I must protect my brother and by that time knew something of the art of fiction. Again I was either believed or appeared to be believed and was given the letter to forward.

Yet surely, surely, I must have told lies dozens of times between these two? Or did each of them mark a step in sophistication, perhaps in liberation, and so become memorable?

One of the nicest things about my young life was my mice. After breakfast I changed into my mouse frock or perhaps pinafore—dark blue it was—and the darling silky mice came out of their cage and wandered over me: I don't know how or why we communicated but presumably we did. Sometimes the mice climbed down me on to the floor and I after them. How pleasing and how large things are from underneath! But there are sadly too many edges and corners on the level of one's head. Being close to the ground gives one a delicious intimate view of flowers, the fine structure of stones and earth and half peeled sticks, and in those days the muddy bottoms of one's elders' skirts.

I spent, as all children do in all cultures, part of my life on my own and part on the fringes of adult culture. As soon as I could be guaranteed not to make awkward remarks or fidget unendurably I was taken out calling. This meant hiring a landau, an open carriage with a small seat opposite the big one, but nicer because nearer the rushing ground, and going the rounds of academic Oxford, leaving the right number of cards and congratulating ourselves when those we called on were 'not at home'. The driver too used to turn round and felicitate us. Later, as we rose in the social scale, we had two carriages of our own and a hard-mouthed mare. For these expeditions I wore white cotton frillies, with broad blue ribbons to match my eyes, catching back my long pale gold hair, and a sun-hat. The difficulty was that these hats tended to be tethered by elastics which were likely to bite one.

At five I wore bunchy white cotton frocks well down below the knee, the neck frill outlined with red cross-stitch. One of these now is in the Langley Moore Collection in Bath. I don't remember finding this interfered with my activities, but my big wish was always for bare feet and sandals, not socks and shoes, and I dis-approved of some of the Flower Fairies in my favourite book, who even wore boots.

My mother certainly had a parasol, black and white, not coloured which would have been vulgar, or even 'fast'. The carriage went at no more than a slow trot, so that the parasol did not blow away but could stay up. The sun was not yet directly welcomed. She would have worn one of her best hats, muslin on a wire frame, with fairly simple flowers or perhaps ostrich feathers. She would not wear any feathers for which birds were specially killed. I think she must have been a beautiful woman at this time, though rather severe-looking; do children make these aesthetic judgements? She never made up, but occasionally, if she was hot and flushed, used *papier poudré*, which came in little books, and mopped up any unseemly damp, after which it left the cheeks and nose delicately pale.

If we were unlucky enough to find someone 'in' I would be allowed to look round the room with my hands behind my back, a habit I still find myself continuing in museums. Many of our friends had curios, some of great fascination. Many ended up in the Pitt Rivers Museum or the Ashmolean, as indeed some of my parents' curios have done. When we got back home we rushed to see who had called on us. The parlour maid would duly have laid out the cards on a Benares brass tray. This ritual involved some deception, but all for the good cause of upper-middle-class solidarity. I call it upper-middle-class which seems to me historically correct. But we would certainly have called ourselves 'upper class'. Now, if I am asked, I shy away and call myself a 'clerc' or use the rather un-pleasing phrase 'professional class' which was not current earlier in the century.

At this time we lived at 4 St Margaret's Road in a detached house of its period, remarkably ugly. There was a great big brass knob on the front door, a circular space in front which we called a drive, and a wide wooden gate on which I was not supposed to swing, with almond trees at both sides. There was also a basement with kitchen, scullery, a servants' WC. Was there perhaps also a servants' bedroom? I was not encouraged to explore, either by parents or servants, though sometimes an amiable cook would let me have bits of dough to make biscuits. The whole basement was dark, lit from a front area which enclosed the windows almost totally and a back area with a slope of rubble or stone on the garden side. One could climb down into this and here my brother and I used to lay trains of gunpowder and have small explosions, sometimes singeing our hair or eyelashes. On the ground floor you went through to the garden; the stairs went straight up and down. There was a largish drawing-room, a study, a dining-room, perhaps a pantry at the head of the back stairs down to the basement, and certainly a gentleman's lavatory. All this was standard in a detached house of the period. There were, rather surprisingly, two bathrooms, one of them rather scruffy, and there was also a water closet with a bottom pan opening down into darkness and smell. This probably induced constipation in everybody. I find, from my mother's book, that they put in the second bathroom; my father had a theory that ordinary baths did not conduct the heat properly so our baths must be made of lead. This certainly warmed up, but was rather cheerless and needed a lot of special cleaning.

The house was lit by gas and from my cot I could see above the nursery screen the pale crocus of dim light and the nasty shadows which could be chased away when some grown-up turned it full on into a bright fish-tail. My father, who was one of the Metropolitan Gas Referees, keeping constant check from the London office which he visited every week on the quality of coal-gas, did not think too well of it and we all had a healthy distrust of leaks and were very careful about turning things on and off. However, we moved to a non-gas house, Cherwell, at the end of Linton Road which at that time ended as a thick-hedged lane, when I was nine. I loved being able to flick on an electric light switch but my mother, in the interests of economy, only had rather low candle-power bulbs in passages, bathrooms and so on, and everything had to be turned off by the last person going to bed.

Talking of my parents' curios, there was a very handsome large scarab which was the pride of their Egyptian collection. Looking at it when I took over the estate, I was doubtful. When I went along with it to the British Museum they, while happily accepting various duller looking bits and pieces, asked me if I could date its acquisition into the family. Knowing when my grandfather went on the Grand Tour (a letter from Lord Cockburn of 1854 dates this) I told them. They were delighted; it was the earliest forgery they had ever met!

II

Real and Not Real

To look at, the doll's house is a solid white cupboard but with windows at the sides. When you unlock it there are six rooms all the same size; from the very beginning they were kitchen, dining-room; one up, drawing-room and best bedroom; two up, nursery and schoolroom. But the furniture is anything but to scale and, alas, in the course of being played with, a lot of it has gone and almost all the Hubbard household, which is very sad. Mrs Hubbard had a china face and hands, as well as feet in black boots and a lovely lilac silk dress; she usually lay on the sofa where I could see her boots. The solid Goan carved chairs and table are still there, too big for the rest, but where is the ivory *chaise percée* and where the work table with its tiny scissors and balls of silk?

In those days, as a literal-minded small girl, I was worried both by the awkwardness of scale and by the problem of the fourth wall. I could pretend that there were other rooms and stairs at the back but I found it very hard to make the open rooms look 'real'. Nor do most doll's furnishings have attractive or well finished backs. I have done a bit of refurnishing since those days but most modern things are too small and flimsy. Nor is there any place for today's bathroom fittings; there used to be a gentleman's hip bath, the kind my mother's father insisted on having in front of the fire in his bedroom long after the Edinburgh house had a bathroom. Duly pails were carried up. My doll's house hot-water can seems to have gone too. It was like the little brass ones that used to be found sitting, a hot towel over them, on one's washstand at suitable times—they were pretty and comforting and someone else emptied the basin of dirty water, while one was out of the room. However, I still have one doll's house washstand with a basin and ewer. People who came to visit my parents often brought me doll's house presents. That little jug came from Niels Bohr, those wooden kitchen things including a churn from an Austrian physiologist—but who? Most of the *décor* dates back to my mother's childhood.

But I was too much of a realist and too little theatre-minded to enjoy it wholeheartedly. How far can realism go? When I cut open one of my dolls, dribbled the contents into a small cauldron and heated it on—real?—imaginary?—flames I can remember my disappointment that it still wasn't edible. My brother and I between us skinned a furry caterpillar for a rug, but it shrivelled up. So many things ought to have worked but didn't. As well perhaps to learn this young.

Once at a picnic up the Cherwell, where we usually went on Sundays and always made a fire for the tea kettle, I simply had to walk through the lovely soft shimmering grey ashes. How delicious they were going to feel on my bare skin! But of course it wasn't like that at all; I still remember the scorch pattern on my feet between the sandal straps.

I do however remember clearly that the goldfish inside the great Famille Rose Chinese bowl that once stood in the corner of the Edinburgh drawing-room used to swim round and eat the crumbs I put in. Sadly these same goldfish are now only painted on the inside of the bowl. This kind of memory makes one just a little uncertain of others. The butterfly that I tamed? Throwing the milk off the tray of my high chair? Probably I did, but I hardly think I can remember it. Or again, that piece of radium my brother convinced me that he had in his desk? And surely he once let me see it sparkling inside a dark cupboard?

I am quite sure all the same about our railway which we had in an empty and no doubt unattractive room at the top of the house. Every birthday or Christmas saw more rails or more trucks. We sent off the clockwork trains, timing them so that they did—or didn't—miss one another on loops which we had constructed. It was terribly exciting being at the points and knowing that the lives of the trains depended on one. Sometimes if we were quite sure we had arranged a train smash, we would put night lights inside the carriages and turn out the lights. That made it all the better. My brother was five years older than me but I tried so hard to keep up and often succeeded.

We had two splendid boxes of bricks, hard-wood with straight edges, cut to size. With these we built mostly castles and forts which we garrisoned with our lead soldiers and then fired at with spring-loaded artillery whose wooden projectiles could make a real dent, in time bringing the whole thing satisfactorily crashing down. For further realism, we sometimes put in cotton-wool soaked in methylated spirits which our mother used for her curling tongs, and lighted it. We were probably safer with naked flames than today's switch-on—switch-off children.

Things seemed to be always cheerful and in the everyday world with my brother Jack—Boy for me. Certainly he did testing things sometimes like making the water in the basin live—off the ordinary house electricity when we finally got it—and putting in pennies for me to snatch. Often he teased me till my temper went and I stamped and screamed, feeling furiously helpless. I hated him for minutes and then suddenly it was all over. But this wasn't the kind of thing which really worried me. This was alive. What I was afraid of was not alive. It was what lay behind the apparent silence and stillness of inanimate objects, including bed knobs, roof finials and the pigeon house—not the pigeons.

There were so many propitiations to go through in my daily life. When I was dressed and my hair brushed and I came down to the drawing-room for tea I used to have to look at the de Morgan tiles and say, 'I'm afraid that hoopoe will eat my dolly'. After that it was all right. The hoopoe still looked fierce but its soul was safely locked into the tile. Nor did I worry much about my dolly which I have now quite forgotten; I was never particularly maternal about them. This propitiation was public; but it was not public that there was a certain chair which I always avoided touching. It was a high-backed *art nouveau* piece and in the end attained a good cash value so I sold it into slavery, getting even with it more than half a century later. The grandfather clocks were equally ominous and likely to become animated, but I put this down to the story someone told me about a clock that ate (or chased) a little boy. This animation of the inanimate strikes me as basically terror-making. At one time I was constantly being taken into old furniture or curiosity shops and kept on having to jump round to see what the chairs, mirrors or suits of armour were up to. I thoroughly hated any story that had this as part of it, and if I was ever asked to a rather grand Christmas party my mother had to make sure there wasn't going to be a ventriloquist, as she knew from dire experience that if there was she might have to take me back screaming and probably wetting my drawers.

Mirrors—looking-glasses (I know that one was a more powerful word than the other, but which?—it was nothing to do with U or non-U), were especially treacherous, most of all tall ones with claw legs like the one in the St Margaret's Road drawing-room which one was aware of even from outside, passing the small window. But I didn't like even the smallest. In all the fairy tales, including George MacDonald's *Phantastes*, which affected me deeply with its concern about beauty and guilt, mirrors were not to be trusted. They told too much or too little. I wrote most of them out of my system in an early verse play.

Of course there were areas of safety; nothing could get at me if I curled up on my father's lap, holding on to his ear with one thumb tucked into it. He had a big brown moustache and a wide Haldane nose with a small lump on it which I liked. When he kissed me it was rough and tickly. Across his front was a gold watch chain with a big tick-tock watch on the end. In my own children's time it also had a chocolate tree which flowered into silver-paper covered chocolates. All about him was safe. And there were areas of laughter and excitement, especially a long saga Boy told me about a family like ourselves and they went along and they went along and suddenly they met—perhaps—a bear and something shatteringly funny always happened. I was a plump little girl and these gales of laughter were quite painful, one felt one was going to come in two. It was almost as shattering as being teased. He was at the Dragon School where I too would go when I was five and the characters in the story were called with exquisite humour the Wagons. That always set us both off. Later on the story had three canoes called The Vagus, The Cornucopia and The Little Mary; but this was a stage on in sophistication.

But there were also lots of ordinary games. The main one, any time, was some form of hide-and-seek. There is a family story of my father bringing back a plague rat from the Lister Institute in a paper bag and leaving it in his overcoat pocket. The hat and coat stand in the front hall was one of my favourite hiding places and I can remember my indignation at being hauled out by a grown-up who wasn't in the game.

My nurse was called Sina; perhaps there had been others before her but she was the only one I remember. When she went away for her holiday she always sent me country butter in a blue cup. Once I wrote to thank her, saying I would soon have a tea set, but my mother told me this was wrong, it looked as if I expected to get more, and perhaps also she didn't like me to be too fond of Sina, whom I now remember as someone who was always nice to me, perhaps because 'a servant' would never be allowed to punish me. She was still there when I first went to school and for several years after that; she comes into my earlier diaries, but I think she must have left in late 1907 when we moved to Cherwell and before I broke my leg. It would have been a good thing if she could have been with me after that instead of some of the professional nurses whom I so hated.

Food in those days was still nursery food. One wasn't allowed for instance cheese, bacon or fried potatoes. There was not so much raw fruit as now, except what we acquired by our own wits. My mother in any case refused to have onions in her house. Much later, when I occasionally cooked for her, I introduced a small amount, particularly in curries which she liked because of Kipling and her romantic view of India, clear in her own book, and she always enjoyed the 'Indian' flavour I had so cleverly put in. Breakfast was porridge, probably a boiled egg and milk. Lunch tended to be stew, cottage pie, tasteless boiled cod with a small pool of egg sauce, and so on, but roast beef on Sundays. There would be milk pudding afterwards, though we did have castle puddings and big fruit pies—not flans which came in much later. On week-days we often had boiled salt beef with carrots; I hated that. Sometimes there were boiling fowls with lumpy white sauce over macaroni. Roast chicken was birthday food. Cooking was much less interesting and varied than it is today. Tea was bread and butter, bread and jam, cake. Biscuits were not as common as they are now; there were none that came my way with chocolate or sugary fillings, but we did have alphabet biscuits and in Scotland 'squashed flies'. There seemed almost always to be an evening spoonful of cod liver oil or something of the kind. Milk was always boiled and I hated it. In spite of this boiled milk I got TB and swollen neck glands which were painted with iodine. I had to wear a collar to cover them.* There must have been other treatments as well, for I remember various doctors poking me and muted quarrels between my father and mother. Finally the glands were operated on and I came out of the nursing home with a nasty scar about which I was very conscious. But at least on TB I was negative.

But there was constant winter illness of a vague kind, coughs and cough mixtures, being sick and having nightmares. Sina slept beside me. But sometimes she didn't wake and the nightmare went on in the dark even though I seemed to be awake myself. I heard the trains hooting in the distance and sometimes the beat of horse hooves but of course never a car. The blinds were drawn down and I waited and waited until, as Stevenson said, 'day shall be blue on the window blind'. Of course there was also standard measles and my brother pretending I was a lion and feeding me through the bars of the cot. It left me with a nice long word: photophobia. There was chicken pox and horrible whooping cough that went on

* My 1905 (seven years old) diary says: 'After breakfast Dr Hale White took me to an instrument maker to be measured for a collar, which he and Sir Alfred Fripp proscribed to keep my glands still. I have got the collar on now, and I have to have my writing proped up because I cannot bend my head forward, so I am afraid my writing is worse than usual. At the instrument maker's I saw an operating sofa where you were X-rayed.'

All quotations from the diaries are *verbatim*.

and on. Illness was something one took for granted and was nothing to do with the terrors of fantasy or the other sharp terror, that one's mother might—some day—die.

Purges were usual for anything and fiercely effective: calomel or castor oil. There were also enemas; any psychologist will point out the deleterious effects of the latter as a punishment fantasy. A few household remedies survive from those days: some quite effective cough mixtures, Eno's and Dr Collis Browne's chlorodyne. But the real jump came first with sulfonamides and then with the antibiotics. We fussed much more about cleanliness at an earlier time. It seems likely that sterilising instruments for an operation was more necessary; one couldn't afford an infection—the kind of thing which is so quickly dealt with now. Iodine always went on cuts; one had to be brave. But doctors came to the house and of course treated us all for nothing, as doctors at that time always did for one another's families. My father had actually been a practising doctor in the wards of the Royal Infirmary at Edinburgh and I think he still felt that bleeding was a good thing though it was never practised on any of us.

But blood was interesting and something to do with physiology —that long word!—and the lab where one could play with fascinating things including of course the original Haldane gas analysis apparatus and those lovely little blobs of mercury that one could chase right across the floor.

By that time my father had done his classic work on sewer gas, mostly in the Dundee sewers, where he knew by the smell of raw jute or bitter oranges which factory effluents were coming in. Now he was working on the physiology of breathing, writing scientific papers alone or in collaboration, but also writing on the philosophical concepts which arose from this work. But it was always solidly based on the experiments which were going on, some of which, rightly and properly, were on himself. He was a Fellow of New College, conscientiously interested in College problems, and usually dined in Hall on Sundays. I grew out of childhood into a healthy respect for scientific curiosity and work, but I never had my brother's early understanding of it, and I wonder, now, whether this was temperamental or whether certain avenues of understanding were closed to me by what was considered suitable or unsuitable for a little girl. Not deliberately closed, I think, since both my parents believed in feminine emancipation, but— there is a difference between theory and practice.

III

The Evidence

There are two ways of writing this kind of book. One is by an act of acute remembrance, sometimes by concentrating on some small object, some tail-end which may, so to speak, be hauled on until the whole animal is revealed. Again, dreams may help, though they may also worry and obscure; one must be careful. A place revisited, although it may have been almost completely changed, still keeps something which will start up the memory train. The smell of gas, the smell of drains, the smell of old-fashioned roses or mignonette, the smell of stables, these can be starters.

But I have something else of a very definite kind. First of all there are the diaries of the summer holidays, which all pupils of the Dragon School were expected to keep, though no doubt not all the juniors did. My mother had ours bound. There they are. Mine date from 1904 (Naomi Haldane age six—Form 1). There are three of my brother's, from 1902 on. The last was written at eleven. At twelve he was doubtless preparing for Eton. We always got prizes for our diaries and no wonder, or so I say now; we were both highly literate. So I can use these to check my memories. Or can I? I try to remember the actual process of writing. 'Have you done your diary?' It was not a welcome activity. Since then I have kept diaries at various periods of stress in my life, including the years of the last war. But these were partly therapeutic, to calm down some of my troubles, or even solve them, by writing about them. These early diaries were holiday tasks with emphasis on the last word.

They are all written on paper with double lines ruled faint. In many ways the handwriting gets worse and worse, curiously more like my brother's which was notoriously bad, though no doubt it went quicker over the years. They are all illustrated, mostly with flowers, though I try people, not very successfully, at a later stage. My brother's illustrations are practically all plans and diagrams. He always refers to his 'pater & mater'. When did that stop? There are picture postcards, but not the photos which one would expect today's children to use. On the other hand in the 1909 diary when I was eleven, there are two or three pencil drawings of considerable aesthetic demerit—let me say quickly!—which recall vividly the dress and even attitudes of train travellers of this date. In my early diaries I was clearly hampered by having to use either crayons or unsatisfactory water colours. But in the 1904 diary at six, there is a drawing of a barley ear which I do remember doing because it was the first time I had really looked at the shape of a barley ear and the twist of the leaf and it was deeply absorbing. A few of these pictures recall their making and the taste of the paint when one accidentally sucked one's brush. There is one of bees on a flower of *buddleia globosa*. There was a big (to me) bush of this in the left-hand bottom corner of the St Margaret's Road garden.

But the content of the diaries? Can I fairly use these for checking my own memories or should they be set down straight without passing through the memory sieve? Clearly the memories, as they come into consciousness sixty or sixty-five years later (sometimes more), have been distorted and censored. There is an element of subconscious choice. But equally there is an element of choice in the diaries, which are all about outside events in the sense that all the ghosts and terrors have been eliminated. I would not have written about those under any compulsion; I doubt if a psychiatrist could have got them out of me, though perhaps careful watching of my play activities might have revealed something. But fear was shameful, and to speak or write might bring 'Them' to life.

So what? Let us see. Page 1, July 23 1904: 'After dinner Boy and Baines went on the River, & Mother & I went to see Miss Northcroft off, & to buy a boat hook. Then we went to Worcester to feed the swans, we found some, & some cygnets. The cygnets were grey, with almost grey beaks & feet; some of them had feather sheaths still on their young feathers. The swans & ducks fed out of our hands, & one swan bit a hole in my thumb. Some boys were fishing close by, & the fish came for the bread which we gave the swans. We had gooseberries & sponge cake for tea which we had under a horsechestnut-tree. We saw a Thrush which was hitting a snailshell against the parth, so as to get the snail out, to eat it.'

The next day the family went on the river. 'We saw a lot of Arrowhead, & flowering-Rush & goldenrod & lithram & Epilobiun & Water Lilies, yelow & white, & creeping-jenny, & tansy in flower. We had dinner in a fairly nettly field, & afterwards Boy bathed, with a fairly good effect. Then we paddled, & got plenty of Plantorbises; they are like flat snail-shells. Then we went home.'

This shows a remarkable degree of observation and the power to write it down,* though I don't much care for so many commas. Clearly I must have asked for a lot of the spellings, but equally clearly I made an attempt at some of them which didn't always come off. I was well used to Latin botanical names though sometimes I got the spelling wrong and didn't know loose-strife or willow-herb. This also shows that flowering rush, now rare, was common only a mile or so up the Cherwell where one no longer finds much in the way of flowers. Over the 'plantorbises', I was keeping up with my elders!

I know that, when I wrote my diary, I was encouraged to describe things I had seen; often I would pick up the words of the grown-ups. But sometimes I rush off on my own. When the British Medical Association came to Oxford 'Mr Lorrain-Smith gave me this:

> 'An owl and a pussy-cat came to me
> In a beautiful rocking boat
>> They took some honey
>> But I couldent see the money
> In a barrel with on it wrote
>> Honey

* My brother's diary says: 'I got some fairly good specimens of *Planorbis corneus, Paludina vivipara, Limnaea auriculata, & Anodonta anatina.* N.B. This year I am going to make Naomi write all the botany, as she is far better at it than I am. We met a good few other chaps up the river.'

27

All this was made of wood,
And on the grass it stood.
And besides that a mouse-trap that
works with a spring.'

And now I can clearly picture the otherwise forgotten owl and pussycat, a wooden toy balancing on a bar with a weighted rod below which made it swing. My finger went out to rock it, often, often.

Sentiment breaks in, 'some dear little pigs', 'a dear little puppy, he was quite brown, though his mother was white and black! his teeth all except the canines were as small as my teeth when I was a baby.' Food is important. 'We found a great many Dewberries, so many we could not eat them all.' There are books which I read: *The Stokesley Secret, Hiawatha, The Treasure Seekers*. But I seem to make few literary comments, in my early diaries at least.

In fact the diaries are, very properly, extroverted. It is only from further away that I can see inside the child. The diary writer sees people through their achievements. In my seven-year-old diary: 'We met Prof D'Arcy Thompson who knows more about whales than anybody else in the world.'

How, then, should I use them now? I can scarcely mix them in, unless a chance word or two brings back a scene or even a state of mind so vividly that it becomes part of adult memory. The fairest thing to do, perhaps, is to add the diaries' comments separately.

What a bore it was to have to get down to writing the day's page, chivvied into it, often at the spare writing table in the Cloan drawing-room which had a very ornate black, cast-iron ink-stand with two inkwells, various pens and a sheet of white blotting paper which one was not supposed to draw on. There were also two short, also rather ornate, silver candlesticks, for sealing, and there may well have been one of the many silver trowels, suitably inscribed, which Uncle Richard was given after laying foundation stones.

Maya collected the written sheets (occasionally making me re-write those which had been hopelessly blotted) which otherwise would have escaped. In the diaries she is always, more formally,

Mother, though in those years I did not think of her like that. But the fact that she read what I had written and that I wanted so much to please her, may account for some of my sentiments. These were second-hand, but my observations on natural history and, occasionally, industrial processes, were genuine, and when I wrote that something was lovely (I didn't use many other praise words) it is probable that I genuinely thought so.

But there are also quite a lot of letters. I turned a bundle of these over to the Edinburgh Central library with various other documents which had started heavily accumulating in the house, and happily forgot all about them. The early letters are in rather worse spelling than the diaries, more blotchy, but full of life. There are some from my brother and one from my father to him, which had somehow got into the bundle. I think my mother must have kept all our childhood letters; some are dated in her hand, especially those from my brother at five or six, sometimes with a proud note they were written without help. In one, to her, he slightly complains: 'Nou wants so much looking after when you're away.' However, I kept myself busy; one of the earlier letters encloses lots of empty seed packets which I had sowed in my own garden, a square in the bottom bed of the St Margaret's Road garden. This was always rather disappointing; they never quite looked like the pictures on the outside of the packet.

There are a number from Jack to me, signed Boydie, which was my baby version of Boy dear. He expected me to understand and sympathise with what he was after. A 1906 letter, when I was eight, tells me in detail about how well he was likely to do in 'Trials' and what prizes he hoped to win. By that time he must have come to terms with Etonian savagery and was determined to get what he could out of the place.

Sometimes the letters recall a definite memory. One from Cornwall is about elvers climbing up a waterfall, and now, reading it, I remember the dark green, wet, hanging, slippery, glancing things. Now and then they recall another name from school days or some specially good ploy. How lucky that I didn't know I was going to re-read them so many years later in so different a world.

Finally, there is my mother's book of memoirs, *Friends and Kindred*. The later chapters overlap the period about which I am writing. She was fifteen years older than I am now when she started writing them, largely at my daughter's and my own instigation. I have gone back from time to time to her book and, so to speak, checked with her, sometimes with a touch of subliminal argument.

IV

Cloan

How cold it was getting out at Auchterarder station! It had been a wearisome journey up, with the wait and change at Rugby, a long gloomy platform. But on the next session we had splendid iron foot-warmers filled with boiling water put into our compartment. Was it a night journey, waking in Scotland and another change, I think, at Larbert? Or did things work out (perhaps when we went over from Edinburgh) so that we got to Auchterarder in the late afternoon and there was a carriage waiting for us with the two horses stamping and tossing their heads? It smelt of straw and fustiness and those with a keen nose would tell every time one of the pair of horses lifted her tail. But as we got up a little, crossing the burn at the stone bridge, the smell sharpened with the scent of pine needles and beech leaves and the horses went slower. As we came through the gate the sound of the hooves and wheels changed and went squashier and grittier as we got on to the gravel drive. I pulled down a window. The leaves rustled; there were sounds different from Oxford. We got to the house and the faintly lit windows high up and the porch and the wall thick with jasmine, then the lights streaming out of the wide door, the horses pulling up and Aunt Bay waiting for us with open arms.

Cloanden (as it was then, but by 1904 Uncle Richard had begun to change the name back to the original Cloan) is half way up the Ochills with a splendid northwest view across Strathearn into the Highlands. It was originally a pleasant little farmhouse with the traditional square of buildings at the back, byres and stables, sheds and bothies. But gradually in the course of the nineteenth century it was built on to, first an enormously inconvenient spiral staircase

31

in a tower from which landings opened out. It had a massive hand-rail with a square-topped newel at each landing for the big oil lamps. The second floor had big sombre bedrooms, each with a four-poster, the red one hung with red curtains and tassels, the blue one in the same style. What might not be crouching on the tops of the canopies or under the ample bed flounces? These, of course, often hid chamber pots, but sometimes I was almost too frightened to pull one out. This is still one of my nightmares. Another is that I find one already too full to use. The marble-topped bedside pedestal table was for the same purpose, with two, but I think, when used, we always hid them under the bed until the latter went modern and ceased to have flounces. The curtains were heavy, with tasselled cords, but could not shut out the owl cries at night. The older dressing-tables had draperies over the mirror.

All the family have had a passion for alterations and improve-ments, not quite so expensive at an earlier time and leading, both at Cloan and at Foswell, where Aunt Edith, a Nelson, was an equally keen alterer, to steps up and down between one level and another. I doubt if an architect was ever consulted until Uncle Richard did his major alterations. The local builder—and ourselves—were good enough. Granniema's bedroom, when I was a child, had a window one could climb out of on to alps of slates with lead ridges and gutters. There was a charming small sitting-room off it, the porch room, all windows, with low window seats and an arched fireplace. Later there was a very large addition to the house, above all Uncle Richard's study and bedroom, in fact a whole suite. The study smelled of leather armchairs, the wood of the bookshelves and his cigars. This was not a place where children were encouraged to go. But there were other, friendlier bedrooms too, and little new turrets and a much nicer WC with a different smell.

From Granniema's little porch room she, or for that matter I, kneeling up with my nose against the window, could look down over the gravel drive, the sweep of green lawn, the hollow hedge of double holly with *tropaeolum* growing through it. Beyond were the cultivated fields, oats, turnips, or hay and pasture ley, and beyond that again the ridge of Auchterarder, and away in the distance across

Strathearn the clefted mountains where the sunsets lost themselves. But in those days there were lots and lots of trains on the main line between us and Auchterarder; on northerly winds we could hear them chugging up the incline, trailing splendid smoke, and always stopping at Auchterarder station which is now grass-grown and desolate.

In one of these cornfields I had very early on a curious adventure. Or had I? The reapers had scythed the oats, the binders following them. I was too small to bind but I was sent out to glean for the old ladies in the Poor House. I would manage an armful of oat stalks and stagger over with them. Probably the end result was that they would be given a bag of oatmeal, but I always thought that my sheaf would be threshed separately. Anyhow, I felt very useful. Then I met a brown hare and we went off and kept house (marriage, as I saw it) inside a corn stook with six oat sheaves propped round us. I certainly did not know that the hare is the Celtic symbol of fertility and perhaps this has no connection at all with what I appeared to be doing in the harvest field. But as I remember it I was married young to the hare.

The difficulty about Cloan was that it was full of ghosts and such. Much of my terror was induced by the elders, my brother and the big Foswell cousins. There was only one younger than me, Foswell Archie, and he was protected by Nana, who would have skelped any of the rest of us. My almost-twin cousin Graeme appeared to be immune to the teasing and frightening. Long afterwards he told me that he too had been scared stiff of the gorgonzola which haunted the tower room, but he had been wise enough to keep his mouth shut. The tower room was round, with the closed-in spiral staircase going up the middle so that if one opened the door into apparent dusty emptiness whatever else there might have been was certainly hiding behind the staircase wall. It still is in my dreams, waiting to come out at me.

Aunt Bay, ordinarily so kind, had invented the gorgonzola probably as a joke, not just to frighten us. Years later when we talked over all this and its dire effect on me, she said I was the only Haldane to have this kind of runaway imagination, something which now she loved and respected. But it was a misery then. And indeed can be still, though without it I would have no wings.

The worst thing the boys did was to take the dummy head on which Granniema's caps were made and put it into my bed. I screamed so loud and long that everyone was concerned, including my brother. He certainly hadn't meant it to be like that. I didn't care for the dressmaker's dummy either; if it started sliding towards me on its three legs . . .

The library with the nice-smelling wooden bookshelves all round and the window opening into the garden, was my favourite place. The big desk, where my father wrote, puffing his pipe, had glass paperweights with a picture of a dog's head inside or somewhere abroad. In the days when suitable Sunday reading was thought to be salutary I found not only *The Pilgrim's Progress*, *The Holy War* and *Foxe's Book of Martyrs* (bloodthirsty all of them) but the *Encyclopaedia Britannica*, which enlightened me on certain puzzling phrases in Leviticus. But there was a room immediately above with games in it. Unreasonably, I hated it, because the steep little stairs had a turn one couldn't see round—and *what* might—? But again, someone may have frightened me deliberately. Uncle Richard's study, a delightful room, and the rest of his suite, were out of bounds until much later.

But outside was different. Here were the peacocks which, if skilfully chased, might be induced to drop a feather. We were allowed to pick these up but not to pull them out, and the temptation of those splendid tails was very strong. I made various houses and forts among and under spruce branches but I was never a good climber. One of our ploys was to steal grapes from the greenhouse; one of the big ones sprawled out so as not to put too much weight on the glass and reached in his arm. We retired up the big lime tree into the summer sound of the bees to eat our spoil, not more than one bunch I think. And I usually had to be hauled up by one of the others. If they didn't I was liable to roam round bleating which might have alerted the grown-ups. All our initials are still up there, growing, with the tree, though some of us are dead and all too old to climb and look.

34

There were beehives in the garden with little beds of bee flowers growing beside them. The sweet strong smell of honey filled that part of the garden which I remember perpetually in warm sun, though no doubt this happened as seldom as it usually does in Scotland. When visitors were walking past being shown round the policies, as one said, another of our ploys was to lob stones over the garden wall at the hives in the hope of irritating the bees into stinging them or at least scaring them into running away. This happened to various distinguished guests and we found it very exhilarating. Was one of them Baden-Powell? I am sure I was pleased if it was, because he kept stopping me to teach me knots, which didn't interest me at the time. When I had to know them because of using them, they became interesting and I was quite quick at them. But not then!

The walled garden at Cloan, about an acre I think, was a kind of Tom Tiddler's ground where we grabbed and hid and dodged the gardeners until such time as we were old enough to be assumed to be responsible members of the family. Meanwhile there were thickets of raspberries, gooseberries and currants, and along the walls dripping purple plums, apples and greengages. Strawberries were more difficult, offering no hiding places. Beyond there were the garden extensions which Aunt Bay had made, with clipped yew hedges, moss roses and the dogs' tombstones. There had been dynasties of large dogs, labradors I think, Bosco, Ben and Tyne, very amiable to small children, allowing us to share their huge wooden kennel with the doorway just large enough to get into, and even to let us eat titbits out of their bowls. Grown-ups were much less pleasant about this, unkindly pulling us out of the big kennel and talking about fleas.

Granniema had various little cairns, intelligent and not always friendly; they liked to lie on the black hearth rug in front of the shining steel of the drawing-room fire. So did I. The big, chilly drawing-room smelt of dogs and potpourri and the great jars of garden flowers which Aunt Bay enjoyed arranging. This was always done in a little pantry in the passage close to the telephone (the kind with a handle one wound) and the gentleman's lavatory. Any large house would have a WC near the door strictly for the men. If one dashed in because one was in a desperate hurry one felt a deep sense of social guilt. It was still worse, if the hurry was such—as I remember once rushing back from school to the Oxford house with a bladder scarcely in control—that one used the servants' WC. That was almost beyond forgiveness. One only hoped not to have been observed.

There were of course masses of shrubberies at Cloan, nothing like the modern shrub garden with special beautiful flowering bushes, but thick and shiny with dark leaves, laurel and rhododendron meant as barriers and excellent for hide-and-seek. Among these were drying greens, small lawns, and a round pond with a fountain in the middle jetting out from a rockery of stones and ferns which, again, if one managed to turn it full on suddenly might on a favourable wind shower a distinguished visitor. There was also the croquet lawn where we had large mixed games of croquet at which I was very seldom chosen as a partner since I was normally very bad, especially if someone stood over me telling me exactly what to do. But this was in general safe ground where the enemy was not supernatural but only the gardeners and then only if one had been in some way naughty. From the garden an upper and lower walk followed the glen, with the burn at the bottom and at the far side steep fields running up to Foswell; here there were dark bits which I didn't like so much. My father was constantly constructing new walks and Boy was allowed to help but not on the whole a small girl, though I helped to knock down nettles with a stick and called myself 'Nou the Nettle-killer'. There was a time when the walk right along the glen was very tiring and one had to be carried piggyback, one's fat legs rubbing against tweed shoulders. Then in how few years one was carrying one's own small ones.

But once Graeme and I ran all the way. It was like this. There was a house party and Margot Asquith was much taken or pretended to be with Graeme and me. She patted our heads, which we didn't like, and then gave us each sixpence, upon which we turned and ran right up the glen, thinking of all the things we could buy—for sixpence was something in those days. But when we were finally out of breath I had lost my sixpence and Graeme wouldn't share his with me. But I don't mind now!

I never liked having my head patted. When I was taken visiting to the Poor House the old ladies used to stroke my hair. Their hands smelt dreadful, so did everything about them. But as soon as I could read properly I used to be sent down to read 'a chapter from the Book' to one of them who was probably blind. There were various village visits we always had to pay. One sat dangling one's legs on one side of a black-leaded cooking stove trying to be good. Perhaps at the end one got a bit of shortbread.

Apart from social do-gooding there was more of a religious atmosphere up north, though I am sure I never went to church until later on. This was partly because it was a longish walk; we didn't drive on Sundays. I don't think I was brought into family prayers until I was of a comparatively untender age. But then I found them very flavoursome. On a Sunday evening we might be sitting in the drawing-room reading or playing draughts and then came the sound of the big gong in the hall. Hastily one sat up, closing one's book, and the deep purple plush benches were brought in. Then in came the servants in order of precedence, Mrs Cook in some sort of dark satin, the butler, my uncle's chauffeur in a smart suit. He was a Methodist and had adapted the horn of the car to play the first few notes of *Lead Kindly Light* so his appearance at family prayers was an act of courtesy. Then came the rest of the staff down to the youngest kitchen maid. The family of course stayed in their chairs, somewhat cut off by a small table with plants on it. The chairs had chintz covers and white crochet antimacassars, though these were later done away with. There were chintz-covered foot-stools as well, for comfortable kneeling.

The senior male member of the family read the Chapter and improvised a prayer in proper Presbyterian style. When it was my father's turn he refused to improvise but read a prayer in such a surprised voice that it sounded improvised. My brother once produced a very Etonian one, even with bits of Latin in it. I always longed to do it but it was never my turn.

Everyone sat during the Lesson, stood to sing and knelt to pray.

Once much later on one of Granniema's cairns leapt on to a kneeling back and walked all the way down along the line, snuffing at necks and ears. The backs stayed splendidly rigid until the turn of the teenage kitchen maid, who heaved with giggles—as I also did.

At first Granniema had been there in charge. Later she was in bed in the room upstairs but she always chose the hymns which Aunt Bay, no musician, played on the seldom-opened black upright piano. They were sad hymns in minor keys, *Sun of My Soul, As Pants the Hart*. I liked them.

Later, when occasionally I went to church with the others, closed in near the back in the family pew, and as a teenager, constantly and painfully afflicted with the giggles, I didn't care for Presbyterianism. There was nothing attractive about building, decoration or congregation. I never even wanted to put the money I had been equipped with in the massive plates at the door under the chilly gaze of the Elders. It was a nice walk back, but Sunday lunch, unless one could quickly get some cold meat, was boiled sheep's head. It had been singed by the blacksmith in the smiddy furnace and cooked with barley. This is something I am very partial to now, but then I hated it, and Uncle Richard would always poke about in it and offer one an eye. That Haldane teasing! How one suffered from it.

But Oxford was utterly different. My parents were among the first generation of agnostics. They had married with the minimal religious service in the Edinburgh drawing-room of my mother's parents, as Scottish custom approved. My brother and I were unbaptised bairns. But the whole family, believers or not, did believe strongly in freedom of conscience for others. When I had something of a fight with my in-laws not to get married in church myself, Granniema backed me up: 'If you're acting according to your conscience.'

I remember being penned in between the back of the sofa and my reclining mother while she read aloud Montefiore's *Bible for Home Reading* which I found dull. There was so little for instance about the animals in the Ark which were surely the most important; they certainly were in my Ark, especially the tigers with string tails.

Noah was in a kind of dull brown dressing-gown clasping a dove.

Sometimes we went to Sunday evening services at New College where the power of the low organ notes seemed to shudder everything. But again I found most of it dull and always involving being properly dressed and sitting still. Above all it had nothing to do with the terrors and propitiations which went on elsewhere. Would an evening prayer have stopped nightmares? One just doesn't know. It would have had to be on the same level of consciousness and the two layers might easily have missed.

When I went to school I was aware with some smug pride that I was in some way different. I bawled the hymns with the others, usually the jolly ones, but did not join in the Amen which I felt would have put me in the wrong camp. But I certainly joined in scripture lessons and indeed got several prizes. One of my first poems was in the first person about being the elephant chief and successfully getting my wife into the Ark.

V

The Cold and the Flower

Both Edinburgh and Cloan were always cold. Central heating was still in the distant future (after a period of being disapproved of as unhealthy and unnatural—look at the Ancient Britons!) and double glazing even more so. Nor is it entirely simple to put central heating into solidly stone-built Scottish houses. In thousands and thousands of these houses the under servants carried the full coal scuttles upstairs and the empty ones down to the cellars and often had coal-smudged faces. I think my parents worried a bit about them, but probably not the older generation. It was after all their place. They were fortunate to be in 'good service' with security and respectability and the chance to move up.

At the beginning of the century the unders still only got a few pounds a year, but the wages of the senior servants were beginning to creep up. All of course wore long aprons over stuff dresses, ankle length, and white caps, but an upper, especially a parlourmaid, might have becoming streamers and her afternoon apron at least would be starched and tucked muslin. I think there must have been a butler in the Edinburgh house who probably among other things warmed *The Scotsman*—and *Times?*—for Grandpapa (my mother's father) who was fussy about his health. There must have been one at Cloan for there was certainly a butler's pantry where the silver was cleaned and I seem to remember green baize aprons, though I am much clearer about the head ploughman who came from the Mearns, as indeed most of the best farm servants did. I think perhaps the butler came up from London with Uncle Richard, while Granniema and Aunt Bay only had women servants.

A fishwife from Cockenzie called at Grandpapa's house, 10

Randolph Crescent, once or perhaps twice a week, splendid in her kilted skirt and striped petticoat, the creel of fish on her back. Of course the horse vans from the shops with which we dealt called every day, not yet having been partly replaced by the telephone. With luck one might be there when the orders were handed in and might find oneself in the way of sugared almonds, biscuits, cookies or French bread. One after another, the 'good' Edinburgh shops disappear and the supermarkets take over now. It isn't even easy to buy really fresh fish. But in those days people rarely ate out; today's coffee houses and cheerful students make up for a lot.

10 Randolph Crescent towered five storeys up in front, but, as it was built on the edge of a cliff above the Water of Leith, dropped down for countless storeys on the west side, past all of which one must climb to get to the gardens; this was a distinctly alarming process which just appears in my six-year-old diary: 'I went down to the cellars where I saw some things that looked like ghosts. The cellars are covered with Stalagtites; under them are stalagmites which are like bumps of India rubber on the floor. Stalagtites are long thin dark black things caused by water with lime in it driping between the stones in the roof.' Thus scientific interest is allowed to mask the terror. Jack describes it in greater detail with a plan and mention of an old well and pipe which I have forgotten. All this was below the kitchens and the wine cellar, far below Grandpapa's study where gentlemen were allowed to smoke, the dining-room, and above it the great double drawing-room and 'boudoir' where there was a singularly horrid picture on an easel of Boy looking good with long ringlets and a hockey stick. The Edinburgh drawing-room must have been beautiful; there was the long, glass-fronted bookcase topped with china, the very best of it in the centre cupboard, pictures, flowers, the gorgeous Worcester tea set and electric light. But, somehow or another, the bulbs done were up in yellow silk bags. Why didn't they get burned? Perhaps they did.

Above them again were the best bedrooms, and the narrower stairs to our rooms above. All has been remodelled inside into unrecognisability. Only the wonderful view remains, north to the pools of the Water of Leith between the high green branches, or down river, and the splendid granite cliffs of the rest of the New Town.

But could Edinburgh in winter have been quite as cold as I remember it outside? Perhaps our clothes were inadequate, though I had a muff on a string and of course gaiters with a row of horrible pinching buttons. Most ladies had muffs and fur necklets for winter, often with an animal's head on one end; these replaced the summer 'boas' of short ostrich feathers, white or dyed, but these were garden-party wear and of little practical merit. Next to us we all wore woollen combinations, thick in winter, thinner and short-sleeved in summer. One had clean ones on Sundays. The difficulty was that the edges round the slit at the bottom tended to get a bit sticky and scratchy. Over these one wore serge knickers, buttoning below the knee, but these had linings which could be changed more often. Men and boys had thick woollen vests and long pants in an unattractive 'natural wool' colour. Combinations went on during all my young life until the early twenties when I cast them off in favour of longish chemises of fine linen or printed silk—and of course I mean real silk—man-made fibres were still rather nasty. But I expect my mother's generation stuck to their ladies' combinations until the end.

Anyway, that should have kept me warm in the east wind of Edinburgh but I didn't. I was taken for walks, my hand held firmly, but I was allowed to run in Prince's Street Gardens or in the Randolph Crescent gardens that sloped steeply to the Water of Leith and St Bernard's Well, repaired by one of my forbears but whose water I was wisely not allowed to drink. I often hoped I would see a would-be suicide floating down from the Dean Bridge, parachuted by a petticoat as the story had it. Edinburgh pavements were particularly appropriate for the lines and squares ritual with their huge granite sets. I avoided the lines as, presumably, most right-thinking people do. Yet there must be some who actually step on the lines. It would be interesting to know with what other abnormality this is correlated.

I think we must usually have spent Christmas at Randolph Crescent until such time as Grandpapa died and Granny moved down to Oxford, when I was turned out of the nursery to an upstairs room, but at least then we had our Christmas tree at home. Still, Christmas was good wherever it was. How long the grey Edinburgh light took to seep through until one could see the shape of one's stocking at the foot of the bed. Was it as big as last time? Bigger? That promising bulge? Boy and I had separately helped to fill one another's stockings but had kept firm secrets. Some of the presents were wrapped, anyhow. I can't think I ever believed in Father Christmas coming down the chimney, but I gave the notion lip service to please my elders as my own children have kindly done for me.

There wasn't nearly such a variety of toys and games in the shops, though of course there was a blissful penny drawer in the arcade where I sometimes went: this had divisions each holding different penny toys: small wooden dolls or animals, tops, marbles, puzzles, single lead soldiers. That was the best place of all when it came to shops. But in Prince's Street, which must have been then partly unspoiled, there was Maule's at the corner by Charlotte Square, where Binns is now, which had 'ballies', round shells into which one's bill and money were put to whizz up on to an overhead rail along which they trundled to a central desk and then back. How deplorable if two purchases were made at the same counter so that both went into one 'ballie'! Jenner's, however, had a lift. Duncan and Flockart had blackcurrant jujubes which made a cold into a treat and there was also the hairdresser where my mother, before her time with short hair which indeed became her well, had it brushed with a rotary machine. I would have thought it would have been very bad for the hair but she kept hers much the same well into her nineties.

These were lovely shops in a way but, apart from the penny drawer, not for their contents. For that there was only one shop, Liberty's in London. They had the Morris materials and the 'modern' hand-made jewellery. I suppose they had the Morris feeling for crafts and, as I remember, the shop assistants wore real dresses and were considered to be 'ladies' in my mother's sense. One of the few things on which my parents agreed, though possibly

43

for different reasons, was their admiration for Morris and de Morgan. We had Morris wallpapers in St Margaret's Road and the downstairs curtains were certainly Morris materials. I think it was the honeysuckle pattern wallpaper in the drawing-room and a dark red version of the palm tree in the dining-room. And of course the hoopoe was a de Morgan tile. And still is. We had a leadless glaze pottery breakfast set in cheerful peasant colours; at that time lead poisoning was a great hazard in the potteries, so my parents made a willing contribution to industrial health. It was also much better designed than most domestic china of the period—was it perhaps by a Morris follower?

Liberty's had all these materials and some of them were so beautiful, *crêpe de chine* and many kinds of silk and velvet. We went there once or twice a year. My best dress was always a Liberty. There was a long magic passage underground with lighted showcases full of beauty. Many years after, in 1953, I had the same feeling of beauty-shock from showcases at the Britain Can Make It exhibition at the Victoria and Albert after the years of making do with rationing and utility goods. When I was around eleven I spent much time with the illustrated Liberty catalogues—few shops went in for colour-printed catalogues in those days. I had invented a family and I chose them presents, allowing myself one in four of the things illustrated. But it was difficult to find presents for the boys. Could a boy possibly want one of those scarves? Would he ever be able to wear it? Wouldn't it be 'cissy'? Of course no gentleman would ever have dreamed of wearing a coloured shirt. Linen must be seen to be clean—and white. It seems extraordinary that men allowed themselves to be bullied for a whole century by the dullest and most uncomfortable of fashions. No wonder they have broken out since.

At least in Edinburgh one still saw the occasional kilt, though mostly on soldiers. Oh, the glory of the pipers leading the march across the Dean Bridge! One rushed out on to the dining-room balcony to see them. The parapet of the Dean Bridge was low enough for one to be able to see the marchers; it has, sadly, been raised since, I suppose because of those suicides—which must have been rare. Sometimes there were Edinburgh fancy dress parties which I loved above everything. Once I went as Little Boy Blue, actually in boy's clothes, but somewhat rationed on how often I might blow up my horn. Boy wore Indian clothes and I think he had a Sikh turban tied by one of the old soldiers who frequented the house, officers in Indian regiments, cousins or from some equally namely family. I helped to put the brown on to his face and hands. These parties would be at the big houses of friends or fairly remote cousins in the New Town but I remember no childhood mates. Boy was enough for me, and, later, my school friends.

There were, of course, the cousins from Foswell, the Fossils we called them, and a series of feuds and alliances with and around them. Other cousins appeared briefly, Nancy from America and several families from New Zealand, nephews and nieces of our dear Rob Makgill, my father's pupil and our playmate, later Medical Officer of Auckland. I was devoted to several of my father's pupils and young colleagues, especially Teddy Boycott.* And they clearly were very nice to me. It was a satisfactory relationship without too much emotion; that was what was exhausting about parents and perhaps can't avoid being. One has so many feelings of guilt and responsibility which make for emotional tensions.

In my time the earlier generation was rather unapproachable. There were various great aunts or perhaps step-great aunts on my father's side, fat Aunt Eliza and thin Aunt Eliza, one of whom gave me some tiny-tiny bright-coloured wooden soldiers. It must have been fat Aunt, Granniema's sister, because I remember sitting on her knee and arranging them along the great ledge of her bosom where also reposed a gold watch on a brooch and various chains. My mother had two uncles, Uncle Philip and Uncle Jim, with whom she feuded, especially after her father's death, when, so she said, one of them—but I can't now remember which was the baddie—had unfairly got away with some pictures or silver which should by rights have been hers. She was very property-conscious.

* He comes into the diaries. 1904: 'It was Mr. Boycott's wedding day & we all drank his health in champaine at dinner.' 1906: 'Mr. Boycott came to tea, we are always very glad to see him. He has got a baby who he showed us the photograph of.'

As I grew up I became much nearer Granniema, who had I think always been interested in me as a potential artist of some kind. She herself did oil paintings, mostly copies of older family pictures. I have one of her 'Raeburns'; it has considerable merit and feeling and one wonders what she might have achieved if the climate of the times had been propitious.

As soon as I could write at all fluently she got me to write to her, especially with descriptions of wild flowers. Then she would explain how I might describe them better. I became more and more ambitious, keen to observe small matters of colour and texture and habitat. The nearer the ground one is the more fun one gets out of small flowers. Under the bracken near the high summerhouse there was soft grass and in it wild pansies, no two quite alike if one looked close enough. There was eyebright and speedwell, blue harebells and sometimes a white one, tiny shining toadstools, scarlet or yellow, and a kingdom of different mosses. Crawling through, there were dark and light patches, smells of sheep and foxes and the lovely earth itself. By the time I was ten I had my own Bentham and Hooker and was on my way to becoming a reasonably good field botanist.

There were two Cloan summerhouses. One went along the terrace walk to get to them, past gnarled wind-blown laburnums and high cedars and larches, and so to the lower plantation, the zig-zag path up among ferns and foxgloves and the low summerhouse built in a rustic style, heather-thatched and much adorned with Auchterarder initials, though not with the *graffiti* one might expect now. It was somewhat overshadowed by the spruces and could be a little alarming. When I dream of it now I cannot be totally sure that something unpleasant may not happen. But one took the path on and up, along a short stretch of dyke and a small pool for the sheep to drink at, which was interestingly populated by moochs. The high summerhouse was in the same style but less overshadowed and with a superb view north-west across the Strath and the other way to the grass hills that backed us. I think most of the big houses must have had this kind of thing, an object for a walk, kept up by the estate workers. Twice in my lifetime the spruce plantations have

46

been cut and replanted. Uncle Willie from Foswell looked after the estates and made some plantations himself quite high on the slopes of the Ochills. The neighbours laughed about this, saying they would never do and in the early years of the Forestry Commission such planting was unheard of. But he was fully justified even before his death when these grand shelter belts made all the difference to the hill cattle.

Today the terrace walk has changed little, though only one laburnum still stretches a single flowering arm from a much aged and doctored trunk and the great larch boles are so grown that they have pushed the path to one side. The diesel trains sound less alive than the old trains and none stop at Auchterarder station. Both summerhouses have gone.

There were other good walks. I can just remember Auchterarder as it used to be, with an open drain flowing down the street and the stone slabs of the bridges over it from the house doors. Then came the sewage plant with the big septic tank, to which we made an expedition on September 7th 1906; it rates a page of the diary with 'bacteria' properly spelled. But Jack was much more scientific and had several pages and some discussion of typhoid. Later the same day he and I walked daringly through the tunnel under the railway line, which the burn still flows through; how far it seemed to the arch of daylight when one was in the middle!

Once at least in the summer holidays there would be the Craig Rossie walk, though at first I had to be pulled or occasionally carried.* But before one got to Craig Rossie there was the Black Swelch where the Perna burn, swelled by the Coul burn, falls over a precipice into a dark and frightening pool, deep down with only a narrow slippery path to cling to and slip along. Once there was a dead sheep, white and shapeless, swirling in it, but I had a feeling that it might be the kelpie. Miss Delf, who was the 'companion' of Aunt Eliza (which one?), had the then very unusual accomplishment of diving and swimming. She dived into the Black Swelch

* Jack's 1902 diary says: 'This was Naomi's first at all high climb (over 1300 feet high) so we had to carry her and haul her a lot of the way.' But not bad for a five-year-old.

47

and measured the depth, a thing I can't imagine myself daring to do.

The first electricity at Cloan came from a turbine worked from the dam a mile or so up the burn. This was when Uncle Richard enlarged the house in 1904. Here was another exciting bit of estate work which visitors, taken round the policies, must not miss. The 1904 diary is full of the thrills of concrete-pouring, though this was less exciting than storming wasps' bikes 'so that they got very angry'. In time the turbine also worked the Cloan sawmill but there were constant problems about how much electricity was being used and difficult moments when the engine raced and the lights glared or dimmed. But in summer the dam sometimes held up the flow below so that there was only a trickle of water, and I minded this because I spent an immense time making dams of my own. Here again it was the closeness that mattered; the matching of surfaces, the swirls that pointed the water's diverted way, the moss, the caddis worm casts, the sailing feather, the dappling of light, the cool live push of the burn against one's groping hands. If I ever found a really suitable rock I would make a fairy's garden, busily adorning it until no sensible fairy could possibly pass it by. Of course one didn't believe in fairies but the pleasure of adornment must have some practical basis.

There was busy house-building as well.* Once someone—Miss Delf?—gave me a real china bell that tinkled, to hang outside my current house. But I had a funny feeling that people in the exploring books did it better.

Sometimes we went high up, perhaps to Ramsay's Loup where a sheep stealer was said to have jumped the burn, cliff to cliff. Here there was bog myrtle, bog asphodel, sundew and pinguicula with the marvellous scent of its violet flowers, and grass of Parnassus, perhaps the most beautiful of all the Scottish wild flowers. But the burn itself was too deep and strong for damming until one got much higher up, beyond a child's walking distance.

* Jack's 1902 diary says: 'Naomi and I are building a house of branches round a tree, and thatching it with hay and leaves.'

VI

Towards School

Once I began to read I gobbled books. One of my favourite reading places at Oxford was the window-seat behind the corner folds of the Morris curtain in the drawing-room. This was also very nice in the evening when the curtains were completely drawn and one could crawl along with the dark garden behind the window panes— for some reason that didn't frighten me at all—and peep through the folds at the lighted room. So much nicer than actually being in it! Like most intelligent children I was omnivorous, and when there was nothing else I tackled books which were much too old for me, including for instance *Dangerous Trades* with its fascinating engravings—not yet photographs—of the ravages of lead poisoning or glass blowers' collapsed chests. I even read the more lurid bits of the BMJ, as well as anything about mine accidents. These were familiar because every time there was a bad mine disaster—and there were a good many in the first decade of the century—my father would take his mine clothes and miner's helmet with the safety lamp and go off to investigate the pit. If after a time we got back a series of telegrams saying 'I am all right', we would know he had got a bad dose of carbon monoxide poisoning which had blotted out the memory of the first telegram. Periodically we would have visits from mine managers and deputies and my mother, who was not too partial to the working classes, welcomed them and fed them. They were—different. So to some extent were others dealing with basic materials, farmers and fishermen.

But to be 'in trade' was the lowest thing, whether you were a shop assistant or a successful contractor—and one or two of these latter shockingly now had sons at the Dragon School which used to

49

be reserved for University children, and also of course whatever parents in the recognised professions, the army, the navy, the church and the bar, might have been found at Oxford. However, University teaching, which was quite badly paid at that time, was not really a thing where one could be certain of finding gentlefolk, though heads of colleges were usually, but not always, acceptable. Their wives were often far from being the people my mother would have considered her social equals in Scotland.

I remember being severely lectured about trade when I was discovered to have made friends behind the counter at the small draper's in North Parade. There were little drawers with buttons and hooks and silk or cotton thread which I had been allowed to look into delightedly and touch, better than a doll's house. I was made to feel naughty, but worst was having to pretend not to be friends with the ladies in the black stuff dresses, to be made to feel they were somehow different, that they 'smelled'.

This trade dislike swept on to include not only managers but directors of large companies. Yet how did this square with early twentieth-century imperialism which my mother believed in so strongly? Joe Chamberlain, her hero? And if she had ever met Rhodes in person? I suppose she managed to surround them with 'the white man's burden' story which she herself took seriously and brought us up on. Which of us don't romanticise otherwise brutal and nasty political realities? But the devoted Briton in an Indian regiment or the ICS or even Africa was the ideal. Her favourite young cousin was actually killed on the North West Frontier and I missed my first ball in Edinburgh. I hardly knew him myself, but had gallons of sympathetic grief for my mother and swallowed my own feelings about the ball. Probably I wouldn't have been allowed to stay late anyhow! I was only sixteen and not properly 'out'. But all this comes very fascinatingly into her own book, *Friends and Kindred*.

My mixed literary diet was reasonably uncensored. It was later on that I was forbidden to read various books, including the works of Anatole France and also *Madame Bovary*. Reading these (as I inevitably did) improved my French but was otherwise disappointing. I did however progress to Balzac's *Contes Drôlatiques*, not forbidden because not known about. Balzac, after all, was supposed to be a respectable writer and there was a complete edition bound in blue leather at Queen Anne's Gate where Uncle Richard had his town house. I do remember that I was considerably shocked by some of the stories, though I was sufficiently curious to go on struggling with their odd French, but they struck me as dreadfully anti-feminist and certainly put me off sex for some time.

But as a child what shocked was entirely different. For instance, I couldn't bear to look at the picture of Alice with the long neck in *Alice in Wonderland* and managed to turn the page quickly so that she couldn't get out. I devoured all the nature books, London and Seton Thompson, and wept over the deaths of Waab (I could still quote that) and the various other animals. If there were children's comics then they were strictly kept away, but I doubt if they had gone far down the age groups yet; rather later I had a Tintin-type picture-book: *Buster Brown and his dog Tige*; I was fascinated by the Americanisms in it. There was *Struwelpeter* which didn't stop me sucking my forefinger—nor did aloes for that matter. There were the *Jungle Books* in which I liked the verse best, and *Peter Rabbit*, though I don't remember any of the other Beatrix Potter books. There was *Little Black Sambo* whom I was delighted to re-meet more than half a century later as a hero figure in a Botswana nursery school. And there were *Flower Fairies*—how I loved those somewhat sentimental pictures! There were other and more genuine fairies in the Jacobs collections with the notes which of course I read. These fairy tales were first read aloud but not *Binnorie* or *Mr Fox*, which it was thought might frighten me. When I read them for myself later they didn't. That wasn't the kind of thing—! Do parents always guess wrong?

I never much cared for the more romantic series of fairytales edited by Andrew Lang in spite of their lovely pictures. Later on when I was eleven or twelve I told him I hadn't liked them and he didn't mind at all; these collections had just been a job. But he liked it enormously when I told him how much I treasured his poems and even quoted some of them to him. Hardly anyone had said anything nice to him about them (and they certainly were minor verse though at the time they rang my bell) but they were, so to speak, his favourite children.

Then there were the first Saga books and *Heroes of Asgard*, as well as a certain amount of perhaps inaccurate anthropology. But there was nothing like the variety of good illustrated popular science and history that there is now. There was also the reading aloud. My mother—Maya to both Boy and me—used to read almost every evening after tea and in this way we went through *The Idylls of the King* and much more Tennyson. I think she must have read very well and I enjoyed it enormously, but prose never quite so much, except for *The Water Babies* where some parts, for instance the descent from the moors into Vendale, are such magnificent Victorian purple patches that they are as memorable as verse. But here the moralities worried me, as in many other books, including most of George MacDonald, though I could treat the early or mid-Victorian moral tales for children with a remarkable degree of contempt and historical interest.

Much of this reading aloud was done while my mother was 'lying down'. I came to accept it as ordinary that ladies did a lot of lying down. That was what sofas were for. Presumably this was part of the routine of menstruation but of this I had no idea. All was completely hidden. I have a notion that at some point my mother had an early miscarriage. All I knew about birth control was that there was such a thing as the Malthusian capsule, presumably an early form of pessary. But this was only hinted at when, shortly before my marriage, my poor mother tried to tell me the facts of life. However, I was determined not to listen. I thought because I had kept guinea pigs for many years and understood Mendelian genetics as far as it had then gone, that I already knew everything.

Reading aloud must have gone right out. I read aloud to my children, and younger grandchildren still like being read aloud to when they are in bed. But I doubt if any right-minded modern child wants to be read to during TV time. Much of my own reading would certainly not have happened if there had been TV or for that matter radio. Even a gramophone was still something quite unusual; we never had one. Newspapers tended to be dull and without pictures, so we never had the awareness of the outside world which a modern child who uses newsprint and TV or radio intelligently would have. We were thrown back much more onto the area of our own imagination, which may or may not be a good thing.

At school we early got on to Macaulay, *The Revenge* and *Lays of Ancient Rome*. How idiotic that one remembers masses of this when things that would be valuable to remember are totally not there. And it is not as if Lordly Volaterrae or even the Forty Prophets were in any way relevant to my life! The multiplication tables should have been drummed in; I had them early. Twice was too easy for colours, but three times was yellow, four orange, five blue. After that they were sombre dark forest tones in which one was lost. Until ten again became clear. But why did I never learn them properly?

Dates elude me still though I am reasonably good on historical sequence and if I am working on a particular period I can manage. But I know where to look things up. That only comes with practice.

I was taught writing in a copy book with 'pot hooks and hangers', the clerkly curves which used thin or thick ink lines which one had to follow. This progressed to copying whole sentences right down a page. But it was dreadfully boring and curiously ink-spreading. One started with a broad-nibbed pen; a fine one would be for later. Fountain pens, still more biros, were very far away. Capital letters might be plain but in the diaries I still tend to make an ornate 'I', 'E' and 'T'.

I found the work in Form 1 of the Dragon School remarkably easy and pleasant and I loved our teacher, Miss Williams, who was small and bright and dark-haired. So I think did everyone else in the class, but how to express it? We were being taught about measures; to make it more fun we were told to guess how big various things were. 'How tall am I?' Miss Williams asked, and I answered 'Eight feet'. Of course I knew perfectly well that she wasn't eight feet, but surely she must want to be and it would give her pleasure if I told her that that was what she was! Alas, no, she was rather cross and told me I was stupid. And how could I explain that it was meant as a compliment?

I think we started Latin almost at once but for a year or two never got beyond the first declension which we all forgot during the holidays, though the early diaries constantly mention 'Doing Latin with Boy'. How long it seemed between one holiday and the next, and endless time till Christmas. One's birthday would never come round again!

The birthday parties were something to look forward to. I was All Saints, Boy was Guy Fawkes. Five years between us, but I liked his friends better than my own age group. We always had a bran pie; for weeks beforehand Maya and I tore up every scrap of coloured paper we could lay hands on and put it into bags until there was enough to fill a tin bath. Then the presents, well wrapped, were put in and a strong cover—oh, the blissful smell of that un-bleached calico—only to be cut open on the day. There was usually another bath where we ducked for apples, since it was also around Hallowe'en time, and I suppose fireworks in the garden for Guy Fawkes. These were lovely and non-lethal compared with today's. I loved holding them and only remember once being slightly scorched. But the main thing was the bran pie and the paper fight that followed, with Maya trying to keep it to one room with the door shut! That made even the tedious hair-brushing I had to put up with afterwards entirely worthwhile. Pleasantly reminding scraps of confettied paper could be found for weeks afterwards in corners and behind cushions.

I suppose we played games like general post, hunt-the-slipper, hide-and-seek, and almost always some of the singing and pulling games, Oranges and Lemons or Nuts in May. It wasn't till much later on at Carradale that I met Dusty Bluebells, Buy Me a Milk Cart, or the Farmer's in his Den. After we moved to Cherwell we started off with an hour or so of out-of-door hide-and-seek with long cross-field chases and dodgings. Tea was always memorable with birthday cake and jellies, crackers and candles. But it wasn't as much fun when Boy was away at Eton. His first year at Oxford he brought friends, including an Etonian friend, Mitch, who had been

Captain of Oppidans and who fell in love with his young sister. But that was far ahead.

For a long time it was mostly one's school friends. School absorbed us. After a term or two, or maybe a year at school, we were told that we were going to learn English grammar. I can't imagine what the mental process was, but it came to me very clearly that this would be in some way damaging and I was not going to touch it. I was quite right in a way; formal grammar would certainly have harmed me as a writer but I had not consciously known I was a writer at that time, nor would the amount of grammar we were likely to learn have been either here or there. A glance at the early diaries shows that I was in little need of it and had a very wide vocabulary. But I refused to learn any of it, which must have been annoying for my dear Miss Williams. However, I did well on the other bits, including as I have said, scripture.

I liked the smell of school, I liked hanging up my coat with the rest. Most of my time I was either the only girl at a boys' school or the only but one, and the other either much older or much younger. But I didn't know or understand other girls—I felt I was a boy who unfairly was not allowed to play rugger (and had no wish to play cricket). The only wretched thing was that when I started school I had also to start wearing black stockings which went right up under my button-below-the-knee knickers. How did they stay up? I think I must have had what was called a liberty bodice with long suspenders attached; I doubt if suspender design has changed very much in half a century. Apart from that I wore a blue serge skirt and a blue jersey, but I did at least have a school blazer with badge. I remember in my first term a boy approaching me with a tin and asking if I would like some bread and cheese. Not being allowed to eat cheese ('It wouldn't agree with you, dear') and supposing myself not to like it, I hesitated. But when he opened the tin it was hawthorn buds which I ate happily and still eat, though they seem rather tasteless now. I felt I was being admitted into the society. It was a nice feeling.

VII

It was True

The Chinnery Haldanes, our cousins at Gleneagles, were all more grown up. We drove over there along the narrow road that skirted the lower slopes of the Ochills with its verges crowded with flowers, the pale Scotch briars and below them banks of wild geranium and St John's wort. One didn't go too far with the carriage horses but one got to know the roads five or ten miles around fairly well. On a hill, any gentleman would get out and walk up, to save the horses; at last I made the point that I could always do this too. Once we got to Gleneagles and had got through the first minutes of polite conversation, there were rooms full of nice things, curiosities or family relics of one kind and another. A family had to have things to show to indoor visitors, just as there were points of interest in the policies for out-of-door ones, and after all, there was always a housemaid to dust them.

The burn was nice, though too tidy for damming; there was St Mungo's well; there was the lime avenue, carpeted in summer with honey-drunk bees; and there was our ruined ancestral castle. It wasn't until I was in my teens that I heard about my back-back-mother, Marjorie Lawson, the Star of Strathearn. My father discovered her in Lindsay and read the poem, which has some remarkably good lines, aloud, somewhat to Aunt Bay's disapproval, since it goes much further than most other poems between then and now. In fact I can't think how this happened: Uffer—my father—was normally rather puritanical in his outlook; I suppose, as Marjorie Lawson was one of the family, whose Haldane husband had been killed at Flodden, it was different. The poem, in fifteenth-century Scots, is probably the first authentic account of a real-life love affair and reads aloud well to this day.

The broken walls of the castle where she played hostess to Squyre Meldrum were fun to climb about and occasionally some-one found an ancient bottle, the main thing my ancestors seem to have left. There is also the tiny chapel and graveyard where many of my Haldane forbears are lying or have had their ashes scattered, as my father's were thirty years later, when, after a non-religious cremation in London, organised by my brother and me, the Auchterarder people had gathered to sing *I to the Hills* over his ashes. Aunt Bay and I had been considerably upset when my brother, in the full tide of Communist conversion, refused on principle to have a sleeper and had insisted on taking the ashes up Third Class, in the luggage rack, having ticked me off for being bourgeois, or something of the kind. Irreligious as I am, after that I appreciated *I to the Hills*. The graveyard is in the mouth of Gleneagles with the great slopes of the Ochills, grass and scree and grass again, rising at either side.

Granniema, when it came to her turn, gave instructions for her own funeral: she had reached a hundred and it would have been something of a let-down to live on to a hundred and one. Luckily I guessed that she would like richly coloured flowers and I brought up an armful of red roses and blue iris. The brown farm horses were harnessed to the big red-wheeled lorry with her coffin; all along the ridge of Auchterarder the blinds were down in houses and shops. We and the coffin caught the Edinburgh train at Gleneagles, then Crieff Junction, a special coach I expect, to take us in for the funeral. My father was at that time much involved in a theory about heat engines; also he had somehow got a top hat two sizes too small for him; both these preoccupations kept him reasonably insulated, while I myself was thinking out a poem. I had borrowed a black coat, but it had a blue lining and I needed to clutch this when the time came for all of us descendants to take the cords of the coffin, while the traffic was held up for us across the Lothian Road outside the Caledonian Station.

But that was far ahead. However, we had constant family funerals during my childhood. My mother took the conventions seriously; she was seldom out of half mourning—grey to mauve—

but women did not go much to funerals in those days. My father used to go and clearly found these occasions quite enjoyable. As we say in Scotland, there's nothing beats a good-going funeral.

I did have one heart-tearing experience of the death of a rather older schoolmate; he had played Mercutio in *Romeo and Juliet* and died of pneumonia. Half the school went to his funeral and wept; we kept remembering his lines. I had presumably been a very small attendant on Lady Capulet.

This was how I started Shakespeare. At six I held the train of the French Princess in *Henry V* and, I'm afraid, wetted my drawers with the excitement of the stage. Occasionally this happened at night; one woke up and there it was, warm and wet, and one would be found out. I don't think I was punished but I was certainly filled with shame. I wore white flannel pyjamas with a buttoned flap behind; I did so want proper boys' pyjamas! My dressing-gowns were thick and grey, inherited from cousins, and I didn't much like them either.

There was always one term which, as soon as one got at all far up in the school, was coloured with Shakespeare. I was never worried by the difficult words; they were swept along in the torrent. It certainly made all the difference seeing and hearing it on stage, even without much illusion, after seeing one's brother and his friends making wooden swords and shields. Only the principal characters had proper stage swords and they didn't cut, as everyone soon found out. My mother didn't like the idea of my wearing hired clothes—germs or moral contagion?—so I was often inappropriately dressed. Later, in my last preparatory school year, as Portia, I was lent a Doctor of Science gown from a small physiologist. I had so much wanted to act Lady Macbeth, but I was too short and round and probably not a good enough actor.

At this point a dreadful thing happened. The Prince of Morocco in the casket scene was a boy with a brown skin—was he Indian or perhaps from the Middle East? My mother objected to the mere notion of a mixed marriage and complained to the school. I don't remember what happened, only that it was one more of those social rules which were invisible until one tripped over them, although there was always the assumption that there were things which a lady, however young, should somehow know by instinct. I could understand, when I aided and abetted some gang which was attacking my brother, that I had committed the worst kind of treachery only for the fun of seeing a fight; but these other rules and expectations of one certain kind of conduct rather than another, were very puzzling and became more so as I grew up into a teenager or, as the word was then, a flapper. This referred of course to our hair which was long and worn down our backs, usually with a large bow, and no doubt flapped. Putting one's hair up was the rite of passage to adulthood and a very difficult and boring process it was for ham-handed ones like myself; we were not encouraged to think that it might make one look more attractive or that it would give one any more privileges. Rather the opposite: yet another and stricter code of behaviour.

I find a photograph of myself as Portia. There appears to be no attempt to make me look Elizabethan, though the other actors would have tried their best. Jimmy de la Hey was worried about his very non-Semitic nose as Shylock, but I think he managed to achieve a beard. But I am just a nice little girl in fancy dress. However, I always looked avidly for the review in the *Draconian* and usually felt they hadn't done me justice. We were all very sympathetic with Shylock; I think I was particularly pro-Jewish because of my godfather, Professor Alexander of Manchester who looked like the very best kind of Old Testament prophet. I called him godfather because this was our relationship, but in strict fact he was a Jew and I an unbaptised bairn. We grew increasingly fond of one another; later on I told him about the people I was in love with, and as he never remembered their unimportant names, it was quite all right when I switched.

But this was far on from Portia and the quality of mercy. I learnt by heart easily and now have that bit of my memory choked like a rubbish dump with anything from Shakespeare to Yipiaddy. How grown-up, how sophisticated one felt when bawling those very innocent music-hall songs! But Portia in her long dress—however one seems to have moved around quite easily in skirts

59

which now appear incredibly hampering, especially for the young. In my last year at school we had work squads in our large top English form and the squad leader had to keep up the squad marks in whatever way seemed likely to succeed. I remember chasing two irritating, mark-losing members of my squad round and round the hall with a fencing foil (fencing was thought to be going to make me graceful, but never did). However, whether or not hampered by a knee-length school skirt, I don't think I ever caught them, which was perhaps just as well.

During my time there the Dragon School only staged Shakespeare. Gilbert and Sullivan came later. The arts in general were somewhat marginal and things like drawing and painting taught in such a way as to put one off for life. Shading, right to left—or was it left to right?—on cones or cylinders, no nonsense about drawing out of one's head. No lovely poster colours, only unsatisfactory pale water colours and if we put it on too thick that was wasteful. But of course the margins of all one's school books were copiously decorated, especially the Latin grammar (though I never drew on or knowingly messed up a proper book). It was mostly pen or pencil, though we did sometimes have crayons which melted dramatically when put onto the radiators. All schools must have been a lot messier in the good old days of inkwells in the desks, not to speak of ink-soaked paper pellets used as missiles. Inkwells in desks came in handy. I had a share in a grass snake once (as well as a share in an unsatisfactory dormouse that died before it woke); there was quite a sensation in class when the grass snake put its head out of the ink hole. The desks of course were copiously carved with initials and the soft wood gouged out for railways. Some were good enough to run small marbles along. There is a story which seems well authenticated, though I don't actually remember it, to the effect that my brother and I, in VI B, had both broken silence with the same remark: 'Please, sir, the ink has gone and spilt itself.'

Music was very definitely an 'extra' at school, apart from our thunderous opening hymn. There was never anything in the nature of musical encouragement, nor did I get it at home. But at one time

—I suppose when I was seven or eight—I went to a house further along St Margaret's Road and 'did' piano. Most of it was five finger exercises and very tedious; all that remains for me is the formal ability to read staff, though not to imagine it in my head as sound. In pre-radio days, but after the death of folk music, there was no musical background to living unless specially provided, and this seldom happened in our household, though I think my father whistled in tune, things like 'Robin Adair'. My mother gave me the impression that music and drawing were accomplishments which it was as well to have, but basically a waste of serious time.

I think I had dancing classes as an extra at the Oxford High School in a large hall with windows looking out on Banbury Road. I cannot remember liking them but I did like the school dance which happened once a year, because of the pattern dances: Lancers and Sir Roger, and still more because of the triumphant final rag of the Gallop when one careered down the hall, bumping as many others as possible and quite likely ending in a joyful heap at the far end.

The school classes I remember most clearly were the best and worst taught. The old Skipper, Lynam, our Headmaster, was a marvellous teacher and encourager in all English subjects. He was usually the first recipient of our attempts at 'creative writing'— poems, plays and even essays. He would ask a chosen few to tea with hot buttered toast and anchovy paste, as well as still-warm fudge, and we had what appeared to be immensely intellectual conversation, touching many subjects. Presumably the real thing he did was to treat us as equals, something we didn't get at home. But those tea parties must have been in my last year, at eleven or twelve, when most of the boys were working for Eton and Winchester scholarships, or failing that the lesser 'public' schools, and we had to write Latin verses. This was a bore, apart from the fact that it suddenly came to me that Ovid had shared certain of my experiences: '*Excutior somno, simulacraque noctis adoro*.' Yes, *simulacra*, those were the nightmares, that was the word for them, the things that forced one to fear and worship.

The Skipper was best. The worst was one term or perhaps more of maths teaching which was so bad that it had a lifelong crippling effect. I remember the name and initials of this teacher. He never explained or helped if we really tried to understand but couldn't. He simply taught rules which were as incomprehensible as the social rules which gave me so much trouble. 'Minus times minus is always plus; the reason for this we need not discuss.' Later, from a simple graph I understood in a moment. But the scars stayed.

When I first came, the school was half its present size, with only a few boarders in the house at the bottom of Bardwell Road. This had a lower room where those whose parents ordained such things had glasses of hot milk with skin on them and a Marie biscuit. Oh, how hateful that milk was! Below the school buildings there were wild hawthorn hedges at both sides of the playing fields where we hollowed ourselves out forts and lived the delightful gang life of school children, jabbering away to one another, climbing and tumbling, making up oaths and rhymes. But what was it we talked about? That escapes me entirely, except that it had something to do with status.

There are, however, a couple of references in the diaries to the forts we made in the ditches on the site of the new house. In the 1906 diary, N. Haldane, aged eight, Form 2, says, 'H. Rambaut came to dinner & imediately after that, Jack and Rodney Slessor came and we all went to the site. We found that the ditch was lovely for a fort. Then we put down the rules in Jack Slessor's pocket book, and we decided who was to be chief. I was queen & Rambaut was to be king consort, Jack Slessor was prime minister, Rodney was not anyone particular. After that we broke down the boughs & made at one end a kind of barrier of sticks and stones. Then we had tea & after that we went to where there is a shed & got a broom & we swept out the fort.' After which much time was spent jumping into gravel holes. A few days later Jack Slessor had a party. 'We went to his fort; it looked lovely, with flags hanging on string across it. We then took our weapons—Slessor took an old rusty toy gun, Rambaut took the banner of the fort, De La Hey took a stick, I took a broom & Rodney took another stick. We marched about & then Rodney fetched a dusting sheet & we went to the pavillion of the cricket field . . .' Here the dusting sheet was spread, there were sentries and a 'snoring competition' and after tea we got the weapons and attacked the nursery and made another camp. Later on, at the site, after someone had caught a dragonfly 'I made a law: there shall be no murder comited in my premises, upon man, nor beast, nor bird, nor fish, nor insect.'

In my last years at school there was much building and enlarging and cutting of the wild hedges and climbing trees with the well-worn hand holes and interesting fallen logs. But I suppose the main hall remains much as it was, though no doubt without the racks of dumbbells and Indian clubs which we used for drill—Indian clubs were great fun to swing, though sometimes we knocked one another on the head with them. 'Sergeant' used to take school drill and taught us some gymnastics, including very enjoyable things like upside-down swinging on the rings.

The western sun streamed into the hall through the large windows at the back of the wooden stage with the piano and the parallel bars standing in front. Here we played our seasonal games, especially in winter when it was cold for playing outside. Conkers gave way to marbles, to whipping tops or sometimes to stilts. But there were always games of He and touch wood going on, with the flee-ers and catchers darting through the rest or jumping over them. Between lessons there was always five minutes of violent play activity allowed, and again at the end of the afternoon. I was bad with tops but fairly good with the various games of marbles and the arguments they gave rise to. Some of the games were simply rolling your marble into little pyramids of the other side's or getting them through bridges cut out of a bit of plank. I got very fond of some of the glassies and there was a terrible thrill in putting them into danger of being captured.

There was one evening in the hall of late golden light and the unmistakable noise of the marbles ringing and rolling on the wood floor, hundreds of them, and the voices of my school mates, all in a state of pleasure and purposeful activity, and I was running round, not even, I think, playing He, just swinging up onto the platform off the parallel bars. I looked down the hall and I thought in a flash, I will remember this all my life. It came to me as certainty on one running foot before the other touched ground, and then I was off again. But it was true.

VIII

Sennen Cove

My father was asked to deal with ankylostomiasis in the Cornish tin mines. He went down to Cornwall and the family followed, looking for a place to stay during the Easter holidays. We got to Penzance and either then or later I went along the causeway to St Michael's Mount and climbed up through more daffodils than I had ever seen. Then from Penzance we started out in a carriage and somehow arrived at Sennen Cove and Mrs Pender looking out of the front window in her stays. At that time the Cove was very much a place on its own with only a few families so that most people were known by their nicknames. Mrs Pender took in a few lodgers and kept the Ship Inn where the fishermen went whenever they had enough money for a glass of beer, which wasn't always. I am quite sure she knew the state of the finances of every family in the village and sent the man home if she knew the wife needed the money more than he did.

Here we went back and back every Easter holidays; I couldn't have borne to go anywhere else. The house had, I think, two small sitting-rooms and the kitchen below and four bedrooms above, one so tiny it just held a bed, no more. If the rooms seemed small to me at five they must indeed have been small; one had to squeeze round the square dining-room table to get into the window bay, or else dive under the table cloth. On the walls there were painted glass rolling pins and the occasional text. There was an earth closet outside; lighting was by lamps. My mother's class prejudices didn't happen at the Cove; these were fishermen and they were different. Mrs Pender spread warmth. I spent a lot of time in the kitchen, helping or hindering her in skimming the Cornish cream from the

65

setting pan on the side of the range or kneading the dough for 'little mansions', small crusty loaves eaten hot with salt butter or cream. When the grey mullet came in we always had mullet baked in milk.

Mullet and pilchards were the money-earners. Watchers from the cliffs and high dunes saw the shoals and signalled to the pair of boats which brought in the two ends of the big seine net; it was all hard rowing. Then every man in the place came down to haul; if it was a big catch it would be all they could do to get it in. At last the bag was in, the fish leaping and dying; they were put into piles as equal as possible, a great circle and a fish left on each pile as the men went round, with half or quarter shares for widows and orphans of fishermen, this being before the days of social insurance. Then everyone, the rowers, the haulers, the watchers, threw some kind of token into a basket, a knotted handkerchief, a root, a piece of seaweed; someone was blindfolded and led round, throwing down a token for every pile. How proud I was when Boy, who had been hauling, got a quarter share! Soon enough I began to feel with the fishermen their hatred and distrust of the middleman, the dealer with his donkey cart who bought their fish and gave them so little for it.

Only a donkey cart, a jingle, could get down to the Cove, slowed on the steepness of the road. That first day we must have left the carriage up at Sennen and walked. Probably I had to be carried up. From that time on, year after year, we went down to Cornwall at Easter and I would know that somewhere in the luggage would be the big cardboard Easter eggs and sometimes Easter presents from other people, including once a cardboard fish full of sweeties with a flap in his side shut by an elastic so that it sounded slock, slock, as one let it spring back: the slock-fish, I kept it for many years. I think we took the night train to the west, for I know once I was sick in the dark. We crossed the bridge from despised Devon to adored Cornwall. I could read the station names: Camborne and now we were near the tin mines where Uffer was working, seeing how his advice was being taken: Dolcoath, West Kitty, Levant, the immensely romantic names of the mines. Then the hill to Gwinnear

Road—have I got the name right?—and the sea, turquoise blue between red cliffs and tunnels, at last Penzance and the drive to Sennen and at once, at once, down to the beach to see if it was altered. There were the two breakwaters of rock and tremendous, squared timbers thick with barnacles, where the Atlantic cable went in, and then a group of great granite rocks with a perpetual spray-fed triangular pool in the middle of one. But how big? Sometimes the sand was washed high round them, sometimes dragged away by the spring tides. But were the rocks five or ten feet high? I suppose they are there still, but how polluted, what would I find? Beyond were other rocks and a series of interlinked rock pools fringed golden brown with seaweed, bottomed with delicate wavering sand patterns. My practised eye looked for dam sites. All that fine sand far along the bay was utterly washed and smoothed, never an oil spot, but along every tide mark an infinity of tiny lovely shells.

Boy had a proper shell collection in a glass-fronted cupboard, his museum; there they were, on cotton wool, in match boxes, labelled with their Latin names. Later on, when I too had a glass-fronted museum, it was full of much more heterogeneous things, though I certainly labelled most of them. There was for instance a stuffed lizard and a kiwi skin, smelling strongly of pepper. Who wants a kiwi skin? I did. And then, later on, suddenly one doesn't.

I collected the shells for their beauty and fragility and especially I loved the small, magic, spotted cowries. Those waves that brought them were the great Atlantic rollers coming strongly, beating themselves out on the sand, so that the air everywhere and especially at high tide was full of a salt luminous mist. The wash and foam of the waves sucked round my ankles and knees; I ran towards them and back; I could not swim, though now, dreaming of Sennen, I often swim or struggle to swim in the great crests and hollows. I was not supposed to get wet through more than once a day, though I can't think why I didn't get wetter, for I wore a school skirt and jersey or a cotton smock to below my knees and usually a hat of some kind, probably a tammy with a toorie on the top where the knitting was held in. Almost everyone wore a hat then. On sunny days my mother wore a straw boater, hatpinned through to a curler in her short hair. For best she had a boater with cherries on it. Boy wore a school cap; my father wore a tweed one and, usually at Sennen, tweed knickerbockers and thick woollen stockings. For years I had a wooden spade, then was promoted to a metal one; immense activity went on all the time. One never walked when one could run. We weren't supposed to play on the rocks in front of the single row of cottages; this was where everything was chucked out and it was probably mucky, though a strong high tide washed everything away. I can't remember the beach or the further rocks ever being dirty, as we know dirt on beaches now.

There was a broken bit on the way down to the beach which was crammed with mesembryanthemums, though we only saw them in flower if we stayed late. But there were sea pinks and scurvy grass with its uncomplicated sweet smell which mixed with the smell of perpetual spray. Behind the beach were long bare sand dunes and marram grass and nobody there. At the far end a small stream edged through the sand and down. Beyond, there was a path up to the cliff tops and along to Genver, the next beach; in later years I followed it on towards the Lizard, again never meeting a soul. On the way there was a small field where someone was grow-ing narcissi for the early London market; there were stone dykes and stiles of upright stones which I was soon big enough to climb by myself. I liked to run along the sheep path at the very edge of the cliff. At this side of Sennen the cliffs were low and climbable; some-times one had to climb if one had tried to walk round from Genver across the rocks and the tide caught one. But at the Land's End side there were tremendous sheer cliffs and the sea boiling on half-submerged rocks far below.

Here too what I liked best was climbing out onto ledges where I could look down on the heaving, creaming waves. It makes my head swing even to think of it now and Maya clearly showed considerable moral courage in letting me do it. But I wasn't bothered by heights until suddenly in my teens that came on me. I thought I would cure it by walking round the slightly sloping parapet of the labora-tory where I was learning as a young Home Student. But when I had made the round I was worse than before. My father didn't like cliff tops and fussed at Boy and me, but luckily was quite without vertigo feelings underground (or in the dark) so that it didn't interfere with his mining activities.

He took Jack to Dolcoath mine and I was very jealous, but probably, at seven or eight, I couldn't have managed the rhythmical stepping on and off a man-engine, the stepped beam going up and down a shaft where the miners clambered in and out of the tin mines.

There is an early letter from my father to Jack, who must have been about ten at the time. He had been down Levant, a very hot mine, and said it had taken three-quarters of an hour to get up or down on the man-engine, being careful to keep to the middle of the step; he ends, 'I think I am going to dream about it all tonight.' They went deep and lost their way in old workings before the mine manager discovered a way out. At that time his temperature was 103. These mines were damp and ill-ventilated, but it appears that they had got to grips with the ankylostomiasis problem, largely through better sanitation. All through the letter, Jack is written to as a fellow scientist.

But there were still a few mines worked from adits, tunnels in the cliff face. Maya and I went into one of them; the red stained water trickled past our feet and the sound of the waves coming in and crashing on the rocks far below the mouth of the adit made a chill, frighteningly enlarged echo.

There were always two or three books for me to read on wet days on holiday and I had to spin them out. Hardbacks of course, and always with pictures. *Captains Courageous* was wonderful to read at Sennen within sound of the sea. So were the Marryats, though the moralising always made me a little uncomfortable. The Nesbits were beginning to come out and one looked forward passionately to the next. There was one at least every two years, but Maya somewhat disapproved of *The Railway Children* where the heroine actually kisses a porter. At this stage I began deliberately identifying, with Alice among the Wouldbegoods and with Anthea in the other family, though I was perhaps more Jane-like. I saw the older boys like my own Boy.

There were holidays tasks for Easter and summer, mostly, apart from the summer diaries, required reading. Certainly *Ivanhoe* and *Quentin Durward*, of which I remember nothing. Some Dickens, probably *A Tale of Two Cities* and *Oliver Twist*. Both these have vanished as well, though I had to pull out *Oliver Twist* again sixty years later in order to help teach it to an English class in Botswana. Here I was struck by its remarkable inapplicability as a school book; in fact I had to spend most of the time telling the class that it was no use learning Dickensian slang to make easier conversation with an Englishman, nor did they have to fear having to eat oysters if they ever came overseas.

At one point—I suppose I was eleven or twelve—Jack tried to get me to read *The Pickwick Papers* which he himself much enjoyed. But I never could like them nor, until many decades later, *Jorrocks*. I think we must have had *Treasure Island* or *Kidnapped* as a holiday task and I never liked them either, though I lapped up plenty more of Stevenson, especially the poetry and the fables and for that matter *Catriona*. Perhaps it was simply that these were set books which put me against them? How universal is that? I see from the diaries that Jack was reading *Gulliver's Travels* aloud to me at five. It might have been his holiday task but I don't think I got much out of it. Isn't it a little hard on Swift to have one bit of his great morality work presented as a children's book?

I read some early Sherlock Holmes but found *The Hound of the Baskervilles* very frightening, and indeed the whole business of fear and capture. I've always been to some extent on the murderer's side so thrillers are not for me. But they had barely started then, though I remember later on a grown-up conversation with Uncle Richard praising *Trent's Last Case*. There was little in the way of what is now called the teenage novel and which in general means a story written straight, in the sense that it has a recognisable beginning, middle and end (which should be fairly happy and conclusive) and without a predominant motive of sex, though the present trendy ones have real-life incidents such as rape, pregnancy, incest and preferably something about racial conflict in which the whites are normally the villains.

This meant that I read a few children's books like *Holiday House*, which had 'morals', as indeed the Nesbits have, though less obviously, and as most books written by socially conscious authors for whatever age group must have. But much was adult, including a lot of exploration books and of course bloodthirsty *Pilgrim's Progress* and *The Holy War*. This led to a lifelong dislike of marmalade since I was taken on a school expedition to Cooper's Oxford marmalade factory and convinced myself that the boiling cauldrons were full of martyrs. Or perhaps I disliked marmalade anyhow and was looking for an excuse not to eat it?

Most years we made an expedition from Sennen to a garden at or beyond St Just where I was told I could pick as many flowers as I wanted; afterwards we sent them off in shoe boxes to friends in Oxford or London; there were fewer flower shops then and better parcel posts. This garden had darkly shining hedges, probably of camellia, and below them daffodils and narcissi so thick that no picking made any difference, hyacinths, early tulips, grape hyacinths, huge umbels of polyanthus primroses, oxlips, and snowflakes, periwinkles; I swung with the bees in the thick scent, close to the texture of the petals. I think we went to other houses, though much later to Eagles' Nest, on my one disconcerting adult visit to Sennen, when I was interested in talking League of Nations politics with Will Arnold-Forster and barely noticed a small boy stalking off into the distance: and coming back from it much, much later, to be my son-in-law.

There were other flowers. Behind Mrs Pender's house a steep path wriggled up the hill towards Sennen Churchtown. There was a great boulder overhanging me and the path, with a trickle of wet through moss and hartstongue fern, and below, under one's delighted eyes, damp silk-smooth violets and furry primroses. The path eased off into a field of daisies, thousands of them and the sweet April smell as one climbed the stone dyke. Near the cliffs there were creeping willows and blue squills and, in the last year or two when I was becoming a passable field botanist, some rarish bog plants.

Most of Cornwall was Methodist, needing a strong religion to tide them over their troubles. (To quote from a sermon, contrasting the welcome for the lax congregation compared with that prepared for the Minister himself: 'Well done, thou good and faithful servant, M. J. Thomas of St Just!') There was a Mission Hall of tarred wood at Sennen. All kept the Sabbath. Once a fisherman with a sick wife, so that money was desperately needed for doctor and medicine, fished on a Sunday and sold his catch. Nobody would speak to him until my father put it to Mrs Pender that he must be forgiven as, for him, it was a work of necessity, and then he and my mother, who also was much liked and respected, went round the Cove, persuading people that he must be taken back. My father did some doctoring himself; these were the days before the Health Service when everything had to be paid for—or begged—and a long illness could cripple a family.

There was little in the way of amusement for the Cove, other than beer: no cinema, no radio. Almost every year we thought up some kind of entertainment, held perhaps in the Mission Hall, which usually centred on our Magic Lantern (also much liked at children's parties at home). This must have worked from an oil burner and magnifying glass. We had coloured slides on which you pulled a lever and changed something, so that a man hammered or shot a tiger, or a dog jumped out of a box; on the nursery rhyme slides there was first Miss Muffet, then (to cheers) the great spider on the next slide. There were also educational slides of foreign countries or British soldiers in acts of gallantry. The show always began with the Flag (a hand-coloured slide of the Union Jack) and ended with the King. And how the audience enjoyed it! Boy and I also thought up tricks like magic writing with lemon juice and there were little presents of striped sweets for the children which I had helped Maya to put into screws of paper folded down. Yet there is a curious contrast with this in Jack's 1903 diary where he goes to 'a kids' party at Strathallon' where there was a cinematograph 'including a coloured film'. Not really a colour film, but perhaps some kind of coloured cartoon? I wonder.

We were down at the harbour often enough, I perhaps carried there by Robbie Pender, blue-eyed and blue-jerseyed, with whom I was in love. I could reach up and just touch his gold ear-rings. The spoken language still used thou and thee; children were childer. It was pleasant on the ear. There were two breakwaters, enclosing arms for the fishing boats; it was exciting to watch them coming home under sail or oars with a gale coming up, hanging back for a wave and then plunging in between the breakwaters on the crest. Once I was taken down at night to see the lifeboat, of which the Cove was so justly proud, launched for a rescue. Every week or fortnight a boat went out to the Longships lighthouse. I was thrown from the tossing boat into arms waiting to catch me on the great rock; there was heaving green water below but nothing to fear. Boy and I showed the lighthouse crew how to feed sea anemones which they had never thought of as living animals, and we explored the lighthouse and the rocks.

Once my mother and I went to the Brizens, the great twin rocks that one saw far out across the bay, the first womenfolk, they said, to land and come off alive, for a ship-wrecked woman had once died there. Every cleft was full of birds' nests, though the species kept well apart. One could stroke the handsome Welsh parrots, the puffins, while they waited on their nests. But the black, snake-necked shags kept strictly to their own part of the rock and jagged with their beaks at anyone who tried to touch them. Cowloe, the skerry just beyond the harbour, was a huge—but how huge was it really?—low-tide island, a whole new area to explore with bigger sea anemones and darting rock fish. One could just wade out through great snaking fronds of kelp, at least Boy did, for one might slip and he could swim.

Some day I supposed I would swim, because in summer I was taken down to the Rhea bathing place in a Cherwell backwater, changed into a musty blue serge bathing dress coming to the elbows and below the knees, with a braided collar which was supposed to hide the figure when one started to have one. I hated being pulled along at the end of a pole and the shallow end was muddy. However I had been promised a canoe of my own, when I could swim, though I don't think I got it till I was eleven or twelve, after my broken leg. By that time I had swum my test (July, 1909) and went

73

swimming whenever and wherever I possibly could, though this was somewhat restricted because the Thames Conservancy in theory did not allow mixed bathing after 8 a.m. However nobody could prevent me falling out of my canoe on a nice sunny afternoon whenever it seemed appropriate.

But not swimming didn't seem to matter at Sennen. Sometimes when my mother and I were sitting out on the cable breakwaters, a wave would break green over our heads and we clung onto the stones. But I was never afraid.

In those days one was always making dares—run round the rocks in the perilous gap between wave and wave, jump, guess, swing, climb! Up to a certain age this goes on. In the thirties Agnes Miller Parker and I swam like porpoises in dangerous waves in the Canaries; I just got back to land out of the sucking surf at Zaraus. But today, at Kovalum, I dodge the crashing breakers, I don't want to get knocked down and hurt. Sadly, one can no longer trust one's nerves and muscles; the balance that made rock-jumping such fun has gone; one becomes less friends with one's body. At last, perhaps, one only remains on terms with certain bits of the brain.

Memory, going back, halts again in 1934, when I went back with my young sons. Mrs Pender was still there then, and so was much of Sennen, though the road had been repaired and there were more visitors' cottages. But the sand was still clean and the great tides only brought in the age-old things of the sea. I wrote this poem then, about Genver.

I am going to find cowries and fan-shells
On a far beach,
Where the sea at half tide breaks, breaks from the clean sands,
Where the spray, blowing and blowing inland, salts the blurred
    cliff,
Blurring and dumbing the sun-light,
As the continual wide rushing of the waves dumbs
Voices of women or sea-birds.

Do I know danger of quicksands, of the footsteps going one way
   only?
On the cliffs Spring is delayed; the heart checks, daunted.
How then shall flower the stonecrop, how the wind-rocked sea pink?
The cave echoes the wind and waves, will echo tonight
When the rushing purposeless high tide has licked my footsteps out,
Flattening the pale sand for dawn.

But I am finding cowries and fan-shells
On the far beach,
Which is beyond the beaches I know or remember or have imagined.
But the beach will cease to have hold of me and the long pounding
   of the waves
Will beat faintly across damp acres of air, and I shall tread
Stonecrop and cliff turf, with my hands closed upon
Cowries and lovely fan-shells.

IX

Surgery

That broken leg after which I learned to swim was not the first accident in the family. The worst was Boy's fractured skull, when he fell off the step of Uffer's bicycle. If it had killed him my parents would both have been heart-broken, but my mother would always have put the blame onto my father—she had said Boy wasn't to ride on the step, and now— But he survived a fracture of the base of the skull, beginning to ask questions about it the moment he was conscious. Absolute quiet in the home, where he lay in bed in the the spare room, was essential. I understood. For him, I fell all the way down a flight of steps and never squeaked.

I myself had an ordinary concussion, being taken out for a walk with my nurse, tumbling and hitting my head on a road crossing. I was only unconscious for a short time, coming to in a chemist's shop, being given something nasty in a glass. We walked back along Woodstock Road and I began to cry with the pain in my head. The one thing that is clear about this is being scolded by my mother for crying in the street, a thing strictly forbidden in the code of courage. My nurse intervened. I was in bed for several days and found the quality of my life subtly changed from before the unconsciousness, which was in some sense a dream period, to after it which was either now and real or a different dream. This wore off, only returning much later, more violently and nastily, when I took mescalin as an experimental guinea pig and felt that the experience had shifted me, so to speak, on base, turning my whole consciousness at an angle to its own past. This took years to wear off completely.

The broken leg was something else again. It must have been in 1905 or 1906 that the Oxford pageant took place; pageants were being held all over England about then, especially in towns with a colourful history. I longed to be in it and was asked for, but it was thought better not. Why? My health, with the TB threat? Or was it that this affair was as much town as gown and I might meet unsuitable people? Instead I was promised a pony, which I didn't much want, though I understood that it was something little girls ought to want.

We were then moving from St Margaret's Road to the large and ugly house, Cherwell, at the bottom of Linton Road. It had fields and hedges, was almost an estate, and was no doubt suitable for riding. But I had to learn to ride side-saddle in a long riding habit. By that time there was a coachman, Crackston, ex-army, rather a brutal man, I think, and not a good teacher.

However, a certain physical toughness was *de rigueur*. My brother was sent to Eton with a broken arm still in a sling and was much teased and tortured by his savage contemporaries for a year and a half. College was a barbarous place and the Master in College had little control over traditional bullying, was probably scared himself. Two seniors for whom Jack fagged, Geoff Wardley and Julian Huxley, saved him to some extent, but he begged to be taken away. When he told me in the next holidays what they had done to him, I tried to get my parents to take his side, but they apparently paid no attention. How could they have taken a son away from Eton and sent him, say, to Radley? The only clue is one letter home, desperately worried because the ten shillings for his fare home had unaccountably disappeared from his 'burry'. Clearly he counted on that leave. He is doing well at school, but 'I am rather sick with people and things in general. Goodbye.'

Certainly he enjoyed Eton later on when he could no longer be bullied, but had made his mark intellectually and quite enjoyed his activities as a wet-bob. But was it something which left permanent scars? I enjoyed Eton too, later on as a visitor, and was once smuggled in and hidden in a cupboard in College during a tremendous battle with Oppidans; the missiles I remember were lump sugar and tin baths. But again, what kind of people is that supposed to produce? I think one knows.

As far as I was concerned, the riding lessons scared me stiff. I was always falling off, never managing to develop the balance or the muscles for side-saddle, and it often hurt a lot, though I didn't cry. I had to go on with them. I don't think Nopy, the pony, was well trained; she was rather an odd creature, with a habit of galloping round and biting off the heads of the ducks. I had a safety stirrup, but in one fall it didn't work. Crackston couldn't catch the pony, which galloped off, dragging and kicking me. I knew I had broken my leg but didn't realise I had also broken one or two ribs and dislocated my neck. It was my tenth birthday.

It was a compound, comminuted fracture of the femur. I dropped out of an entirely new dimension of pain into chloroformed dark, woke immobilised and sick, my head held in place by hard pillows. I was at home, in the big spare room and perhaps safer than at any hospital of that period. One must remember that treatment at home was still usual until at least the middle thirties; my children and husband all had tonsils out at home. One son had an appendix out. The well-scrubbed kitchen table, mackintosh-sheeted, was usual. Nurses would come in, but servants cleared up.

The surgeon came in almost every day, adjusted the weights on my broken leg and tried to help where the cast chafed; his breath smelt of whisky but he often had a small orchid in his buttonhole—he grew them—and would usually give it to me. He had to have a good look at the top of the cast on my femur, but my mother in the curious interests of decency, always hid my very immature sexual parts with a large handkerchief. Perhaps also a surgeon was still considered a social inferior, nearer a barber than a doctor. I don't know what analgesics were in use; I remember none. But perhaps they existed.

An X-ray machine was brought to the house to see what was happening to the broken bone. This must have been fairly early in X-ray development. It took a long, painful time, with the leg being moved and nobody scolding me for crying. Perhaps they X-rayed my neck too. Nobody then thought of screening X-ray operations; the damage was yet to become apparent.

I had a succession of nurses whom I hated, who frightened me in dreams. I fell from one nightmare into another. The leg was re-set under open ether; one struggled against the stinking suffocation. I was extremely sick afterwards, but was given some kind of opium mixture which cured this. Two months went by. At last the weights were taken off; the ribs and dislocation had mended. I was carried down. There was a Christmas tree in the hall and the branches were swung over me with the lovely once-a-year spruce smell so that I could decorate them with tinsel and beautiful birds with spun glass tails.

But in the end the cast was taken off; some of it had stuck and the skin was pulled off too; I still carry the scars. The surgeon tried to bend the knee. It had been immobilised for three months or so and of course was almost a hundred per cent stiff. So I must do exercises, and now I was in the hands of a physiotherapist, Jo Phelps, who bicycled in every day. She must have been very good; in spite of the fact that it hurt like mad, I liked her enormously. But little movement returned. I remember the surgeon saying to my mother: 'This child will never run again', and I made up my mind that whatever I had to stand, this was not going to be my future.

They decided to break the adhesions under an anaesthetic; this time it was nitrous oxide without oxygen, a new kind of suffocation and plunging into a pit of diminishing lights. One struggled and died. Coming to, the knee hurt enormously, but the exercises went better. I was left with an oddly misshapen right patella which, however, gave no trouble for over sixty years, and one leg two inches shorter than the other. They were always measuring them and there was talk of a boot. But I made this difference up on a laterally tilted pelvis which made childbirth slightly more difficult. But for weeks and weeks I went on with the exercises every day, the knee being bent over a table at first, then kneeling or otherwise getting flexure. I could walk. At last I could run. Clearly some bad effects went on. For many years afterwards I was constantly spraining my ankles, both that of the broken leg and of the other, which took the extra strain. These were never bad sprains, but did land me with unpleasantly thick and misshapen ankles.

After the first few days of the accident I read and read, all sorts of books, or else I was read to. I didn't want to slip back at school, nor did I. But I read unexpurgated Grimm which was nightmare stuff and all Hans Andersen, some dreadfully sad, but beautiful. It must have been then that I was first enchanted by Dulac's pictures; I think the Skipper gave me the first of these, probably the Kipling poems. I don't know what happened to them, but I remember the pictures in detail. I also read eagerly the bound volumes of *Aunt Judy's Magazine*, especially the part about the poor little girl in the Aunt Judy cot at the Children's Hospital, with 'hip disease'.

Then they decided to operate on my neck glands, which had got worse with the dislocation and appeared likely to burst. For this I was taken to a London nursing home, which must have been very expensive. I begged not to be given open ether, but of course that was exactly what I was given, and without pre-medication, although at that time and for much later, an enema was standard. The anaesthetising was as unpleasant as ever though I tried not to struggle, but it left me sick for days; this strained the stitches and opened the wounds. I begged for some kind of opium, remembering how it had helped the last time, but did not get it. The surgeon was away for the week-end. I recovered physically with great speed, but it took much longer for the mental effects to wear off. If they ever did.

While I was getting well I did a lot of cutting out pictures for scrap books. This is a form of occupational therapy I still enjoy. At this time the old Edinburgh scrap books lived inside red flannel cases in the middle drawer of the drawing-room bureau. These had some enchanting pictures dating from the period when much trouble was taken with naturalistic detail and any kind of impressionism was still far in the future; there were also genuine scraps, the kind one bought in sheets and separated with scissors, soldiers and children and flowers all in shiny colours. There was much patriotism; there was Bugler Dunne, a young hero of the Boer War. Even with those very unpleasant and somewhat shaming two years in the memory of many, soldiering was still thought of as 'fun' or at least a supreme adventure. But then war at that time was still fairly likely to produce a few heroic situations and emotions among the combatants. Perhaps it helped to have illustrators rather than photographers to do the recording. One of my other favourite reads was the bound back numbers of *Punch* with plenty of noble Britannias.

April at Sennen and then I went back to school and had two good years in the upper forms, and watched the new boarding house being put up. The Skipper wanted to take me on one of his Blue Dragon cruises but again I was not allowed. Instead of 'Games' —and I really would have liked playing rugger—I used to go rowing on the Cherwell with Jack Slessor. The river was empty enough for rowing boats in those days; we rather despised punts. He too was out of school games, since he had a lame leg, almost certainly polio, though my mother, typically enough, said his nurse had dropped him and this came of leaving children in the care of servants. I suppose polio, then undiagnosed, was often blamed on someone in this way. Jack and I were very good friends and talked a lot between rowing; I'm sure the British Empire came into it. Both of us read Kipling. Jack desperately wanted to go into the Army, following his father, but this ambition was thought to be hopeless. But his elders and advisers had not reckoned with modern technology, so Jack is now Marshal of the Royal Air Force and covered with medals, all well deserved.

There were other friends, Richards and Rankin—we surnamed one another in those days—Carline (whom we somewhat looked down on because his father was a painter and he wanted to be one) Jack Smyth, later a V.C., and one or two others in our gang. Occasionally we played Devil-in-the-Dark, groaning and flashing lights at passers-by out of hedges, delighted if they ran, and sometimes we were intellectual and devised plays. Mine (like Shakespeare's) were usually in blank verse with a rhyming couplet at the end of each act, but often had difficult stage instructions, like the one about Hannibal in which his brother's head, bleeding, was thrown in for him to soliloquise over. Of course this might have been quite the thing for the Royal Court if it hadn't been two generations too soon.

At one time Jack Slessor and I formed a kind of literary partnership. We wrote a who-dunnit play with revolvers and detectives and carefully designed exits and entrances, which perhaps were a wee bit tricky. It never actually got into production, but involved lots of pleasurable and exciting meetings and conversations. We could be so enviably single-minded about such things, not letting any other aspects of the world interrupt, the way they do now.

I didn't try riding again for some fifty-five years, and then not side-saddle. But I was quite attached to the pony and, later on, used to drive her in a four-wheeled open pony carriage. I often took this down-town into Oxford and either knotted her reins onto a lamp post or gave them to some small boy to hold while I did the shopping. This was a perfectly safe and sensible thing to do pre World War I. In the end, after much wear and tear, the pony carriage came in two in the middle, leaving my governess (for by that time I had left school and was being governessed) in an undignified posture in the back seat, still clutching the reins. How I laughed!

What I really liked was driving the big hard-mouthed carriage horse from the coachman's box, twirling the whip in approved style, especially on the country roads round Oxford. They were not tarred yet and no doubt the carriage wheels stirred up dust or mud. But what did this even more were the early motor cars which we were beginning to see towards the end of the first decade of the century.* I used to shout at them 'Paap-paap! Stinker!' Probably they were quite used to that. Bicycle traffic was growing steadily, but my mother, again, was not keen that I should learn, having some obscure fear that it might damage my sexual organs. I ended, annoyingly, not able to ride a bike, though this was partly because when, in 1914, I at last had one and had begun to learn to ride it, the war came and with it the Belgian refugees. In a flood of sentiment I gave my bike to a girl called Yvonne. In theory it was a loan, but in practice, of course, not. She gave me a rather badly made flowered dress with a lacing of yellow ribbons. But my bike was gone.

---

* Jack's 1902 diary: they had been driving from Glencraig colliery near Loch Leven. Jack had been down with Uffer and writes full and interesting notes, showing the main differences between a colliery and a Cornish tin mine. Then Mr Wilson, the 'proprietor' of the mine, drove them back through the Yetts of Muckhart where the car began to heat and they had tea at Kippen while it cooled down: 'We didn't break the law badly, as we only once, I believe, reached 24 miles an hour! However we averaged about 17 on level ground.'

In time of course, we ourselves succumbed to buying a car, partly so as to get my father to the station quicker. He was by now going up and down to London fairly often, as a Gas Referee and also in connection with various Government enquiries and Royal Commissions. These meant a special black briefcase as well as many pencils and notebooks, in some of which I wrote my early novels later on. One got the feeling from his anger, talking things over with my mother, that the Home Office constantly had to be prodded into making any kind of move over industrial safety. Probably this was so. I think by this time, too, he may have been starting some connection with Birmingham.

He was taking longer and longer to lace his boots in the morning; he always wore thick, knitted socks and black laced boots which he carried down to breakfast with him, clonking them at any child on the stairs, and did not start putting them on till he had finished the tea and eggs and bacon and marmalade. They held the train for him at Oxford if they could see the carriage turning almost at a gallop up the station incline. It was clear that a motor car would halve the time. They bought a Daimler in 1913: it was supposed to be the most reliable and of course there was a chauffeur, replacing Crackston who by now was extremely alcoholic. But the chauffeur was called up in 1914 and the car was given, I think, to the Officers' Hospital.

X

Politics and People

I took it for granted that my mother's views on everything were right, including her great worship of the British Empire. In one general election I refused to wear my new red flannel coat because it was the Liberals' colour. My father never spoke of his views—or not till many years later—but I did know that my parroting of her political slogans annoyed him, making him frown and shake one foot. It was many years afterwards and my own political views were then not hers; we were walking up the glen at Cloan together, and he said, 'You can imagine what was said when I married an Edinburgh Tory.' I don't propose to consider what 'being in love' is or was, but I believe this had happened to him. I also think that she had made some kind of agreement with him about not expressing his political views. However, as a child, I put enormous enthusiasm into trying to understand hers and if possible going one better. This is clear from the diaries after about 1906.

There would be political pamphlets which I could put into envelopes or deliver to the neighbours. I remember collecting for some earthquake fund—in the West Indies perhaps?—and saying 'They are people like us.' That is to say not mere natives. However, this was not entirely a matter of colour. When the Russo-Japanese war got into the British press, several of the boys at the Dragon School, including my brother, drafted a letter to show their sympathy with the brave little Japs. No doubt this was a matter of unsympathy with our rivals or enemies, the Russians, whom we thought of as bearlike and constantly throwing babies out of sledges to feed the ravening wolves of the boundless steppes. Now, I wanted to sign the letter too; I must have been six and it was a real

84

matter of status. So they all questioned me on what I knew about the war. I had heard so much that my answers were thought adequate and I was allowed to sign. In due course a letter came back, I suppose from the Japanese Embassy, and was taken in triumph to school to be handed round and admired.

From here came playing Japs. I quote from a 1905 letter, describing yet another happy day with the Slessors. 'We went down to the towpath at Iffley & played Japs . . . & went on board an old barge . . . & played murderers after tea—black crape masks, cloaks & slouch hats.' I feel fairly certain that murderers were envisaged as having daggers or possibly garotting their victims—all very hand-to-hand.

My mother was Oxford's staunchest pillar of the Victoria League, which was in those days much more actively political in the sense of being British Empire orientated, and probably part of Conservative Party background, though it also organised some hospitality, which is its main function today. Among other activities it held an annual bazaar; here I went around in my best frock with a tray of sweets to sell, and I was allowed to buy things for my museum, kauri gum from New Zealand, Zulu beads, a tiny birch bark canoe from Canada, treasures of all sorts. I am sure I was given the money specially, as I had no pocket money until much later; it wasn't at all universal for school children.

One got tips from uncles, but these were usually saved up for something special. Uncle Richard—Haldane of Cloan—used to give Boy a golden half sovereign and me the same when I was past childhood. But I was well aware of my mother's deep political disapproval of him, which I now find sad because I am almost sure he realised that she was remarkably intelligent and he treasured intelligent female company; but he never got near having a rational political discussion with her. He must have found my political imitations of her views singularly trying. I note these from time to time in the later diaries, where there is much about Empire, Compulsory Military Service and similar subjects; I never had any doubts on the correctness of her and my views, though I now find myself unreasonably ashamed and embarrassed when I re-read

85

them. Had I arrived at this earlier, the later break might have been less painful.

Uncle Richard and Aunt Bay were Liberals and in practice deep in party politics. The Liberals were then an official and powerful party, against what they considered Conservative privilege and injustice. The voters (no women) were sufficiently evenly divided for alternate governments to take power, so that there was a democratic structure. Although most of the old traditional upper class were Conservative, with a few mavericks, below that it split class-wise. Today the two old parties may look much the same; it was, for instance, only the radical wing of the Liberals that was genuinely anti-imperialist.

But there was a real difference of opinion over Ireland, where the Conservatives approved of using force to put down 'rebels', while the Liberals favoured reasonable, unarmed discussion, though perhaps with almost the same end in mind. But it was a difference of approach and that was perhaps the dividing line elsewhere. As a child I would always be pleased to hear that we had 'sent a gunboat' to 'show the flag' to dissidents. Oddly enough, this type of phrase is still used emotively to justify enormous expenditure on armaments and still gets the childish response. My mother would accuse her Liberal relations of having caused the death of Britons by not immediately sending soldiers to enforce British rule. Gladstone, the G.O.M. (Grand Old Man) could be called the M.O.G. (Murderer of Gordon). I remember repeating this gibe to my father who responded with pain and anger that scared me into silence.

The other dividing line that I remember was between Free Trade and Tariff Reform, the latter being, I think, Imperial Preference, helping to build up Australian wool and New Zealand butter. Again, people felt passionately about it, though the main thing that sticks in my mind is a Liberal slogan: Tariff Reform means happier Dukes. Presumably, too, the Labour Party was lifting its ugly head. And yet I think my mother and quite a number of fellow Tories would have been as much in favour as any Liberal of social legislation for the amending of obviously bad conditions of work or housing. But for both main parties it was done benevolently, from above. The same was true of education. Board Schools should be improved but they were different in kind from the schools to which one's own children went.

The Victoria League meant parties for Rhodes scholars, who might well find themselves rather friendless, considering how far from home most of them were. But, for my mother at least, they must be suitable ones. She did not, for instance, like Afrikaner accents. But young Fairbridge, with his child emigration schemes, was one of her favourites; the Fairbridge farm schools probably owe much to her backing. I am almost sure that, with hindsight, I am being unfair about this. Let me add that her feminism was very real. She always supported women in the professions, went to a woman doctor when possible and encouraged me to think of medicine as a career. But this was somewhat marred by the counter-force of being a lady. Thus, it was wrong that women should not have the vote, but suffragettes had behaved in a deeply unladylike way. She was therefore a *suffragist*.

It is hard to be accurate or dispassionate about all this. It seems that my father was a quiet Liberal, only drawn into direct politics over an occasional issue such as the Boer War, but in general a believer in social justice, naturally on his own valuation. Like many honourable men he was not 'advanced' in the permissive society sense; he was much easier to shock than my mother was, though this only became apparent to me at a later stage in my life.

It seems also that my mother was an active and constant propagandist for Tory imperialism, as exemplified by Chamberlain, Kipling, her uncle General Keatinge and many public figures of the time. This comes constantly into my brother's diaries: clearly she took him with her whenever possible to League of the Empire meetings, especially those for children or young people, where she spoke and showed 'things from the colonies', including Samoan war clubs and kava bowls brought back by her father (the best of which are now in the Pitt Rivers Museum), Canadian birch bark models, African beadwork and so on. I don't remember any of this but it sounds as if she was a highly competent speaker. Jack in his 1902 diary writes: 'Mother told us very much what is put in the papers, that it is a society for making people more able to fight for their country, and to be useful if they emigrate to the colonies, & to let them know about colonial life by a system of couples of correspondents in England and a colony, or two colonies, and that the Empire isn't a lot of little countries, but one big one, in fact to teach them to be good citizens of the Empire. We enrolled about 10.' Some of these were 'village boys and girls' for whom he had a certain contempt, less social than intellectual—even in Scotland the village school wasn't up to the Dragons!

This reminds me of a laborious correspondence I had with a girl in Mauritius whom I finally met many, many years later. She was one of a huge French family, few of whom had managed to get married; it was all rather sad.

My mother's desk at Oxford was large, with locked drawers, and a great many sheets of facts and figures of the kind with which we propagandists are all too familiar. Clearly she was completely successful with both her children. In Jack's ten-year-old diary he says: 'My mater and I are very sorry to hear of Mr Chamberlain's resignation but hope he will get into office again soon.' Indeed I think there is evidence that he was even more deeply involved in her politics than I was which of course made the inevitable break all the more painful.

Did the fact that we loved her and she—not of course deliberately—used this to bring us into her line of feeling (naturally for what she thought was right and noble) make us more bitter when the time of disagreement came? What else, considering her deep involvement, could she have done with her loved children? And what, I ask you, parents or children, is the moral of that?

She had, meanwhile, a cousin, Charles ffoulkes, who was a somewhat unsuccessful artist and lived with his mother in a house at the corner of Bevington Road. I am sure he sympathised with my mother's political views. He did a lot of work in copper and bronze, good craftsmanship, all of it; he knew a great deal about armour and organised all that side of the Oxford pageant: he bound books. Today such of his work as survives is very fashionable, as it was the better kind of *art nouveau*; he also did drawings for me when I was ill and, I think, helped over the many difficulties that followed my parents' unwise decision not to employ a real architect for their new house, Cherwell, at the end of Linton Road, but instead a building contractor who claimed to be an architect. Gardiner his name was, another of the baddies. But my father disliked Charles ffoulkes; I think he was somewhat jealous and probably my mother did get some affection and sympathy of a kind which she needed from Charlie. His workshop was a very nice place, but I couldn't bear Aunt Annie, his mother, who had probably kept him, her only son, from marrying. He taught me to make chains of butterflies and little people out of folded paper and to make paper dresses for cardboard dolls which had lovely faces when he painted them up, but not when I did.

Oxford held plenty of my mother's fellow imperialists, including believers in the League of the Empire, more political than the Victoria League, with a constant flow of pamphlets which I read eagerly and distributed. Many were non-University people, like the Slessors. They had, I thought, nicer houses than ours, first up Woodstock Road, then Iffley Road. This was almost certainly because they had newer furniture and curtains and light fittings. I liked things new and shiny, in spite of or perhaps because of, my Morris upbringing. At the Hale Whites' house in Harley Street, where Sir William practised as a consultant, my mother and I had a room with shiningly polished wooden bedsteads with curved ends, no iron frames and knobs; they had new, glistening, silk-covered quilts; the dressing-table had a glass top and three mirrors and there were meringues for lunch. Dear Lady Hale White always insisted that I should have a second.

Another nice house was Miss Townshend's up Banbury Road; it was built a decade or so after St Margaret's Road on a much pleasanter plan, with no basement or top floor and the garden had a mound at the bottom nicely planted with rock shrubs and rareties, while in front a thick shrubbery shut off the traffic. Miss Townshend was Irish, wrote fairy tales and did one book with a photo of me as the frontispiece. She told stories and induced me to help with them, and there was an Indian hanging in her drawing-room with a great tree and quantities of beasts and birds among the branches. Here again I was neither talked down to nor owned.

When, at eleven or twelve, I became a serious field botanist and member of the Wild Flower Society, I used to go and visit Mr Druce, the great authority. He had a highly reputable chemist's shop in the High, and round his North Oxford house a garden wholly taken up with wild flowers. He was very kind to me and when, in my early teens, I found one of the *Muscari* in the middle of a spruce plantation, he put it under my name into the Berkshire flora. What happiness!

Naturally, Mr Druce was his own gardener, though perhaps he had someone to cut the lawn. Most professional class people had gardeners and consequently were much less knowledgable and interested than the same social group are nowadays, when they do it all, or most of it, themselves. Among the owners of great gardens, there were a few, fortunately perhaps, who were keen landscapers, planters and breeders, with equally keen gardeners, but others did little but show off their gardeners' work. The real difference was among those with small gardens, who nowadays produce such fine and often unexpected results. Many plants which we grow fairly easily were supposed to be tender or difficult; there were few viburnums other than *laurustinus*; I don't remember the early species crocus or winter cyclamens. Admirers of Morris felt that bedding-out was vulgar, though I loved the flower clock in Prince's Street Gardens in Edinburgh, as surely all right-thinking children must. I doubt if there were many of the really good rhododendrons at Cloan, but it would have been too cold for most of them. But it was in the conservatory, there that I started eating fuchsia berries, not quite so nice now, perhaps, as they used to be.

Our Oxford next-door neighbours on one side of 4 St Margaret's Road had a boy and a dachshund with whom I was vaguely friends, so that we met across the wall, but on the other side were the Murrays in a much bigger house and garden, but I was not supposed to climb in because they were Liberals. This was an emotive word, like Communist is now in some countries or to some people, and had no real meaning for me. Later it faded away; probably by then my mother had come to the conclusion that there were worse bogeys than Liberals. I went back to the house in my late teens and did a few thought-reading experiments with Gilbert Murray; my father thought they were nonsense, but I didn't. Once he caught what I was thinking but said it came out of a Russian novel; he may have got that by picking up the image in my mind which I was concentrating on in the same way I would have done if I had been writing it. It would have been fascinating to go on, perhaps getting in tune with him, but he found it extremely exhausting, as people who can do these things usually find it. Much later my mother and Lady Mary Murray seem somehow to have made friends.

There were always a few people who had something special which made me look forward to seeing them: Miss Legge and her Asian curios, most of which, I believe, ended in the Pitt Rivers Museum: Alice Raleigh and her delicate drawings—she lived in London Place when there was still a block of slummy, elderly houses between her and the main road and there was no inside WC, so I thought she ought to feel poor and unhappy, though I don't think she did. In one letter I had been to tea there and had a lovely time sorting buttons. And at Dr Collier's house, there was a bay window, one end of which looked out onto the High. When going into a new house one tended (and indeed I do still) to give it a quick look over for its hide-and-seek possibilities.

Uncle John, the Professor of Physiology, whose hatred of nepotism led him to be very unfair to my father and unforgiven by my mother, lived in a large ugly house in Banbury Road; I found him impressive, partly because he was in a Holman Hunt picture (May Morning), but I was scared of Aunt Ghetal. However, they had a typewriter and occasionally I was allowed to use it. Thus, my ambition of having a typewriter of my own. But this ties up with something I have long forgotten; the presence of 'Aunt Florence'— Florence Buchanan, a distinguished physiologist whom my mother approved of as a feminist, and felt she must look after, since Florence had a detached retina and her sight became increasingly bad. But I disapproved of her because she was unkempt, had large hairs on her face and smelled bad (if I remember hard I get that smell back). She almost always had lunch with us and I am sure she disapproved of me as much as I did of her.

I had school friends in and around Park Town, including Miss Poynter, sister of a then-famous painter, whose home was full of pictures; I used to blow bubbles there, from a big soapy bowl held on my knees. There were the Starks who lived, I think, in St Giles and then moved out to a low, rambling farmhouse at Noke. They had a model railway in the garden, the same gauge as ours, but still more fascinating, since it went over a miniscule lake and through a tunnel. There was a station with various home-made miniatures in it. How the Stark family, Boy and I, used to gloat over the Basset Lowke catalogues of model trains and all that went with them! At Noke, the 1906 diary mentions two hound puppies, 'one black puppy about a foot long, 8 inches high at his head & one foot round, it had short curly heair and it looked like a bear.' Also a pink bunny and a hen with many chickens, 'they were very clever for thier size I caught 3 & put them in a house I made. They imediately got out, I found through a secret passage into the railway cutting!'

The 1909 diary talks of the splendid hiding places at Noke, especially the loft. I hid there long enough to scare all the others most gratifyingly. Jack's schoolmate, J. D. Walker, came out that time and when he was there too 'it is awfully jolly because there are 6 of us all liking the same things, from J.D. at one end & me at the other.'

Beyond the railway was a tangly unpruned orchard where a friendly donkey wandered, while golden plums dropped lushly from old trees. It seemed to me that in order to have enough of them one must start at dawn, so I laid in plenty of plums under my pillow. And then slept on them. They were very ripe. Mrs Stark was dying of open tuberculosis; her dreadful cough rang through the house. I looked with interest at the blood on the handkerchief she held to her mouth. Did that have anything to do with my own TB? I have an idea that we suddenly stopped going there.

I think there was still a certain feeling that gently brought up children should also be made aware of the realities of human suffering, though this was not as strong as it was a generation earlier. My Foswell cousins were regularly taken to visit an old lady at Auchterarder with lupus-cancer of the face; not pretty. We were more familiar than today's children with death, which tended to take place at home rather than in hospital, and certainly with the idea of the sought-after 'good death'. But we were less familiar with killing and genuine violence, and would have been desperately upset by many of today's news items.

Without quite remembering who they were, I know there were families with whom we took Sunday afternoon picnics with wicker picnic baskets and kettles, well up the Cherwell in fields which were then completely remote except for the cows. If we went downstream there was the fun of Maya and me putting our hands over our eyes as we passed the naked University gentlemen bathing at Parson's Pleasure. There were water rats in plenty and sometimes kingfishers; a mile or two up and the river might be blocked with fallen trees, which our New Zealand cousin Rob Makgill helped us to move; there was one, the Great Snag, which took most of the summer, or so it seems now. My father, in shirt sleeves and braces, rowed, and sometimes I was allowed to steer, but was discouraged from the fascinating sport of bumping other boats. Punts came later, when the river was too crowded for rowing boats. But early in the century everyone knew almost everyone else. The Colleges had their boat houses, but there was no casual hiring and we were all affronted when Timms started the hiring business on 'our' river.

One went more rarely on the Upper Thames, but there was one expedition every year, either by boat or carriage. This was to Wytham to eat strawberries. If we drove there we went by a road now blotted out by the by-pass, with gates here and there and children who opened them and to whom we threw pennies. If we came by river we walked past Fair Rosamund's nunnery, and along a raised path between hedges and above road level, no doubt built that way because of the yearly floods. Traditionally one squashed the strawberries with the bottom of a wine glass before digging in.

Every year, too, we went on brambling expeditions, often on the

93

little train to one of the stations beyond Islip where there was waste land with great bramble thickets where we could easily fill our baskets. We got them in our own hedges too, near at hand. Every year there were crab apples and sloes. Have all those splendid hedges been tidied up now, so that there is no longer the great wealth of autumn fruit? Or do people just not bother about it?

XI

Polly and Others

I begin to wonder about our pets, once I had outgrown the mice. I don't think my mother held with them very much: she hated the smell of carnivores. But our desires were strong. There was a fox terrier called Spot about whom I have no fond feeling; he definitely belonged to the males of the family. And there were the white fantail pigeons, who lived in a pigeon house on the top of a pole at St Margaret's Road; Boy used to lie on the ground with maize up his shorts so that the pigeons could wriggle in to get it. Later, at Cherwell, there were more pigeons and different kinds. That was where I first heard the phrase: 'simple, stable Mendelian population'. Rarely, there were red maize grains among the yellow. I collected them for one drawer of a Japanese toy writing desk in which I kept other collections, including my own milk teeth, out of which I intended to make a necklace, but they were too difficult to bore holes in.

For how many years I have forgotten Timothy Titus of Tavistock! And yet he must have occupied my mind during most of out-of-school time for a whole summer. Someone gave me a yellow duckling, the weakling of a batch which would probably not survive in farm conditions. He drooped in my hands, his eyes shut. But we gave him whisky and he never looked back. I think he was imprinted on me; he followed me everywhere round the St Margaret's Road house and garden, first carried, then wriggling upstairs, step after step. I quickly learned to interpret his various duck noises and was only able to support the idea of an almost adult and non-house-trained duck going back to the farmyard by being told that he would be king. The 1904 (six-year-old) diary has pages about Timothy Titus, including a poem beginning,

> 'There is a duck called Tim
> None other equales him.'

and three rather peculiar drawings. Descending to prose, I write, 'Tim has grown very much since he came here. When he came there was a sort of skin on his beak but it has pealed of now. It is coloured browny-gray, but his beak is pink. When he is in the garden alone he usualy squekes, but when we talk to him out of the window he stops; he follows you about the garden, and when you go into the house he evan follows there, he some-times goes into the study & sits in the middle of the floor. Tim always squeaks when he wants food; the more hungry he is the louder he squeaks. If at tea anybody puts down on the grass their cup of tea, Tim, before they can see Tim, begins to drink it.'

It was well after my broken leg that I started to keep guinea pigs. I was around twelve and it was the first pair, precursors of hundreds, whom I successfully induced to nibble off a wart on the first finger of my right hand by holding it against the netting where I usually put carrots. The wart never came back. But the guinea pigs, whose language, again, I began to interpret and imitate, and their many descendants, went on far beyond childhood, taking me into the almost adult world of early genetics.

And then there was Polly! I never thought of Polly as a pet. Polly was a person and died in my arms. He (we thought he was a he) was left to us by my cousin Alys Trotter—with whom he had lived for many years and where I had first got to know him; we never knew how old he was. He was immensely affectionate and, I thought, understanding. When I had my broken leg, Polly walked gently, carefully, so as not to hurt and came to my face and kissed me with open beak and little soft dry tongue. That was what he did, or, if he felt exceptionally friendly, he sicked up pellets of food to offer one. While he was with us I was able to communicate with the macaws at the Zoo, even the great red and yellow ones (Polly was blue-green), and get them to respond, to sit on my wrist and let me tickle them.

Polly did not care for other non-humans and could easily put a

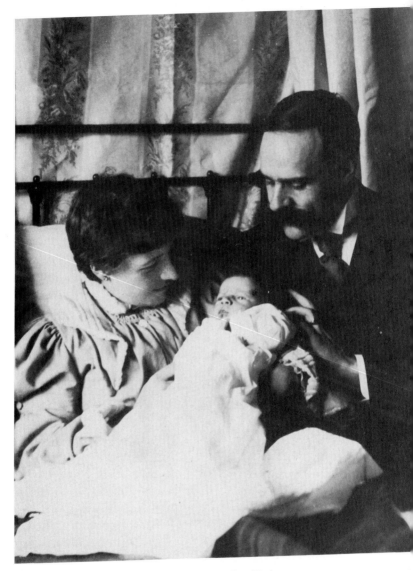

The first photograph — Mother
Father and me, 1897

Father

The dangers of a mine. Father and
a miner having been trapped underground
for three days.

My brother Jack and me, November 1898.

Jack aged 11   *Me*

*Mother, Jack and me on a picnic with
a cousin from New Zealand*

Mother and me

*Mother, Father, Jack
and me at Cloan*

The Dragon School, Oxford — in Sunday best

Sidesaddle on Nopy — before the fall

The Dragon School — tree games

Cloan
(Courtesy of R W Haldane)

dog or cat to flight by threatening behaviour, dancing up and down with his wings open and yelling. He did not care for the tits hanging upside down on the coconuts outside the drawing-room window and flapped his wings at them too. But he could not see immediately in front of him and if one put a clockwork mouse so that it would run directly in the line of his beak, he would leap upwards with a prodigious squawk. Boy and I knew this was disapproved of, but once or twice we even made him drunk and he became remarkably human, lurching about and talking a lot, though his vocabulary was not very large. He liked to be in on meal times, climbing up one's chair, pulling my hair or nibbling at Maya's specs. Her somewhat disapproving attitude towards pets, especially carnivores, was completely reversed with Polly, who liked best to go round on her shoulder and was forgiven for tearing a piece of lace when holding on or for feeding her ear with food pellets.

What I didn't like was his habit of grinding his beak while I was doing my prep in the dining-room, where his perch was. It may be that he was simply trying to communicate and that he didn't much like the half-dark of the dining-room with only the reading lamp at the desk where I was trying to do Latin translations or, sometimes, playing my Liberty catalogue game. If I put him down on the floor to roam around he would go to the sand tray below his perch and scatter the sand with his beak, which was equally interrupting.

I don't think I had much homework until I was ten or so, but in the top forms we had a lot, usually two hours. It was less homework in today's sense, when the object is to acquire relevant knowledge out of school, than a test of what one knew, to be marked the next day. So one wasn't allowed help. It was Latin prose, French verbs and sentences, counties and rivers, dates. If it was an essay I had no trouble. Arithmetic was worse, especially Euclid. Later I did solid geometry for fun with my brother and found it very pleasurable.

We had lots of exams and I usually enjoyed them. I was extremely competitive and exams set me off like jumping hurdles. Not that I was ever a hurdler! I was useless at school sports, or at organised games, other than the obstacle race. Later, in my early teens, I was in a North Oxford lacrosse team. This was enjoyable, though I remember how, egged on by my mother, I was against their very sensible suggestion of allowing one's gym tunic to finish just above the knee instead of below it. I still either believed in her total rightness in such matters or was afraid of the bother and disapproval if I had to get the tunic altered. Finally it was solved because I was thrown out of the team for playing foul whenever I got excited.

I think, though, that I learned to skate fairly young. Were winters colder then? Probably not, but I remember the meadow at Magdalen frozen over, and Port Meadow too, and the excitement of getting on one's skates and wobbling out and then sailing clear away. Nor was falling too uncomfortable. The floods, preceding the frost, were always something to watch and talk about and compare. Soon I began to realise how much they were doing for the fertility of the water meadows. Port Meadow itself was special at all times; we went there a lot from St Margaret's Road, an easy walk, over the railway bridge, dragging one's feet if a train was in sight so as to be in the very middle of splendid billows of dark smoke; there was a corrugated iron barrier too, to run along with a stick. I was expert with a wooden hoop about my own height and could run in and out of it while I bowled it along. It was Johnny. But a dreadful thing happened. I was bowling in the field near the site of the new house and my little hoop-boy Johnny fell into the river and was carried away, white and calm and round, down stream, and nobody came to rescue him. After that I played no more with hoops.

The canals and the canal boats with their painted castles and flowers were fun. So were the drawbridges, most of all standing on one, holding on, while it was pulled up. We poked endlessly with sticks in canals and ditches. Once Boy and I pulled out a huge river mussel; we watched, fascinated, when we put it into a jar and it gradually opened and extruded a foot. But when finally it died there was no pearl.

One year there was a thrush's nest in one of the pair of small cypresses which finished off the bridge over the 'back area' from the garden door of St Margaret's Road down to the garden itself and the bushes of pink La France roses. Once a day I was lifted up to feed the gaping nestlings with small pieces of meat. Later, I thought they knew me. Occasionally we found other birds' nests and watched for the parents; whatever else we collected it was never birds' eggs or stamps, though I had an album full of picture postcards of foreign countries. There were magnificent dragonflies up the Cherwell. Earthworms too were sympathetically viewed.

The diaries are full of animals: my own rabbits and bantams, other people's puppies, the seaside donkeys I rode. When Grannie took a small house on Boar's Hill there were rabbits to track and watch and a new lot of birds, jays and woodpeckers. Even the insects were different; I was observant on moths. And the Cherwell had its own animals, birds and water dwellers; there were water rats all along the banks, going about their business.

House rats, however, got no sympathy. We had great rat-hunts at Cloan, with the cairns, good ratters, and Kaiser, the St Bernard, less agile, as long-stop. We and the Foswells were all armed with sticks and hit one another as often as not. We threw the dead rats into the pigsty and the old sow crunched them up, the rat tails hanging out of her mouth at both sides.

Both parents encouraged scientific curiosity, though there was a rule that we did not talk about anything below the diaphragm at meals. But there were other kinds of curiosity, too. I used to spend much time in the Pitt Rivers Museum, partly with the prehistoric skeletons, with which I was always on good terms, and partly with the anthropology section, but not forgetting the plaster duck with protective coloration. Parts of the museum were unfinished and one could watch the stone-carvers at work on the capitals of the small stone pillars of the gallery, sometimes with a sprig of oak leaves or some such thing which they were perpetuating in stone.

I did not care much for the Ashmolean, except for some of the Pre-Raphaelite pictures: Holman Hunt's 'Dovecot', the rescue of the Christian Martyr by well-combed Britons, 'Home from the Sea', all with the detail one always hoped for in pictures but so often didn't get, and with real, vital colours. Wherever I found them later on, in other galleries, these were the ones I stared and stared at. Rossetti was boring with those stupid-looking girls, but Millais and his gardens were always beautiful and one knew at once what

99

the picture was about. There was only one other picture in the Ashmolean that was satisfactory in the same way; that was Uccello's 'Hunt'. Piero di Cosimo's forest fire, with the good but anxious bear rescuing his cubs, was not yet there; if it had been I would have tugged at anyone's hand to stop and look at it. I was moderately interested in Alfred's jewel, but not at all in the casts of classical sculpture.

The Botanical Gardens were a good place, either from land or going in by boat; at ten or eleven I was an adept stealer of cactus shoots and offsets, hiding them under bread for the swans, then growing them successfully to flowering size. In Magdalen there were the deer to feed and the odd little statues of the virtues and vices round the inner quad to identify, or try to. St John's garden had the best rockery, but New College was of course our own. Boy and I scooted up the forbidden Mound in the garden there, and then not again until the year of our father's centenary, when there were lectures and celebrations at his old laboratory and college, and we came back as ghosts.

For a short time there was a private big game museum about opposite the Radcliffe, which I much liked. I used to go there and try to paint kudus. If there had been anything like a science museum I would have loved it. I don't remember being taken to museums in London, only to Madame Tussaud's where I was scared stiff—here were serried nightmares, dead but almost alive. We did go to the Zoo, several times, in the days when, for a small tip, the keepers took out the kinkajous to climb round our necks, or the beautiful, ripple-bodied snakes. We knew what not to give the animals to eat and probably did no harm.

In Edinburgh my great treat was the *camera oscura* in High Street, where, on a great round magic sheet one could watch the moving people, tiny and coloured. But again I don't remember being taken to any museums, though I was sometimes taken to the National Gallery and always wanted to see Paton's 'Oberon and Titania', with all the fairies, good and bad, and again, again, the clear detail. It is again becoming fashionable, but oddly, it has become quite a small picture; I remember it as very big.

XII

The Underpinning

While my mother's father was still alive, that is, before I was seven, the Edinburgh family and servants used to take a house each holiday somewhere in the Lothians. These would be two-storey houses with spacious rooms, a good garden including a kitchen garden and perhaps a conservatory where I was not allowed to pick the flowers. There must, above all, be plenty of opportunities for nice drives. I think my mother was totally bored; her role appeared to be that of dutiful daughter helping with the housekeeping and servants, writing notes; sometimes she and her mother played cribbage; I might be called in to help with winding a skein of silk or wool, holding it between my hands while my grandmother wound. Grandpapa had considerable correspondence, I think about geography; he was a member of several learned societies. There were occasional distinguished visitors. It seems almost certain that Grandpapa took his own horses and trusted coachman, but I remember being taken by the more interesting train.

One house was at Inveresk. I was not allowed to dam any of the streams or set foot in the Esk, already much polluted from the paper mills. Nor was I allowed to play on the sand at North Berwick for the same reason. In fact, we were getting into the modern world. All this comes into the 1904 and 1905 diaries. There were walks to the churchyard 'where some tomb stones have been left lying about'. There were expeditions, for instance to Stirling by boat, going under the Forth Bridge, and an attempt to get to the Belhaven sands past the 'drainy, rocky' Dunbar beach. Later Sina and I went there, or to the Portobello pier, or to fish—there is a drawing of a flounder. There was one great expedition to the Bass

Rock which takes pages of the diary, what with the engine of the launch that took us there, the sea birds, the landing ('not as difficult as landing on the Longships') and the lighthouse mechanisms. Other expeditions were to Dalkeith, Rosslyn, to Miss Wauchope 'who has been all over the world', to a flower show at Pinkie, and to Miss Wardrop who had a pony called Mysie 'which I drove myself; I do like driving with Mysie in a pony cart'. I fed her with apples and rode her, more or less.

On both years when Grannie and Grandpapa were at Inveresk we drove over to Preston Pans. The salt pans where the sea water was evaporated were still there and still one got the big scrunchy crystals of Sunday salt when the evaporation went on over the Sabbath. But there was also the Preston Pans pottery, where I was allowed to make a clay bowl on a wheel and to buy myself a penny money box shaped like a monkey. The 1904 diary goes into the industrial process with great care, starting with the clay ('I have seen white clay works near Penzance'), going on to, 'They used to make more interesting things than teapots & pie dishes, they showed us an old china man, he was 300 years old and beautifully painted. They smash a awfull lot of things, and through the broken bits onto the shore, when mother heard this she turned round like a —— and said "to cut the children's feet upon!" '

There was also Cockenzie House where Colonel Cadell and his daughters lived. That was the best place. There was a long drawing-room stretching right across the house. As I remember, one window looked north over the harbour with storms louring and wind and fishing boats and bustle, and the other south over the garden with clipped hedges and richly flowering roses in quiet sunshine and white fantails parading on green grass. Between the windows were cabinets, one with mirrors at the back, tortoiseshell panels and little inlaid drawers; there was fine china behind glass; there was ivory and sandalwood, camphorwood chests and worked brass from India; there were pictures, which I liked, also full of storms and sunshine—early Cadells perhaps, for this distinguished Scottish painter was first cousin once removed to the Colonel. And above, running the length of the house, was a corridor with a springdale, a thin board that one sat on and it jumped one up. In the garden a swing was set between ivy-run whales' jawbones and a white marble Nandi, an Indian temple or palace bull, reclined calmly in a very Scottish grotto.*

All this and more comes into the diaries. There is a drawing of the springdale. But the most enthusiastic description is in 1908 when we actually stayed there, and now I recall Colonel Cadell feeding the black and white fantails that crowded onto his head and shoulders, though I don't remember the Persian cats. Nor yet the 'great collection of daggers, taken from Indian convicts, each of which is said to have murdered at least one man', nor even the Indian prince's baby clothes given by the Maharani of Ulwar. There was an Indian inlaid jewel case and a long sword, as well as things from the Nicobars. Colonel Cadell had been Governor of the Andamans, where he and his daughters had rowed out to caves full of the edible swifts' nests, which had never been visited before, so that the swifts were quite tame and could be stroked; one supposes that is all over now. The Miss Findlaters were there too, 'authoresses whose books I have seen reviewed in Punch'.

We stayed at Woodhouselea where the 'walls are quite 8 feet thick' with the Fraser Tytlers; it is a notoriously haunted house, but that kind of haunting didn't bother me. Trotters and Fraser Tytlers had been friends for five generations and my mother and

* Jack's diary tells a lot more about the bull, which had been brought over by Colonel Cadell's brother who was a gunner and was able to take it away on his gun carriage, presumably after the 'Mutiny' in which Colonel Cadell won his V.C. It is of course taken for granted that loot is loot. He goes on, 'As soon as the bull was safely installed at Cockenzie, a letter came from the Duke of Somerset's son, saying the bull was his property! He declared that the Colonel of the 17th Lancers had given it to him, however on investigation it was found that he had *asked* the Colonel if he could take it, and as no-one else wanted it, his request was granted. However, having no gun carriage, he was unable to take him away, and Capt. Cadell of the artillery, who came next, bagged it, and by the laws of loot, it belonged to the man who could carry it off. The Duke of Somerset's son then wrote for "his bull" to Captain Cadell who replied that he had given it to his father. Old Commander Cadell was then asked by the Duke of Somerset to name his legal adviser; he replied that that was a luxury in which he could not afford to indulge, and also that he knew more of the laws of loot than any London lawyer! So the bull remains at Cockenzie in a grotto built of lava from Hekla, brought home by herring boats as ballast.' Those were the days.

'Aunt Christian', who had been a Kerr, tended to have second sight about whatever the other one was doing or thinking. I painted the trunk of a tree with just one branch sticking out and called it 'Last of the Kings of the Forest'. That was really rather grand! I think I only liked painting flowers and plants, which led me to look at them rather carefully. At Inveresk there were begonias in the conservatory, some with stamens, others with the curiously convoluted style which is typical; these I immortalised at six in coloured chalk, a he begonia and a she begonia.

We may have stayed with the cousins my mother loved at Colinton among the lawns and great sixty-foot holly hedges against which the summer annuals blazed. But I remember it as gloomy, the end foreshadowed. There were other houses near Edinburgh with relations or friends, and so often one of them was a bit 'wowffy'. There was a very fair girl a little older than me with epilepsy—but what was that? I wasn't told.

By now my brother was in his teens and had got over the worst of his early time at Eton; he did the normal upper-class things, rode, shot—quite well—and, apparently, was a fairly good boxer. There were various boy cousins and I suppose my mother was beginning to think of a suitable match for me. But I remember none of them and few survived the first war.

From Cloan we visited a few big houses. Miss Christie had a Japanese garden with all the trimmings, a little bridge and a temple, incongruously set in a Highland landscape where the view was all wrong. And everywhere we went there was the accepted underpinning of servants. This might mean a happy and comfortable relationship, probably on both sides, as it usually seems to have been at Cloan. The servants were almost always local people, their parents respected and often intelligent members of the same church. There was never any need to lock things up, as one might have to do elsewhere.

It was a funny business, really. Here were people living in the same house, walking through the same rooms, but thought of differently. Yet isn't this to some extent true of all groups? People give one another different kinds of understanding. Scrubbing and emptying other people's chamber pots were thought of as inferior work, but it led to higher things and one could only admire skilled ironing and pleating or silver cleaning, and the upper servants at least would, in Scotland, have insisted on a relation of mutual respect and would never have stood for impertinence by the young. And again, when we think back to a set-up of nominal—at least—servants and masters, we have to remember that what seems odd and even shocking today, was not so yesterday. We can't be sure which of the actions and habits and relationships of today will seem all wrong tomorrow; don't let's be too certain who to blame for what. Sixty years ago, a young girl and her parents were probably very happy when she was taken 'into service' at Cloan where perhaps her mother had been before her; she learnt a number of skills and was proud of them; she had a position; she had friends. That was what mattered.

But even so the servants were different. Formal relationships were entailed; from babyhood, almost, I was Miss Naomi, putting a distance between us. If a new kitchen maid came she was watched and commented on; she might be discussed between Granniema or Aunt Bay and Mrs Cook, like allied generals. And of course the servants had their domain, into which one didn't go unless invited—or at one's peril, the main peril being that the grown-ups on one's own side of the boundary might be told and then one was in for a scolding—worse if one was a boy.

The servants exerted a powerful influence on the household, perhaps stronger than was ever admitted. Sabbath-keeping became increasingly something one did as an example to the servants, though some of the adults still believed in it—but perhaps in a different sense. Certainly the servants imposed ideas on the children whom they saw most of, though sensible children might translate the language when talking it back to their mothers. These would be class ideas, what was 'common'. They enhanced the ideas of ladyhood and what was expected of one, and the unwritten rules. From below, one was told that one must not descend.

Sometimes we went to other large houses where there were real nannies. Sina was not in any sense a 'nanny'; she did not have complete charge, nor was she a mother substitute, but I was very fond of her and so, I think, was Jack. These others were more formidable than ordinary grown-ups: grace was said, which made me uncomfortable, and there was insistence on table manners. I was always offended if I had to have a 'nursery' meal; my status was being questioned. And I was certain the grown-ups who had brought me were having something lovely, like roast chicken or hot-house grapes, while we had boiled fowl and milk pudding.

But there were other odd things. Here for instance is an incident from slightly later. I was having a bath and forgot to bolt the door. The then-butler almost came in, but stopped as soon as he became aware there was someone towelling; I thought it funny and made some remark to Maya. Her reaction was 'Did he see you? If so he must leave the house at once!' Of course he didn't, I said, yes, I'm sure, no, of course not, and so on. I was horrified at this threat held over the poor man who had in fact merely and innocently opened a door a few inches. Nor could I really see what this new fuss was about. But it was a lesson to me—not to talk.

There was a staircase at Cloan, leading up from near the back door to the servants' bedrooms. I never went up and I doubt if Granniema would have gone up except in case of dire illness or some similar mishap. I tried to guess at the rooms by counting the windows from the outside, but could never be sure. In the new house at Oxford, built 1905–1906, there was a servants' flat at the top with its own bathroom. It had a door which opened into the schoolroom and I knew it fairly well, as I often ran down that way, going by the back stairs to avoid those I might meet on the front ones. The rooms were under the roof with sloping ceilings, but were very nice, with gorgeous views over the river. My daughter had it as a flat in the fifties and sixties. Two of the bedrooms certainly were meant to be shared. There was a servants' hall below, opposite the kitchen, which also held the linen cupboard. It seemed quite a friendly place and I knew more or less what went on in that world by then. But I still never did any cooking.

The bigger the house, the higher the barrier. But one must modify this in one way. In the one-servant house with the 'slavey', usually young and easily put upon, sometimes old and cross, there must have been a really cruel barrier, isolating the wretched woman and asserting the superiority of the employer. But I don't think I knew any such households. Later, of course, the household with a single 'help' was common, but by then, already, the relationship had changed.

At Cloan the barrier meant a certain provocation to raiding from our side, when one of us took a dash into Tom Tiddler's Ground usually for goodies of some kind, though it was more practical to be on friendly terms with Mrs Cook or, for grown-up dinner party leftovers, with the butler. I suppose Granniema, or, later, Aunt Bay, had daily discussions, talked over meals, though not necessarily in detail, and the state of the stores. Aunt Bay certainly did the books—going over the household accounts at her desk, where she was also writing the life of Descartes.

My mother did the same. It was careful accounting, down to the halfpennies, with everything she had spent. I rather think that my parents had a joint account at an Oxford bank in the High where people behind counters weighed and shovelled shining pennies and half-crowns, but my mother had a personal account at Coutts where the ladies of the Trotter family have banked for a couple of hundred years and where I and my daughters, equally, keep our accounts.

My mother had a bunch of keys and was always locking things up. This is not a compulsion I have inherited. I think she was always more suspicious of her servants who were, after all, English. How happy she was that the furniture removal men, who brought the things down from Edinburgh after my grandfather's death, were Scots! A Scottish accent in the lower classes meant a proper attitude: not fawning but knowing what was what. Both she and my father were sometimes taken in by hard cases with Scots tongues in their heads. My own accent was groomed to upper-class standards, a pity in these days when a regional accent is such an asset for TV or radio! All that is left of my native country is that I pronounce both letters in 'wh' and 'ch' and 'r' sound in mid-word are still perceptible. Oddly enough my mother herself used certain

Scotticisms which I inherited, ashet, gigot, redd, for instance. Often I deliberately use 'will' instead of the English 'shall' when it seems to sound better in a sentence.

Oxford servants were much discussed in drawing-rooms. If one didn't have some kind of local source, like farmers' daughters, whom one might know something about, then there was nothing for it but a registry office. Then there was the business of written references and reading between the lines. What had been left out? Ladies were often asked for references for someone who had been with them years before, if, say, the most recent employer had died.

I think most Oxford households tended to have a relationship with some professional waitress who came in to help for a big do of any kind. Such people were also in demand for College garden parties or children's Christmas parties, where extra help was needed. After World War One this kind of thing probably increased, as regular parlour maids became fewer and more expensive, but Miss Williamson's coming in was a fairly early memory and my mother's relief when she turned up, took off her hat and coat and took charge. She was always 'Miss' which showed she was not a servant but could be trusted. She saw to the silver and the table setting and dealt with any little *contretemps* like my father gazing absentmindedly at a joint or bird and forgetting to carve. When there was no butler she saw to it that the right wines went into the right glasses.

These were mostly grown-up dinner parties, to which I didn't go till much later, but Miss Williamson could sometimes be found at New College or other parties, and would manage to slip me that extra ice or bit of cake. We ourselves had a garden party once every summer at least. It was the Oxford thing to do and was a good way of polishing people off. The ladies wore frothy dresses, big hats and white gloves, the men often looked cool in white flannels and there were usually other children. I expect the idea was to have it at a time when the garden looked nicest, but the garden at St Margaret's Road was small and the garden at Cherwell not very imaginative or well laid out. My mother was much more interested in the vegetables than the flowers! Its chief merit was some fine walnut trees.

Some years these produced massively and we picked baskets and baskets of walnuts and I was perpetually stained with walnut juice. In one of the later World War One years, chopped walnuts made the flour nicer as well as making it go further.

We had various gardeners who came in, but none were friends. I did a lot of weeding and also berry picking. There were more varieties of strawberries and gooseberries at that time, both in gardens and for sale, but the raspberries, though flavoury, had more caterpillars in them. I don't remember nearly as many winter-flowering plants, nor were there more than a few iris hybrids. I doubt if the species iris or tulips were grown. Probably the College gardens were well ahead of the dons' gardens when it came to new or difficult plants.

My father usually dined in College on Sunday evening, rather a relief perhaps, because we tended to have quite a lot of under-graduates coming in for Sunday tea. This meant the silver tray and tea set, including the hot water urn with the little lamp lighted below it and the silver dish for the hot buttered scones. The silver was polished by the parlour maid into a real glitter with plate polish; there was no 'long-lasting'. Knives were ground in a knife machine with a handle one turned round. Napkins were folded, either plain mitre shape for ordinary meals, or into various fancy shapes for a party. An experienced parlourmaid was good at this.

I got a lot of fun from the damask tablecloths and napkins to match. Sometimes I even helped to set them on the polished mahogany table over, I think, a green baize foundation. Maya wasn't good at flower arrangement, and when I left school and she got a governess for me, I know she was interested in Miss Blockey's ability to 'do' the flowers. However I very soon took that on myself. We had a kind of Victorian mosaic tray in the drawing-room, in-herited from Randolph Crescent, where Granny used to have azaleas in pots on it, which seemed to me the height of luxury. It would take pot plants or else large jars in the middle with smaller ones on the outside. In fact it was remarkably ugly and I did not grudge it later on to Sotheby's.

We are so accustomed to certain kinds of conveniences and

gadgets that, in Euro-America at least, we have rather forgotten what things were like before. There was, of course, no mechanical help in the kitchen nor with washing. Servants were used to going on their knees and scrubbing floors. It was the period before disposables. Soap is harder to wash out of one's hair than a shampoo! When I began to menstruate, rather early and alarmingly, for I had not taken in any of the tactful hints which my mother had made on the subject, there were no disposable sanitary towels. They were made of towelling or thick linen damask and one had to learn to fold them into a kind of pocket. When finished with, one rolled them up, put their own loop round them and dropped them into the dirty clothes basket. I *think* they went to a laundry at the end of the week and were soaked in cold water, for the stains came out of them. But it must have been someone's job to undo and sort them. Probably things like stained knicker linings were washed at home. But not by the wearer.

This seems now to be strangely barbarous. But we took it for granted and so, on the other side of the dividing line, did they.

XIII

The Doings of the Grown-ups

Breakfast at Cloan always started with porridge—good porridge made with salt—and sometimes cream. Following tradition we supped it standing, which meant we could observe the grown-ups and even read their letters over their shoulders. The most interesting of the grown-ups was Uncle Richard, though we had to be a little careful about breathing down his neck; he could scatter us. His correspondence came in large, stiff new envelopes with the lion and unicorn on the back and big red seals. These were real seals, none of your phony wafers. One learnt young, in the days before sellotape, to seal a parcel or letter securely and tidily, spreading the wax in a nice round pool, then quickly, before it hardened, pressing down the well-licked seal for just long enough. Many people had seal rings; my father's was a gold seal with his coat of arms, my mother, being an heiress, that is an only child, having hers quartered on his. I have forgotten it all now, but at eight or nine I was fascinated by heraldry, the words and the usages. Charlie ffoulkes taught me all this and gave me the books. I could reel off the rigmaroles and amused myself making up 'correct' coats of arms for my friends. It blended in, too, with *Idylls of the King*, which was my favourite reading aloud at that period.

But of course the best seal of all, with the coat of arms which I knew by heart, was the Great Seal of England, with which we became familiar. As Lord Chancellor, Uncle Richard had to take the Great Seal about with him under his personal charge. I suppose he got a direct sleeper from London to Crieff Junction, now Gleneagles and steadily going down in the world, fewer trains stopping, fewer flowers and less paint. He would have had to have at least one meal on the train, and had to carry along to the dining-car the case with the Great Seal in it, which looked light, but wasn't. Then it lived in his room at Cloan.

When a document actually had to be sealed, the man whose job it was, the keeper perhaps, came up in a neat business suit, but with a mysterious bag like a doctor. We all went off to the old laundry, for this was a messy business. Any piles of sheets were cleared into a corner and made to wait.

The procedure was for a large cake of wax, red or green, depending on the kind of document, to be thoroughly soaped. There was usually a silk cord to be passed through the seal and in fact I think it was done with two cakes pressed together. The seal itself was fitted face down into a kind of screw press, the wax was heated on a small burner and the screw turned down until the wax was squashed and the soap bubbled out. This was always a pleasure and we were given bits of wax—just the thing, naturally, for my museum.

This cannot have been before 1911, so it is not really a childhood memory, but I seem to have had the same direct visual appreciation of the scene; I remember the smell of the wax. Uncle Richard also brought back some of the expensive things Lord Chancellors had to buy, especially the embroidered purse, which hung on a chair back. But on his second term he managed to start the custom that these were to be handed over to the successor, thus saving future Lord Chancellors a considerable sum.

One of my father's colleagues, Professor Boyes, one of the other Gas Referees, knew all about soap films and had invented a cup which could be twirled round on a stem; one drew a thin film of soap across it and as one spun it the colours ran into exquisite tiny patterns of blobs and whirls. In the middle where it was thinnest a dark area gradually developed and spread until the whole film collapsed. I played with this for hours, as also with a kind of simple wooden pantograph which produced patterns which seemed to me to relate to the soap films.

But what exactly were the grown-ups? Another version of Them? Something not quite understood and therefore frightening as well as having authority? One could dodge and outwit, but probably in the end they won. Death the ultimate grown-up? I wonder.

There were some grown-up professions which one supposed one understood; I played orchid-collecting in the Himalayas, especially on the Sennen cliffs. But of course I never thought of the orchids as being objects of commerce. Equally, when I thought about the East India Company with which many of my forbears on my mother's side had been connected, I imagined it as some kind of noble agency, governing and helping the poor Indians. One got the idea, not utterly bad, that one must help those in worse situations than oneself. Uffer, I well knew, worked so hard and was so often in danger to help miners and sewermen and divers. If I had considered the mine owners at all, I suppose I would have taken what is, basically, the Tory point of view, that they had been helping the miners by opening and equipping the pits. But the profit motive entirely escaped me for a long time.

Doctors were simple. So were soldiers and sailors (who were, naturally, always defending the Flag) and civil engineers who built bridges and railways. All science was good, but one must be kind to animals though, regrettably, some scientists weren't. But if one had been in the lab and seen Uffer handling animals, one knew that he was kind. Fairly soon I began to make comparisons between farm practice, especially cattle markets and such things as castration and dehorning, and scientific practice with the cheerful cagefuls of guinea pigs and darling mice.

But I had absolutely no consciousness of economic facts, nor was this even mentioned at school and barely in any history book I read in my teens. None went further than the Diamond Jubilee or possibly the lamented death of Queen Victoria, who had not yet been subjected to any kind of critical process. If one thought about economics at all, it was money, of which some people had more than others. But why? That hadn't occurred to me. I am quite sure this state of mind was common to most upper-class children, most of all the girls. It was all very Freudian in a curious way: money was dirt. It should be no concern of ladies except in such small quantities as not really to count: what would go into a purse was harmless. The difficulty of this point of view is that if and as money must at some point be dealt with, it assumes an unnecessary and ugly importance, like a pile of shit in a drawing-room. Teaching of simple economics would have helped, but there was nothing of the kind in our schooling in those days. Besides, it might have been disturbing.

I don't think I, or any of my contemporaries, ever read a daily newspaper unless there was something very special that we were made to read. Neither of my parents had any use for the 'popular' press, which was considered only fit for the servants (my mother had exactly the same feeling about religion). With no radio, children were far more isolated from world events than they are today. There were no 'current events' or similar school classes. Nor were we aware of the prices of ordinary things; we were taken shopping; we never did it on our own. It was often, however, pleasantly basic and untinned; there was no polythene or plastic problem. I always enjoyed a small shop in the Cornmarket at Oxford where there were great open sacks of flour and maize and other cereals that one could run one's fingers through. At that time, of course, there was a real weekly market at Oxford with beasts driven through the streets; it was very definitely a country market town as well as a university town and remained so until the Morris works started. Elliston's was the big shop, but my 'sensible' shoes came from Freeman, Hardy & Willis at the corner. On the whole we did not take our purchases away; they were delivered at the back door. If a new errand boy unwittingly went to the front door, he was sharply reproved. In Auchterarder, however, we would pick up the singed sheep's head from the smiddy by the bridge. The only prices I knew at all were for boxes of soldiers or spares for our railway.

Without economics, politics don't mean much. Yet *Harding's Luck*, published in 1909, stirred up the beginnings of political doubt. I think I know when something in the nature of real political illumination happened to me, and it is rather odd. In the interests of my education in my early teens, Maya took me to hear Lansbury and Larkin speak at an Oxford meeting in aid of the Dublin dock strike. I am sure she felt that these were people who were being unfairly treated and whom we ought to 'help', the more so perhaps as it showed that the poor Irish must continue to be looked after by the good English. Yet I think this is unfair; she was never quite as *simpliste* as I have made out. She knew (and disapproved of) the Webbs, but had certainly read some of the early Fabian essays, if only to refute them. Also, her own brand of help could be extremely practical, involving her in personal effort and expenditure. The only criterion seemed to be that whoever was to be helped must show courage in a difficult situation; this again may have been part of the reason why she felt the Irish dockers deserved—something.

So there was certainly for her, at that meeting, an element of philanthropy. But I, for my part, experienced something in the nature of conversion. In tears I put all my pocket money into the collection, a thing I had never felt impelled to do in church.

Historical research was something adults did, especially the Professor—Hume Brown, who at one stage of his career was tutor to the Haldane boys, as well as their sister, Aunt Bay, since she, unusually, shared much of their education. I thought I knew the kind of thing he did and why he didn't want to be interrupted when he was working in the dog-smelling, pipe-smelling library.

From time to time there were theologians and churchmen at Cloan. I remember the fascinating clobber of the two Archbishops, and also how Kaiser, Uncle Richard's beautiful St Bernard, putting up an amiable paw, laddered two pairs of ecclesiastical silk stockings. After that they took to duller gaiters. Kaiser was an immensely friendly dog, but his tail was just on the level of the tea table and a good wag sent the cups flying. I did not much like him in his puppy days, since, true to form, he always wanted someone to rescue and this was usually me, but, to make the rescue plausible, he had to knock me down first, often onto scratchy gravel. Later, when I could swim, I got my own back by dodging him in the chill waters of the dam, or even pulling him round by the tail. In 1914 there was an attempt to change his name to Albert (of the Belgians), but he never responded and maybe there was something in it, for he took to killing sheep. There was the terrible baying that showed he was after one, and we all poured out of the house, trying to stop him. Once, all the same, he charged at a group of black-face tups and one of them knocked him over; black-face tups don't care to be pushed around. He hated being chained, but was given a long wire and ample leash so that he could gallop in the 'Kaiser-feld'.

Later still, I remember Inge, the Gloomy Dean, coming to stay at Cloan, and one evening when I had left my elders to their arguments, but came down afterwards and found my father in a state of deep irritation, jerking his foot as he did when feeling like that, I asked what had happened, and where was the Dean? My father answered, 'I have been trying to teach the elements of Christianity to that man!'

Granniema looked very keenly on the visitors. When she was approaching her century and had taken to her bed, they were summoned to be inspected and talked with. I asked her once what she had thought of Ramsay MacDonald. 'A very agile-minded young man, my dear,' she answered.

It was a pity that my mother's and Aunt Bay's feminism never coalesced, but politics stood in the way, perhaps a touch of jealousy. However, Maya was devoted to Granniema, who enjoyed a certain liveliness in her which did not always come out in the serious Haldanes and Nelsons. Besides, Granniema's immense breadth of human sympathy easily included her daughters-in-law, though neither Maya nor Aunt Edith came to the formal New Year prayers. Nor was I in on them until much later when I was more or less grown up myself.

At this time all Granniema's available descendants, but not the in-laws, gathered at her bedside. Then Uncle Richard addressed the Absolute, explaining what the family had been doing and thinking over the year. After that Granniema asked a blessing on all of us, and we all kissed her. She looked wonderful with her two long white plaits tied with her favourite pink ribbon, her specially knitted bed jacket, and the lace and lightest of Shetland shawls over her head.

Meanwhile in Auchterarder the heidyers and futyers from the two ends of the village met and fought in a perhaps older New Year rite. I could see the lights on the ridge from Granniema's window and wished I was there. But that would not have been the right thing.

The Professor would not have come to the intimate family prayers. Dear Hume Brown, one of the last of the Whig historians of Scotland, what a nice man he was! Among the grown-ups, he was the one who was most likely not to be cross if one asked questions or showed off. He always had his own bedroom kept for him and his special armchairs in the library: the dogs loved him. But there were so many distinguished visitors at Cloan round whom we children skirmished, among dogs, politicians, philosophers, soldiers —Uncle Richard had after all organised both the Expeditionary Force and the Territorial Army in the teeth of Conservative disapproval—scientists and historians. For them the table in the hall was spread with newspapers and learned journals; I dipped into them and sometimes found something I wanted to read. A few, like *Blackwood's*, even had stories. But they had to be put back tidily.

My favourite place was the window-seat in the drawing-room behind the table with the books and the marble doves drinking. One could observe from there and absorb whatever seemed absorbable. Best of all the books, I think, was *Adventures of a Young Naturalist*. The people, chatting away in their grown-up clothes with Aunt Bay and whoever else was there, were somewhat cut off; I seldom wanted to be routed out of my hidey-hole.

There were occasional writers, like Marie Belloc Lowndes, a nice, friendly person, but the only one with whom I had a real friendship was Andrew Lang, although in my 1909 diary, at our first meeting, I found him 'silly but amusing'. We got on much better the next year, when we talked to one another about poetry and he did not, like the rest, snub me when I said that I wanted most of all to be a poet. We also talked about fairies and such. These he encouraged me to see (or think I saw). Looking back on this, it seems to me that what I perhaps perceived, rarely and fleetingly, but most commonly between the ages of about twelve and thirty-five, was as though any present moment of time consisted of something like two sheets of paper, each with a pinhole, moving against one another. If the pinholes accidentally coincided and one happened to be looking, one saw through. This was always interesting and pleasant. Twice, much later, I have seen something of the kind, but once I was in a state of great stress. One doesn't know.

However, all this led to an incident at Oxford where a poor young man from Jesus had written a Ph.D. thesis to prove the existence of fairies, and Andrew asked me to sit in as an expert on the oral examination. It was clear to me that at one point he had mixed up *voler*, to fly, and *voler*, to steal, in the French version of the Fairy Ointment story. But I was very sorry for him and realised how embarrassing it must have been for him to have me there. But what fun for Andrew Lang!

XIV

The Diving Days

I was eight years old when my father did his classic deep diving experiments for the Admiralty in the Kyles of Bute. I remember this patchily, but there is plenty about it in my 1906 diary which starts with the boat trip from Greenock in the *Mercury*, with the long loch and the hills folding and unfolding, and the obsolete battleships which were 'waiting in the water for someone to buy them'. The next two days were spent exploring the burns above the hotel at Colintraive where we stayed and about which I have somewhat dubious memories. Highland hotels were not all that good in those days. I know Boy and I played sources of the Nile, going further and further up but never quite getting to where even the smaller burns really began.

The vegetation was very different from Oxford or the Lothians, or even Cloan: dwarf oaks and birches, heather and ling; it might have been more like Cornwall but I had never been at Sennen so late in the year. I was fully aware of these differences and enjoying them. There was high heather and the bracken over my head. Apparently we saw a great many grouse—I wonder if we would now. Then 'we climbed up a quarry but at the top the midges bit so that we came down. Then we went to the beach and watched the barnacles opening and shutting their shells; a barnacle opens with slits like this.' Here a little pencil drawing of a barnacle. 'When it opens it puts out a little brown arm and sweeps the water in and gets food from the water. I found a shell with water in it and some little beasts were swimming in the water. They looked like tiny slaters, only they were blue. They seemed to be able to swim and to walk, they had a great many legs.'

When one was half one's adult height, that much nearer the surface of things, there was always something near the ground to look at. But what I now remember best were the great nests of the wood ants in the pine woods. There is only a short mention in the diary, but whenever I see them now I go back for a moment to being the me then. We were on the way to a house with a lovely garden sloping down to the sea; from the diary I identify the owners as Mr and Mrs Mackenzie—but what Mackenzies are there now in a lovely garden 'which I think is almost perfect' near Colintraive?

I also remember our expedition to the vitrified fort on Burnt Island. None of the grown-ups seemed to have had an adequate explanation of what a vitrified fort is. Clearly I was fascinated. 'We *all* wanted to take some stone away but we called one another trippers and we did not (except me).' But I was equally fascinated by the hermit crabs which walked about on our hands. At that time we had Arthur Makgill, one of the New Zealand cousins, staying with us. He must have been in his early twenties and I was clearly very devoted. I can just remember playing Consequences with him and finding him exquisitely witty.

Reminded by the diary, I recollect gazing down through very clear water at a wrecked boat with starfish and flat fish 'lying at the bottom and blinking at us'. Clearly there were two expeditions, one by ourselves, the others with the sailors from the *Spanker*, the gunboat sent by the Admiralty for my father's deep diving experiments, with Mr Catto, the diving instructor. 'He says he will take Boy down. I wish I were a boy.' These two expeditions run together in my head, but what I remember best is not even mentioned in the diary. I was steering the sailing cutter between Burnt Island and the wreck, steered too close to the wind, jibbed and the boom swept off the cap of a sailor from the *Spanker*. I was both convulsed with laughter and terrified of having done this both to a grown-up and to an adored sailor. And his cap looked so funny bobbing on the water!

There are pages and pages about the *Spanker*. My father and Boy went off to Rothesay. Maya and I followed the next day by steamer. I remember the smell of dead fish on Rothesay pier and looking over the side to see them in masses at the bottom. Possibly they were herring, which had been dumped by the fishing boats because there was no market for them, but nothing comes into the diary. We went on board and were introduced to the officers and were just in time to see Mr Catto having his diving dress put on. There is a careful description of this old type of diving dress which we got to know so well. My father even had a pipe given to him with the bowl made like a diver's helmet. At the end of the description I say, 'I cannot explain the pumps because I do not understand them, but they are each worked by six sailors turning wheels.' After that we went round with Mr Henson, the first lieutenant, who seems to have shown us everything, starting with the bridge and going on to the conning tower where I seem to have been allowed to work the foghorn. We went on to the anchors. 'I found it was like Earls Court exhibition. It is pulled up by a windlass as they do big sailing boats at Sennen.'

Then we went down to the sailors' quarters, the hammocks and the mess room. Finally we had the 4.7 guns explained. We seem to have gone into it all very thoroughly. Then 'the gunner brought a shell case and the fuse and loaded the gun and we pointed it at a boat which Father did not like at all and he said "Oh, no, wait a minute" but Boy fired! It gave the people in the boat a big jump but it could not have hurt them because there were no shells in the gun. I fired another one. Boy and I ran round to the muzzle of the gun before the nitrous fumes of the cordite came out but Father told us not to breathe it as it was poison. We looked down the inside of the gun and saw the rifling which is for the shell to go through more easily. Mr Catto came up after he had been down two and a half hours. He brought me a sea urchin, two starfish and one whelk, a very large one, all alive. The whelk's aperculum was like tortoiseshell.'

After that 'we had tea in the wardroom which is the dining-room and drawing-room of all the officers except the commander, who has a room all to himself, which must be very dull. Father had tea with him and talked business. Boy slept on board last night beside a row of rifles and pistols and he could reach to draw a dirk from his hammock. Father slept at Rothesay which cannot have been half so nice.' Clearly this was a wonderful day and I end, 'It is very nice to think we are not trippers but have come to Colintraive on business for the Admiralty.'

There is a glimpse of another side of it in a letter from Boy to Grannie. This describes how Uffer, the Owner, and the Bloke dived and then he dived himself. He tells of the pain in his ears which felt as though they were bursting 'but they didn't burst' and then he gets to the bottom, fixes the distance line and explores the bottom. 'The same beautiful light green from the sky down to the dust clouds, or as one should say mud clouds, that one kicked up.' What he doesn't mention is that as he was in a grown-up diving dress the cuffs on the sleeve were much too big for him and the water seeped in so that when he was finally brought up he was in water to the waist. But how I envied him!

There is one other thing I remember very well. It takes a lot of the diary and a drawing. 'We saw a tiny bat hanging on a little tree just outside the front door. It looked like a little mouse with wings. He hung on to the branch with little hooks at the end of his wings. He had Chain Stokes respiration which means that he left off breathing and then went on again. Father timed it and it left off breathing for ten minutes and then went on again. We cut off the branch it was on and put it into a jar. After supper it gradually woke and soon began to walk up the branch. We put in a leaf with green fly on it which it ate and Mother poured in some milk which it drank immediately. We saw its little tongue and its eyes. We put it out and in the morning it had gone.'

From then on we used to see Lieutenant, later Captain, Guy Damant quite often coming for consultations at Oxford. He was part of ordinary life and always willing to join me in my ploys. The deep diving experiments went on as well as those on submarines. Again there was Uffer's acute indignation when someone disobeyed orders, brought a diver up too quickly and let him get 'bends'. Then it was a case of telephone calls and the decompression chamber quick. The Navy had all this taped but it took longer for commercial diving firms to realise what had to be done. Later there was close contact with Siebe Gorman, who built an artificial diving tank where more experiments could be carried out. At the same time there was always work going on to improve mine rescue apparatus and methods. My father's study at Cherwell opened into an inner laboratory and a larger outer one with airtight chambers for work on various gases and pressures and the general paraphernalia of a lab, sinks and fume cupboards, glassware and balances and labelled bottles, a familiar world without ghosts.

From the beginning there were young colleagues working with Uffer, sometimes on hints from earlier unpublished and sometimes unfinished papers which my father had stuck into a drawer and not gone back to because the immediate work he was on had become so fascinating. Rob Makgill sorted them out with Douglas, Priestley, and Mavro, all young, with my father as S.P.—the Senior Partner. I don't know what the economic basis of all this was. Perhaps the University provided some finance but I don't know. That wasn't talked about. There are still masses of unsorted Haldane papers. One day—but it was the scientific excitement that came through most to my brother with a small spill-over to me.

I was expected to understand more or less what was going on and to take it seriously. There was something very heartening about the study, with its incredible litter of papers spreading from a great central oak table over the floor, and yet Uffer could usually lay hands on what he wanted. It all seemed to have a purpose. Sometimes I went in and there would be an opportune moment to ask questions, sometimes not. What mattered was never measured by a money standard; it was an idea spreading out to new conclusions, it was devising a piece of apparatus, it was convincing the Admiralty, the Home Office, the Institute of Mining Engineers or whatever it might be that something had to be done. It was a saving and bettering of human life.

Yet for me outside that there were huge areas of fantasy. The builders of the new house had left piles of gravelly sand. Here I made roads and railways and towns. Sometimes I found a stone which was in some way special. Perhaps it would become the focus of one of the constructions. It all appeared to be very important, though it would never have gone into a diary. Did the grown-ups think it was all a waste of time? One doesn't know. I remember a calm happiness about this; presumably I was playing God. As perhaps one is when one is assembling a book.

XV

Celebrations and Shows

It was certainly 'Mafeking Night'—popular celebrations for the relief of Mafeking in May 1900. My mother was an ardent imperialist, my father a pro-Boer. The Africans themselves didn't come into it one way or the other. At two and a half none of this affected me. I think Maya must have wanted me to remember this wonderful moment all my life—as indeed, in a way, I have. We were in a crowd which was probably by today's standards sufficiently orderly and gentle, although some of the crowd's methods of rejoicing brought a new word into the English vocabulary—mafficking. No doubt my hand was firmly grasped but for a moment I somehow escaped. Probably for less than a minute but I remember the feeling of sudden freedom, losing myself among strangers' legs. And that is all I do remember.

Boy and I tended to be taken to celebrations, lengthy and decorative Oxford ones, but usually with ices. After I went to school I got into the ice-eating competitors' ranks and once, in Eights Week I expect, won with fourteen. They were pink strawberry and probably smaller than today's, though perhaps made with real fruit and cream. I know I was taken later to various public occasions, royal funerals and coronations, flags and illuminations, crowds watched from windows. Nothing remains except my father telling me that the new neon lights were dangerous. And those crowds. Yes, I liked them. But I enjoyed much more going out from the cousin's house where we were staying in London and playing Indians in Campden Hill Square garden with no grown-ups about.

An important Oxford celebration was the yearly Encaenia. This was supposed to be good for my Latin and also my knowledge of the fairly famous: Empire builders were pointed out. But I only liked the gowns. What did improve my Latin were the carol services at New College which I really did enjoy; there was always a lovely theatrical feeling about them.

However, the main Oxford festivity was Eights Week, walking down through beautiful Christ Church and the meadows, hopping in anticipation, then the barge and how long till the first pink ice? One crowded to the edge, peering over, hoping one would see a boat overturned or some incident on the towpath. Everyone was cheerful, full of Eights Week gossip, what bumps were likely. This being the College barge, I was assumed to be safe, so nobody kept grabbing me. Then came the start, the wait till one could see and hear the first of the race, and almost at once one could start yelling oneself, occasionally for some crew which was doing well or with which one felt some kind of alliance, but rising to the climax of 'Well rowed, New College!' when our own boat shot past, usually well up on the cards which one filled in for the bumps. Then the runners on the towpath going by, the bicycles and the megaphones and the exciting wait for the final results.

The British Medical *soirée* in the Oxford museum was very enjoyable; there were experiments laid on, new types of apparatus and photographs. In Jack's 1904 diary—but Naomi was too young to go that year!—it was great fun: 'My pater was showing a new portable gas analysis apparatus and an apparatus for measuring dust and photographs illustrating miners' phthisis in Cornwall.' Also, after the show the high frequency current machine was made to make sparks. Later *soirées* which I remember were full of equally enthralling things.

The Edinburgh Festival was far in the future and also, I suppose, the fireworks on Calton Hill. There was of course the Auchterarder flower show, when I didn't win a prize for the best bunch of flowers, though mine had more different kinds that anyone else's. But it was all right because Granniema agreed that my bunch was the best and I think gave me a consolation prize.

The early diaries have long and careful descriptions of shows of various kinds to which Boy and I were taken. Sometimes these remind me of what had almost been forgotten, sometimes not a memory trace has been left. The earliest is 1904, when we all, including Sina, my nurse, went to see Buffalo Bill in Edinburgh, after having lunch at Jenner's, an event in itself. There was trick-shooting, the lassooing of a 'horse-thief', rough riders and Red Indians. And then the sideshows with a tiny little lady, another 'with an alive snake round her neck' and above all the performing cockatoos with their castle—yes, I think this does just come back, rather grubby white cockatoos.

It comes back more when I read Jack's diary, increasingly badly written every year. He details the Jenner's lunch: 'strawberries, sugar & cream, scones & lemon squash'. He too liked the lady snake charmer, but also mentioned a giant and a dwarf—Princess Noumahawa. He describes twenty-two different scenes and goes into technical detail about the military ones, but with a certain fine contempt for Yankee methods. There seem also to have been English cavalry, Mexicans, Arabs and Japanese, as well as a replica of the battle of Little Big Horn.

The next year we went to Hengler's Royal Italian Circus: 'I am going to tell only about the performances I was interested in.' These were all animals, including a baby elephant, 'the smallest ever seen in Europe'. After the circus 'we went behind the scenes and fed the beasts'. This was clearly just one better than the Zoo.

The same year we went to Earl's Court, where there must have been some kind of permanent show, where we went on board 'the cruiser' with moving pictures at each side. Then there was the moving staircase—strange to think how unknown this was!—and a diver in a tank: 'very interesting because father is going to Portsmouth to help the Admiralty divers to find out how to work at lower levels.' Last and best was the water chute, something I still love.

This was just before my father took Boy to work with him on his first serious set of experiments: 'Father said he was better than a laboratory boy, he made soda-lime.' We stayed with the Harcourts at their huge house, St Clair, Ryde, and had peaches after breakfast. Vernon Harcourt, the distinguished old chemist, had been one of my father's predecessors as a Gas Referee: he was an FRS of the generation who still had private laboratories for their own work.

Here I was allowed to blow my first glass, undeterred by Sina. Like most really good scientists, Vernon Harcourt was always ready to explain things, even to a child.

Sina and I stayed on at the Seaview Hotel from which I wrote: 'I went to Seaview pier this afternoon, it is a sort of suspension pier, it wiggles when several people go along it.' I have a notion that it also wiggled when firmly jumped upon by me.

We used to go from Cloan to an occasional fair or market, at one of which my mother, nodding to an auctioneer friend, inadvertently bought a flock of lambs. And we went to the library at Innerpeffray where they keep Montrose's sword and Bible, to be shown to and handled by relations, of whom I was one, through descent from Montrose's sister married to a Haldane. That gave one a great feeling of status. Yet I found industrial processes equally fascinating; the day Colonel Hally took us round the Auchterarder cloth mill gets four pages of diary, though I confessed to not quite understanding every bit of the process.

I don't think I now remember anything about the Edinburgh International Exhibition, but at ten I found it deeply satisfactory. 'First we did all the whirligigs, the figure of eight railway, the water chute and the flying boats; then we did the maze.' There were also Jacobite relics, communion tickets and 'a village of West Africans from Sierra Leone. They were very black and horribly ugly. They ran on a far flatter foot than a European and they kicked up their legs in front of them.' They were all doing something, a woman was twisting up her hair into braids 'which looked just like very old boot laces'. The men who were dancing 'were evidently witch doctors'. So much for the imperial point of view! The second day we went to the Exhibition it seems that the main attraction was pictures: 'Some of them were very interesting to me, as I have seen their engravings so often.'

In 1909 we went to the Marine Gardens at Portobello, where there were switchbacks, a roller-skating rink and, best of all, a menagerie with three baby lions, the first to be born in Edinburgh. There was also a small circus with performing animals. Finally tea at a public house managed by the East of Scotland Public House

Trust. The publican got no profit on his alcohol sales, only on the food sales; clearly this interested me; I had already seen too many drunks in Scotland. We seem to have had a very good tea.

As the years go by, while my brother became more deeply interested in science, I seem to be more stirred by visual beauty, storms and sunsets: 'a golden sunset with the Forth Bridge looking like spider's web hung across it'. I was ten when Uncle Richard got a car for Cloan, a Daimler, I expect, and of course with a driver. My great treat was sitting in front next to him with everything pouring by. There were still flocks of sheep which were quite un-used to motor traffic and ran in front without trying to get away. But there were also children playing Last Over, a game which must have accounted for a few accidents. One day we drove right across the strath to Loch Earn. I write: 'Loch Earn is about the most beautiful place I have ever seen; the further end was hidden by a golden haze, so that it looked unended as if it was the sea.' All was made still better by the Stuarts of Ard Vorlich who showed me their black fantails 'iridescent with green and purple'. Colour and form had begun to beat on me, to need to be written about.

Of course the best show of all was St Giles' Fair at Oxford, though we were not often back from Scotland in time for it. In 1907 'first Boy and I went on a merry-go-round for which they only charged ½ penny, but it was not much fun, but the next one was splendid as the horses went up and down as well as round and round. We went up the lighthouse and slid down again on a mat.' Then we and the Slessors went on the great wheel and after that the whole family engaged in shooting, which must have been rather fairer in those days as 'Mother and I got a bottle down almost every time.' In the end 'Mother went home and Boy and I went to some more shows.'

Although the later diaries found me in Scotland, I had over the years several more days of St Giles' Fair, which have coalesced. One year they started whirling platforms which centrifuged people off. However I managed to stay in the middle, shutting my eyes and carefully spreading my weight in different directions; this impressed the proprietor so much that I got several free rides. We usually came back with coconuts and probably other 'prizes'; the cost of anything was still in pennies and still the top of the great wheel showed the glorious crowded streets and the fair noises coming up, mixed and transmuted. It seems to me, but I may be wrong, that the fair folk were friendlier than they are now, interested not only in collecting the money, but in helping everyone to have a good time.

For me, however, the supreme show seems to have been soldiers. Now, I get this out of the diaries. Otherwise I am sure I would have forgotten it, which only shows what tricks one's subconscious can get up to if one's political convictions are allowed to interfere. I have forgotten quite a number of large areas of imagination, of which army manoeuvres, something very far removed from real life, is one. The other which I know about but cannot get a clue onto which I can latch, is the vast area of stories told to myself which I know went on for years and finally turned into writing story books. There is of course nothing about this in the diaries; it was no part of the outside world. It was as secret as They. But why can't I remember it? Especially as it must have been very much a major part of the Me who is still Me. I think, but with no real certainty, that the stories had no real background in time or place and that they involved long conversations which gave me great pleasure to devise; some may have risen out of the books I read; it is also possible that some may have been a dip into a changed state of consciousness. If this was so, it is quite possible that I might not remember unless I could get back into that particular 'high'. I would not like to be definite about this, but certainly I could get somewhere, so to speak, else, and might have to be recalled and told I was dreaming.

I think sometimes I involved other people in the stories, especially in recognisable activities like the 'orchid-collecting' which gradually merged into the daylight world of real field botany. Boy or my mother might be someone in the story as well as themselves. But what zones of fancy I wandered in and whether—as is probable—they were erotic zones, that door is shut. I may have had fantasies of war, violence, torture, Mazeppa bound on wild horses, but all completely unreal and ready to vanish with my first knowledge of real war and, in the surgical wards of St Thomas's, real wounds and real, stinking gangrene.

That, then, has gone, unless some chance turning over of a stone leaves it uncovered. But the soldiers? There were Territorial camps near Cloan, and an occasional mention in the diaries; but I remember how exciting it was to see the tents and the fires and all the paraphernalia of soldiering. In 1907, in London, 'We passed a battery of Royal Horse Artillery with 6 guns. They looked splendid.' Then there were the O.T.C. camps which Boy clearly enjoyed as he grew older and tougher; they were full of physical tests which he tended to pass with pride and pleasure. But in 1909, in my last but one year at school, we ran into some big army manoeuvres and I write page after excited page. My mother was deep in it; her involvement with army matters and people is clear from her own book.

The diary gets tremendously detailed and excited. They seem to have been the biggest manoeuvres ever to take place in England and it sounds as though everyone had enjoyed them vastly. Boy and I went to the camp at Wolvercote, and two days later the whole family drove out beyond Woodstock. We nearly found ourselves in a flower and dog show and I remark smugly, 'I wonder anyone could go and see a flower show with troops so near.' Soon we found the Gordon Highlanders playing football and some field artillery drawn by cart horses, as well as telephone mules with the coils of wire. The next day we went in another direction, hiring a pony cart at Kingham, and delightedly watched a 'white' scout being captured by the 'browns'. 'Boy, whom we met afterwards, told us that he had seen a man captured by some Highlanders. He had managed to escape, but one of the Highlanders took the safety pin out of his kilt and punctured both tyres of his bicycle, which he had left behind him. Boy lent him some rubber solution to mend the tyres with after the Highlander had gone.'

Then we climbed Ickham Hill and listened excitedly to the rifle fire, 'the pop-popping of the pompoms and the distant roar of big guns'. Boy and I came close to the artillery and watched the whole process. Then there was a battle for Ickham station attacked by the 'whites' and defended by the Gordons. 'They charged down hill into the whites and took about a dozen prisoners. They often got very excited, especially at close quarters, and I saw one man pull his officer down into the ditch beside him, saying "You're not out of their fire, Sir". Altogether I think this was about the nicest day I have had yet. I found *Senecio Erucifolius*, rare.'

That night Boy slept under a hedge and had brambles, chocolate and cider for breakfast 'as the troops had eaten everything else'. The next morning we were out there again, but it was foggy, and I was, I think, a little disappointed to see lancers in their ordinary khaki service clothes 'without pennons on their lances or any of the usual colour on their horses' harness or their own clothes. They looked very businesslike and real.' The next day there was a tremendous hailstorm. I write about the havoc in the garden, and note, 'I am collecting the seeds of the thorn apple in the garden, which can be made into stuff nearly as valuable as opium.' However I think I was aware that it was highly poisonous. I did a lot of experimenting in those days, nibbling away at various plants and occasionally finding something which did me no good. But later the family went off again to look at the soaked troops; I think: 'it must be terribly unwholesome work lying out in the wet all night'. The diary ends with the same smug note: 'We seem to have seen more of the manoeuvres than most civilians.'

This was the diary which, on another page, records that I had been 'reading More's "Utopia" as you advised me'—this no doubt being pointed at the Skipper! 'It strikes me as being a most horribly socialistic place, where it would be impossible to live in peace.' A rather odd comment.

But why, until I looked at the diaries again, had I so totally forgotten the manoeuvres? I suppose all that was completely blotted out by real war, the first excitement almost like manoeuvres, imagined as being the same, except that the British army seemed inexplicably to be retreating. And then the repeated shock of the killings when one after the other of my friends were killed—gone for always—and I went to Nigg to see Boy in the Black Watch and knew I would do anything in the world to avert it from him but knew also that I was utterly powerless to do anything at all.

All Change Here

Girlhood and Marriage

CONTENTS

I

Boy into Girl

This book is, I am afraid, less factual and more self-centred than its predecessor, *Small Talk*. It seems as though one's clear memory of how things looked and smelled and sounded and tasted, which goes back into childhood, gets twisted and obscured with the coming of puberty. It is not one's self one looks back on but a teenager or, as we said then, a flapper. What affinity have I with this creature? I can fit quite well into the six-year-old, not into the sixteen-year-old. As in the earlier book certain things stand out, but often in a different way to how they did when I was a child; where the child can be an individualist, the essential thing for a teenager is to conform. So I must write about myself as the perceiver, but largely the conformer, sometimes rebelling a bit, but never quite enough. Again, if I am to be honest about a book of 'memories', I ought only to put in what I can actually remember; and as one gets out of one's hardheaded childhood with its factual curiosity about the adult world, the main thing one remembers is one's self. So this book is not so much social history, those taken-for-granted differences which are so curious now; there is more about the development of a writer and that is something which is perhaps of interest. It begins in 1910.

And here I had better firmly mark in the family: my father, John Scott Haldane, whom I sometimes called Uffer, the physiologist and philosopher, a Fellow of New College, but working mostly in his own laboratory, built onto our house, Cherwell, at the end of Linton Road in Oxford, with his own team of young scientists. Behind him Cloan, the family house on the

9

north-western slope of the Ochills. There lived his mother—Granniema to me—his brothers, Richard, then War Minister in the Liberal Government, and Willie, father of the Foswell cousins, and his sister Elizabeth—Aunt Bay to me. Then there was my mother, whom I called Maya, with an Edinburgh background, but her mother—Grannie to me—was now a widow living with us, having brought much of the Edinburgh furniture down with her. Above all there was my brother Jack in his last year at Eton and then at New College.

But now let us look for a moment at the process of finding one's way back in time. Apart from memories, what evidence have I for what I am going to write? The school diaries which I used in *Small Talk* came to an end after I left the Dragon School. There would have been little incentive to write a diary without competition and the almost certainty of getting a prize! I missed the school prizegivings, the hall filled with parents who probably did one credit and one's proud walk up to the platform; the number of times one managed this in one prizegiving was comparable to the number of pink ices one could manage at a party.

But just a diary for its own sake? No. I wrote them occasionally later in periods of great stress and during the whole of World War Two, but for the six years from 1910 to 1916 my written evidence is in letters to, by or about me and occasionally the *Draconian* itself, the school magazine, for I still kept up with it and sent in my poems. It was sad for me now to pass the Dragon School but no longer to be part of it. So many loyalties were involved, most of all perhaps to the Skipper, C. C. Lynam. Clearly he was a marvellous teacher, green-fingered with children, but dull organisation was not his line. Hum, his brother, was the organiser and I, instinctively feeling myself on the side of chaos, was indignant on the Skipper's behalf whenever Hum appeared to be superseding him and bringing a lot more order into an ever-growing school, gradually spreading over more and more North Oxford fields.

For some reason my brother, J. B. S. Haldane, and I were allowed for a few years to set an annual general paper for the school. It was full of questions and catches, mostly on modern events or trends (*vers libre*—at that time one never said 'free verse' although I suppose unrhymed verse had really started in America—was translated either as bookworm or 'towards freedom —motto of a political party'). But we ranged through the ages ('Virgil was the mother of Our Lord; there is a picture called the Virgil and Child'). I expect brother Jack must have put in some scientific questions. We marked the papers, wrote a report and enjoyed ourselves. I felt that with this I was still in touch. But how I longed to be once again in one of the Shakespeare plays! How much I wanted the smell of the greasepaint, the lights and the poetry! Sometimes still I dream of this, and great swatches of Shakespeare come back, but I am always afraid of getting my cues wrong.

As for other outside evidence of what we were all like, there are photographs. It isn't always easy to get inside them or remember the occasion, but I know I was taken to be photographed once a year at least. It was the same for Jack. My mother's big desk which had been in the family for two or three generations had a kind of fence of photographs and these also gradually crept all over her walls. It was as though one was forever being pegged down. Yet they quickly ceased to be really me. From the family letters about me it appears that I was admired, encouraged and protected, too much of all three I expect. It gave me a certain kind of over-confidence—so long as I did the right and acceptable thing. Sooner or later if I was ever to be or do anything on my own, this over-confidence had to be reconsidered and broken. But how was one to know?

One thing did break a part of it. I had enjoyed myself very much at the Dragon School. I was for all practical purposes a boy until the awful thing happened. I was twelve, still at the Dragon School, unsuspecting. I had little or no pubic hair; my breasts were ungrown and did not in fact develop until my mid-teens. And then there was blood on my blue serge knickers. I was quickly pulled out of school and I never went back. I couldn't quite understand why, only it seemed that it was something about me which was shameful and must above all never be mentioned to a school friend. It had been a complete surprise, because I had not taken in my mother's carefully veiled and no doubt physiologically inaccurate information. The process was not at all well known at that time, and there were many superstitions about it and little medical help. Even for unbelievers a reading of the Old Testament (those bits of *Leviticus* probably gobbled while one was supposed to be merely taking in the bloodthirsty tribal adventures in *Kings*) with its perpetual reference to uncleanness added to one's unpleasant feelings. For many years I had monthly pain, distress and acute embarrassment; I was taken to various doctors, but, as nobody understood the physiological process, this did not help. The curse, as it was always called, was a main trouble most of my life. After all, it is only in the last twenty years or so that all this has been taken seriously and without embarrassment. In my day men knew nothing or next to nothing about it. Soon after we were married Dick told me that he had been given to understand that ladies had something in the nature of headache every month. Girls of my age were not allowed to swim at these times, which for me sometimes went on for ten days, and were discouraged from many other activities. Tampax did not come in till I was in my thirties, though at least disposables must have arrived with or soon after World War One.

It was all very discouraging and I acquiesced in it, as indeed in other discouragements, but no doubt resentments and determinations built up inside. At a jumble sale I bought a small jug for a penny. It had 'Adventure to the Adventurous' written on it. That, some day, was to be my motto. But meanwhile I went on being what was expected of me. What then, would happen after the end of being a boy at the Dragon School?

If I had been sufficiently determined, I suppose I might have gone away to boarding school, in fact to Priorsfield which, because Mrs Huxley had been headmistress, was acceptable. But two things intervened. My brother would be at New College in a year's time, and I wouldn't want to miss being with him in

Oxford, would I? And did I really want to leave home? Although this was not said in so many words, it was apparent that, if I chose the boarding school, I would hurt the feelings of Those Who Loved One Best. Another solution must be found.

Thus, at twelve I left the Dragon School and found myself with four of those strange beings, girls of my own age. For years in my later life I completely lost touch with all of them; I didn't know if they were alive or dead. They were part of something which had ceased to be real. But in the past, which is the reality about which I write, they are very much alive. Frances, with whom I was friends longest, and whom, only lately, I surprisingly re-found, was grand-daughter of the Warden of Wadham, with two younger sisters, Gwenny and Lily. Shirley too had University parents. Both of these had rather large noses, which would have been no disadvantage with today's fashions and hair-do's, but probably was then, when delicacy of features was more admired. Mary Cooke had this; she was, I think, the niece of J. A. R. Marriott, at one time Conservative candidate for the University, and she had two very pretty, red-haired younger sisters. Her mother was quite a talented painter; she did a romantic water-colour of me, all long fair hair and blue eyes. Finally there was Geraldine, who was plumper, had darker, rather fuzzy hair and lots of freckles. All were definitely young ladies whose brothers or male cousins went to reputable and expensive public schools, where various kinds of learning were shovelled into them, if necessary by the cane, but whose own education was mainly in the hands of a governess with no particular qualifications as a teacher, but possibly the ability to please their mothers, her employers. She stayed with us, in the smallest, north-facing guest room, with her small wardrobe and her few photographs. Her name was Miss Blockey, quickly turned into Blockywox. After we all grew up I went on writing to her occasionally, since by then I had ceased to blame her for my own lack of education; I think in the end she died in some kind of 'home'. I am sure she did her best with five potentially rather bright girls and possibly did less harm than some of the public school masters did to their brothers. But as I came into my teens I was worriedly aware of how far I had slipped behind my old school contemporaries like Jack Slessor, in actual learning of basic school material, though, all the same, I could put no effort into learning on my own.

We had lessons in the school-room at Cherwell, the large new house my parents had built in 1906 at the end of Linton Road, where the hedges had already been cut down and newer houses had been built, in a style slightly more 'rustic' than Cherwell, with lower ceilings and more bay windows with smaller panes, which I thought much nicer than our own big sash windows. The school-room on the top floor was pleasant, with a bit of slope on the ceiling, and plenty of windows to west and north. In the big toy cupboard there were still the boxes of bricks, the rails and rolling stock of the railways that we had played with so often, but suddenly didn't want to. My brother was clearly too old for them; it was no good without him. I never got them out for my classmates; they had to wait for my own children. The old doll's house stood on the landing outside, but again, I hardly ever looked at it now.

Below the school-room was Maya's—my mother's—bedroom, also facing north-west, but the large window mostly blocked by a dressing-table with a full-length mirror and sets of drawers, in one of which were my many hair ribbons; behind was a wicker shoe basket. Here I used to sit in front of the mirror while my hair was brushed and, uncomfortably, combed for scurf, which I felt was somehow shameful and unladylike. Many remedies, suggested by doctors or hairdressers, were tried and had little effect, but some were greasy and meant I had to wear a cap out of doors. These silk caps were quite pretty, but they were not what other girls wore. Naturally, I grew out of scurf in a year or two, so there was really no need to have made me so uncomfortable or ashamed.

Now, Maya's bedroom was one of the least nice of the rooms at Cherwell. The two best, facing south, were for Grannie, her mother, as bedroom and sitting-room, though there was another, smaller and badly proportioned room with windows south and north, which was Maya's own sitting-room or study and where, later, I had a small bureau and bookshelves. When we first moved to Cherwell I had a room of my own, facing over the fields and the river. But after my childhood troubles, a broken leg and after that an operation for a TB neck gland, I had a bed in my mother's room, just under the smaller window; fresh air was thought to be basic for TB. Yet also I am fairly certain that my presence was to ensure that my father should not be allowed in. His room, a rather meagre slice, always smelling of pipe tobacco, was opposite on the other side of the passage, but that side of the marriage was definitely over. She would have been forty-five or so and he some five years older. In her room and in that bed I stayed and dreamed into adolescence.

There was a marble-topped washstand with matching jugs, basins and small ware, above it a medicine cupboard, beyond it a very large dark, carved wardrobe with ample hanging space and deep drawers. The main decoration of my mother's mantelpiece was a large frame of family photographs on a green velvet background—her side of the family. It seemed a crowded room and it is odd, now, to think that she did not move, after Grannie's death, into the big bedroom with the broad south-facing bow, though she did move into the equally pleasant sitting-room. There was a small bedroom between Grannie's bedroom and the bathroom, which had been for Grannie's lady's maid. Perhaps my mother felt that it would be in some way wrong—a deviation from her increasingly spartan way of personal life—to take the nicer bedroom; but at the same time she may have had an undercurrent of resentment at not having a lady's maid of her own.

On the large landing, whose main decoration was a huge gilt-framed pier glass and a marble-topped, gilt-edged sideboard, there was a rather strange WC. It had an outer and inner door. From inside I could hear Grannie shuffling in slow slippers across the landing, opening the outer door and trying the inner, while I stayed very quiet; the brass hook rattled. If she came in? Now, in nightmares, she does. What is the connection? I liked Grannie on the whole and wasn't afraid of her. Was it simply that the shuffle was the approach of old age which I feared desperately? It has come, certainly, and it is very annoying. Why? Villon said it all. But it has brought long experience; it is not simply something that has pounced on me quite unaware between the opening of two doors. In a child's fable I read once, a boy, wanting to be grown-up, unrolls the magic reel and *is*— irrecoverably. I want to go back and forth, as, in a way, I am doing now.

However, there were several other loos in the new house, including the servants' on the back stairs and the 'gentlemen's' through the bicycle-smelling cloakroom off the outer hall, where hats and coats hung. It was down two steps and the only place in the house with a fixed basin—except of course for the lab sinks. It had a red-tiled floor where a drop or two of menstrual blood did not show, as they tended to on the upstairs lino. There was also a faintly forbidden flavour about using it.

But upstairs in the school-room, what did I and the other girls talk about? Plans for games, I suppose, or picnics. Possibly we discussed our parents, swapped stories about them. What, if anything, did we learn? Miss Blockey took us through some history books, asking questions no doubt; nothing remains. History bored me deeply. If she tried to teach English grammar, as she may have done, I was already perfectly capable of handling the language and, usually, the spelling. All of us could write a reasonably good essay. Her own reading was limited and cautious; she was no leader. French progressed slowly. Arithmetic? No doubt it continued. Lately I was asked how one did long division; all I could remember was that one put on two ears. Music lessons went on; there was a piano in the school-room and Miss Blockey played, I suppose, fairly well, and saw to it that I practised scales, easy pieces and singing. The nicest things were the settings of the *Just So* songs. But, apart from College carols, I don't remember ever being taken to a concert or recital.

I doubt if we got anything from any of her other lessons except some smatterings of German; I quite enjoyed reciting bits of Schiller, but *Faust* was proving difficult and perhaps, although a classic, not quite nice. When we were released from the school-

16

room we simply bounded off, running downstairs and out. By this time there was quite a farm at Cherwell, Jersey cows, poultry, pigeons and my own families of guinea pigs. There were the carriage horses and my pony—I suppose nobody ever rode her again after my riding accident—and the pony carriage. There were lots of old hedges—hawthorn and sloe and crab-apple—and it was a good hide-and-seek place.

At first I had been shy of the other girls, never having thought of myself as anything but another boy, but later I got to know them, especially Frances. We went to tea with one another and played versions of the games I had always played, with an element of make-believe, of being someone else, someone more interesting; and we bullied younger sisters and kept them out of our games. Tea in Wadham with Frances was best; we used to have it in a kind of pantry room—or so it was much later in Maurice Bowra's time—from which there was supposed to be a secret passage into Trinity, though we never could find it, even after we moved all the furniture in those back rooms. Afterwards we played in the huge beautiful Fellows' garden, full of great trees, enclosed by mellowed stone walls. I do remember playing prisoners and captives under one of the dark, spreading yew trees and making Frances tie my wrists, though this was perhaps a little later, at fifteen or sixteen. There was a deep excitement about this, not recognisable or at least not nameable at this time. If a grown-up had found us and asked: 'What do you children think you are doing?' we would have collapsed into sullen shame. Sexual shame? Maybe. For me it was all connected with the stories which I still told myself and of which, I suppose, versions persisted into my earlier books and are perhaps recognised by some of the young who are given *The Conquered* to read so as to improve their ancient history. Bedside books, clearly!

But, as for lessons, it must have been apparent that Miss Blockey's amiability and capacity for being put upon concealed serious deficiencies. Perhaps my brother may have pointed this out. I don't know if my father paid any attention to my education or if it was quite outside his world. I went for Latin to Jack Denniston, then a young don. Latin bored me, but I was willing to do a bit of work to please him. I was set for Junior Locals, presumably something in the nature of 'O' Levels, though I am sure on a lower standard in most subjects except perhaps classics; I supposed I would go to university, but with little idea of what this was about; it was just something one did. For a few weeks I was coached in maths by a young woman whose name I have forgotten, but who undid some of the harm of my earlier maths teaching. With her, horizons expanded; I was very happy. One can teach oneself history, geography, some science and some elements of a foreign language, but for maths I think one needs a certain amount of leadership and explanation. I wish I could have gone on, but perhaps that would have been thought silly and extravagant. Later, Jack did some solid geometry with me, which I enjoyed equally.

I missed the excitement and competition of school exams. I had always enjoyed them, especially when they happened, not in the classrooms, but in the school hall. One limbered up for them and then went all out. When, occasionally, I dream about exams, it is usually pleasurable and exciting. So, would this ambitious, competitive young thing have done better at a large school? Would she have been better directed? One thing is clear. Whatever education parents provide for their children, it is always wrong.

II

Rouen to Doncaster

I still had minimal pocket money, sixpence a week perhaps; I never went shopping on my own, even if it was I who harnessed the pony and drove the pony carriage down into Oxford. I never went alone to the Rhea bathing place. When I went out to tea I was usually taken and fetched, except for the Cookes who only lived a few houses up Linton Road. Above all I must never be alone in the Parks, especially not on any of the small paths, nor yet in the lane beyond the Dragon School, because there might be a Man. The lane had in large letters on one wall 'Commit No Nuisance'; it was no use asking what this meant but it had something to do with the Man. I think I was more carefully shepherded now than when I was at school.

At home I never brushed my own hair and was dissuaded from trying. I am not sure when I was 'allowed up' for dinner, but even when this started I was always sent to bed early and obediently went. Above all, I must tell everything I did and if possible everything I thought. Yet it would be entirely wrong to say that I really minded this; it was talking about oneself, always a favourite occupation, and so long as it was in the right direction, my mother was tremendously understanding and encouraging. Not being Truthful, not being Frank with Me, that could be very unpleasant. I doubt if I was punished, only sadness and disapproval were felt. But nobody knew what stories I told myself; I was never asked about them; they were a world.

However, for all this babying, some other quite adult social activities were encouraged. From my early teens I was one of the badged Victoria League guides to the parties of overseas visitors, who came mostly in the Summer Term and who were shepherded round the colleges in groups. I always took mine up New College tower, probably at a brisk trot. The porter always gave me the keys, safer with me than with my father who once inadvertently carried them off to Scotland. I am not at all sure how much actual history of the colleges I knew, but I don't think I was ever at a loss to produce something interesting. At some point in summer there was always a river steamer excursion down to Iffley and beyond; sometimes the Harcourts gave a party in the beautiful garden of Stanton Harcourt, for I remember a tumble of small roses down the terraces and wishing we had anything like that in our flat Cherwell garden with its remarkably unsatisfactory built-up rockery.

This was the pleasantest part of my continuing involvement with Maya's imperialist politics. I did not so much care for the Rhodes scholars, nor for blind 'Trooper Molloy', much used for Empire propaganda and again, at a later stage, for recruiting. There were other young Tory favourites whom I was supposed to look on as extra brothers; no doubt I went along with this after a fashion. I am rather surprised that I never became a Girl Guide; perhaps this would have been in some way unladylike.

In term time there were Sunday tea parties in the hall at Cherwell, with undergraduates, including Rhodes scholars and various cousins who turned up from time to time. The hall had Chinese willow-pattern plates hung on one wall, de Morgan tiles round the fireplace, some splendid bits of furniture and a portrait of Uncle John, Regius Professor of Physiology and first of the family scientists. It also had a grandfather clock whose loud tick sounded through the house at night, apparently chasing one upstairs. There was another in the drawing-room, with a gentler tick, brought south by Grannie with other Edinburgh furnishings. The oldest of the white-aproned removers chided my mother over this: 'Och, Mistress Haldane, what are you thinking on, to put the hall clock in the drawing-room?' But it looked well there.

The drawing-room with the heavy Morris curtains was beautiful. The marble fireplace was carved with laurel wreaths and on the wide shelf were Chinese vases and bowls; the hearth was hand-beaten copper—made, like many of the furnishings, by Charlie ffoulkes, my mother's artistic cousin—and here were the crested fire irons which, unhappily, disappeared at some point; they are somewhat rare. The long bookcase was crowded with china and glass, as was the glass-fronted cupboard above one of the bureaux. Much of this was the very handsome but un-marked Trotter china, probably ordered in quantity by several branches of the family, most likely Worcester. There were also the Lowestoft bowls and jugs, painted in China (many years later we found the crest and directions for painting in Chinese characters) which my mother's grandmother had consigned to the dairy.

The bow-fronted satinwood chest of drawers had the Samoan things which my grandfather had collected when he was consul (being the only English Gentleman—although Scottish—about in those parts at that time) and a few boomerangs which my brother and I got hold of. We were practising with them in the field outside the house when he threw one which decided to come for me. I had seen them dig their sharp points into the ground so decided not to lie down but to hold my own boomerang across my face; the thrown one flickered at me across the space between us; I had time to register what a good war weapon its zigzagging near-invisibility made it; then it hit the one I was holding and slid down it, cutting my finger open. Jack was really upset, but I felt I had been sensible and was pleased with myself.

The other big bureau, made by French prisoners-of-war at Edinburgh Castle during the Napoleonic wars and beautifully inlaid, had much family material, books and documents and the scrap books in red flannel covers. I have it now. It has a secret drawer at the back, but what is exciting enough to put into it? At my age, nothing. But maybe I shall think of something yet.

The drawing-room had a door, always kept locked, into an unsatisfactory little greenhouse, where I tried to grow things. All I was successful with were the cactuses which I stole, as buds or leaves, from the Botanic Gardens and which would suddenly produce astonishing flowers. We never had a gardener who was any good; that would have been an extravagance. Besides, Maya liked to give orders and have them carried out without question, a thing no good gardener could have put up with; she could never have got onto good terms with an Oxfordshire gardener; he would have had to be a Scot, and one never turned up.

I was still a passionately keen wild flower collector. Sometimes the Wild Flower Society, which provided the diaries in which one wrote names and dates, queried my entries, but I would never have cheated over this, whatever else I might have cheated over. I knew all the special wild flower places, the shallow lake and woodland of Ruskin's Plot, Cowley Marsh, now built over, where one used to find some of the rarer orchises; Bessel's Leigh, where I once taught a Sunday School class about Noah's ark; the heights above Hinksey and, further on, the beginnings of the chalk and the rare haunts of *anemone pulsatilla*. Some of these expeditions must have been excessively boring for those who were with me and couldn't possibly have shared my enthusiasm. I suppose it was mostly my mother, and it was the price of keeping an eye on me. There were interesting plants up-river in the edges of water meadow and copse, and then there was Cloan in the summer holidays, with Granniema, my father's mother, who shared my interest and encouraged me to find parsley fern in the screes of Craig Rossie. She was now approaching her nineties and becoming, for me at least, an increasingly genial and interesting figure, with good stories of her young days if one got her to talk about them.

However, we never went back to Cornwall for our lovely, magic holidays at Sennen Cove and I resented this, always asking why couldn't we go. Instead there were Easter holidays in what were supposed to be more educational places. Once we stayed in Dover and went over to Calais on a day trip. But it wasn't like going out with the Sennen boats. Yet one thing stands out; these were the days of early cinema. Jack and I went as often as we possibly could and watched entranced the improbable, captioned adventures of various characters, for these were the days of serials, including the Exploits of Elaine, also of the cinema piano or even orchestra, the pounding of hooves, the chug-chug of the absorbingly oncoming train. As yet the splendid disappearing cinema organ was not with us and many of the cinema halls were somewhat flea-pittish, but if Jack was looking after me it was assumed that all was well.

During Jack's last year at Eton, however, when I was fourteen, it was arranged that in order to improve my French I should stay a fortnight or so with a family at Le Havre, but duly chaperoned by Miss Blockey, and then rejoin Maya and Jack at Rouen en route for Paris. I had one of the Victor Hugo's to read, in fact I was supposed only to read and speak French. Probably I had a Dumas as well. It put me off Dumas and Victor Hugo for life. It seems odd, considering the general censorship, that I should be pushed, at fourteen, into reading *Les Misérables*; however, it was a classic, and in a foreign language. A little later I was also pushed through *War and Peace* in French; it was only when I re-read it, much later and suspiciously, in English, that I realised what sort of book it was. But I was not encouraged to read some of the English classics. *Tom Jones* was strictly kept from me until the time Aldous Huxley came to stay and persuaded my mother that this was Eng. Lit. and an essential part of my education.

However, I ploughed through three or four pages a day at Le Havre. The family also had a couple of young Germans staying—perhaps indeed it was some sort of semi-educational establishment?—and I picked up a little German from them; they always referred to Madame as *die alte Hexe*. I quite liked the harbour area, but mostly we went for walks in the dull suburbs. Perhaps it was more fun for Miss Blockey; she might even have had a mild flirtation.

However, she took me over to Rouen and here an explosive aesthetic experience overtook me. You might think that, living in Oxford, I ought to have been used to Gothic; there is good stained glass in various college windows, including New College. But no. Rouen Cathedral, St Ouen, the clock, the *patisserie*, the thought of Joan of Arc, bound to the stake by soldiers, all combined into a riot of feeling, an alteration of consciousness which I find hard to explain and cannot recover or describe; I only know it happened and that, from time to time in my life, something of the same sort has happened. I drank and drank in the colours of the glass, twined myself into the traceries, quite unable to express any of it, especially to poor old Blockywox who must have wondered what had come over me.

Then we went on to Paris and stayed in a respectable North Bank hotel and ate an excellent *table d'hôte*, but suffered a bit from the current French loos in little corners of the landings. My mother insisted on paper seat covers; I think she always took these about with her, as well as various myths about catching loathsome but anonymous diseases.

Jack and I went to Luna Park and naturally on all the switchbacks and slides and water chutes. At one point we became slightly detached and I was approached by a Man. In fact I think he may have tried to kiss me and I hit him. It was exciting but rather guilt-making, though good for my French. But somehow, if I had behaved as a real lady at all times, it would not have happened, so it was my fault. But why was our mother told? Confession? Or me just wanting to describe something that interested me, a habit I still have but have tried to sublimate in writing books? Or just because we had been brought up to Tell Mother Everything, a very bad principle? Apart from that, we did some shopping at the Bon Marché, ribbons at least.

This business of being a lady was continually besetting me. There were things which, apparently, I should have known by instinct, or if I had listened attentively to what I was told. But I didn't and hadn't. Sometimes I felt as if I was netted by invisible rules, then I would forget. Jack's last year at Eton, when he was nineteen and I was fourteen, seemed to be very full of these invisible rules for a visiting sister. He was by now Captain of the school, multiple prize winner, wielder of a Pop cane. He duly wore a carnation in his buttonhole. For a long time afterwards, the rules of Pop, framed by pale blue-ribboned canes, adorned the school-room. I had of course shared in the general prep school sadism, when one listened outside the headmaster's study for the swish of 'a juicy one'. Normally this went with the bravado of coming out with a swagger but this was not possible for me, although when I had my hair judicially pulled as an equivalent punishment I managed the swagger all right. I think Jack may well have enjoyed an occasional ritual beating, but it was probably going out even in his time, and I doubt if he did it much.

Maya and I went down for the Fourth of June and watched Jack as Lord Burleigh in *The Critics*, though the dramatic performance I still remember was by an earnest young Catholic reciting Heine: *Die Mutter Gottes zu Kevlaar tragt heut' ihr bestes Kleid*. Jack was not one for cricket and my one visit to Lords was only assuaged by many pink ices. He played wall game and was celebrated in verse over this, as well as in one of Ronnie Knox's alphabets with 'H is for Haldane who has a white spot On the back of his head where others have not.' For he had this patch of white hair which occasionally seems to turn up in the family. He was Captain of the Boats too, rowing in the decorated first eight. I longed to swim in the foaming rapids of Boulter's Lock and he had promised to take me, but alas, the curse, coming a few days early, frustrated this. I cried and cried in our hotel room. Clearly there would never be another chance, and I knew, oh yes, I knew, that it would have been as tremendously deep an experience as Rouen.

But the fireworks were fun and the sudden illumination of Windsor Castle. Jack's coevals, who came to gorgeous buttery teas in his study, seemed infinitely witty and interesting. Trev Huxley was one of them, but Julian Huxley, Geoff Wardley and Dick Mitchison, all a year older, had already left. We did an expedition to Burnham Beeches where of course I found a few new plants to look up in the Bentham and Hooker that was always part of the luggage. Eton was still in deep country then, with beautiful walks all round. This Bentham and Hooker obsession has left me permanently with a wish to look things up, to note down plants or birds and when I can't find them I feel faintly undressed. One tangles with the Portuguese of *Flora Zambesiaca* and probably fails to get even the family. But I think I have by now nailed down the immediate flora of Carradale!

Education went on. At home I was in and out of my father's lab a great deal and picked up a little physiology, eked out by reading the small Huxley text book, already, I expect, out of date, and whatever else came my way or was explained by his pupils and colleagues. There were amusing phenomena, including what happened to people's voices after a breath of pure nitrogen. In the inner lab were rows of bottles; one knew about them, more or less. Jack and I administered chloroform to one another, for the delightful sensation of falling among stars. But we sensibly always did this standing up and when we became unable to stand we always stopped.

My father was at this time deeply involved in mine safety and much of his work lay in the central English pits where the main colliery workings were. As a treat I was allowed to go by train to Doncaster to go down Bentley's, one of the deep pits, with him. I knew a certain amount about it, including some of the technical words; I had been shown the capped flame in a miner's safety lamp that spells danger. But actually to go underground was as exciting as Rouen. I wore a black dress, one of those, I am sure, made for me during periods of acute family mourning, I had my own safety lamp. The miners were nice to me, though there was a little teasing during the drop down the deep shaft, where, if one jumped, one shot up. But there was no swearing! They all knew 'the doctor', my father, and respected him for their own virtues: courage and loyalty, hard work and expert knowledge of conditions.

We walked along to the face, saw, smelled, touched, everything. Once I heard singing in the dark distance. I suppose Jack was there too, as I spent the evening with him; we went to the Doncaster music-hall, my first time in such a place, and laughed and laughed. It was totally delightful, a raising of the level of excitement already set off underground among the darknesses and small lights and echoes.

Now, looking back, it seems to me that in the main I only

remember accurately and in any detail the times in my life when there has been this tension of delight, of fear, of pain, of action, when I have been most clearly myself. Yet what is remembered is not the content of the tension, but the facts that aroused it, the people and places, the sounds and smells. Why did some things trigger it off, others not? Psychologists might answer according to different theories. It also means asking oneself about this funny business of memory. What is the process of dredging down, taking off the lids of the memory boxes, recalling smudgily in dreams, sharply through smells? The written word is there, my own letters to Granniema, to Maya, to Aunt Bay, a few to Dick, in upright, legible, ungrown-up handwriting, fluent and full of things observed and set down, mostly natural or personal rather than artefacts, and with a sad amount of clichès about patriotism and all that. There are also my early poems, plays and what-have-you, all too many of which still survive. In these there is an occasional echo of this heightening of feeling, where it breaks through into something written down—and, in a sense, through being put into words, externalised and lost.

III

No Padding on the Bust

I am not quite sure when Grannie died, but it was certainly several years after we moved to Cherwell. I had been old enough to talk with her about books and it was she who introduced me to *The Golden Bough*. She was a great collector of fine lace, and her dresses and caps foamed with it. In looks she was distinctly Jewish, but we never knew of any of the Irish-Jewish relations whom we must have had; there was only the mysterious Miss Joseph, a sudden name in the family tree.

Now she was dead, white and dignified with her silver hair, my first introduction to that mystery. We had to play quietly for a few days and there were comings and goings. We all wore black and arm bands were sewn onto all male jackets. I have no idea where my mother's parents, Grannie and Grandpapa, were buried, presumably in Edinburgh, for I know Maya disappeared for a few days. I only know about my father's mother, Granniema, because, many years later, I was one of the bearers at her funeral and it was somewhat of a state occasion. Later, cremation was normal, though I suppose bits of my brother's body are still around, carefully labelled in Indian academic handwriting. The Oxford Department of Anatomy asked not to have to dissect my father, who had left them his body in his will, as those who would have done it had been his colleagues and pupils. We don't, as a family, hold with material memorials, supposing, with a certain arrogance, that by our works ye shall know us.

In time, Maya moved into Grannie's sitting-room and the old one became full of boxes, files, chairs waiting to be mended and so on. Most of the rooms still had the distemper which, as an economy, had been first put on when the house was built, with the intention of having Morris papers when the walls were thoroughly dried out at a later date which never came. Many years after, I repapered the spare room which I'd lain in during the months of my broken leg, and a few others were done, more or less under protest. We all have our favourite economies.

Much had already silted up in the huge boxroom under the slope of two tile roofs which gradually began to leak; the cross beams constantly knocked our heads as we groped among trunks and screens and mouldering games, plaster busts of the Prince Consort or our own forebears, unliked wedding presents or inheritances, large pictures with broken glass, rolled rugs, things which might come in usefully at some point, and stacks of books, though many that filled the bookcases all over the house might just as well have been stacked—or thrown out. But one didn't throw out in those days. Inexorably things were kept; sometimes they would be just what was needed for a bazaar or jumble sale. However, immediately in front of the boxroom door was the dressing-up box, a very good one with all sorts of gorgeous bits and pieces, hats and parasols and swords. Much had accrued after the deaths of the original owners. (How could a really 'good' piece of material be thrown away?) That didn't worry us. I became more and more addicted to dressing-up games which finally turned into Nebuchadnezzar, that splendid version of charades in which one acted a character who was then one letter of the total word. It was a bit dull being audience, but the grown-ups were always conscripted. I liked being the chief character, Salome or Boadicea or Europa, but we had to have turns.

There was a period of months when all I wanted was to 'go on the stage', which struck me as being perennial dressing-up. The delightful Dowson family lived just round the corner: the twins had been Viola and Olivia in the Dragon School *Twelfth Night*, my last school play, where I was Maria. Their mother, dear Rosina Philippi, had started 'dramatic classes'. We learnt quantities of verse; she taught us how to breathe through rapid declamation; from those days I still know most of *L'Allegro* by heart. But I am sure I was much too self-centred to be a good actor and in time that ambition died, though Frances, who shared it, did go on to act a bit at the Old Vic. For that matter I appeared there once as a troll girl in a raffia skirt for an early production of *Peer Gynt*.

How different dressing-up was from the annual visit of the dressmaker! Before World War One it was most unusual to buy ready-made dresses in shops. Maya paid an occasional visit to her *corsetière* in London and was very distressed when she died and there was no successor. Shops often had dresses in the windows, but if one wanted one it was made to measure, though this was more expensive than making it at home; there were no exact standards of size and almost anything would have to be altered. Once a year, I think, I was allowed a Liberty dress. I had one in a golden rough silk with a square neck cut a little bit low and hand-embroidered in shades of green. With this I wore stagshorn moss in my hair, collected on Craig Rossie, a romantic conception. I think I wore this when I was fifteen or so, perhaps at the dance we had in the house, when all the furniture was taken out of the hall and the floor polished. Miss Williamson, the much-loved waitress who organised all good Oxford parties, arrived to put out the silver and take charge; cakes and jellies and some kind of cup as well as orangeade were laid out in the dining-room. For best I usually had some kind of special thing for my hair, perhaps a spray or circlet of gilt wire, pretty enough and probably ending in the acting box. I had no valuable jewellery but quite a lot of beads, including one very handsome long Chinese necklace of green glass, which Aunt Bay had given me for Christmas in 1912 and which I loved dearly.

But all my ordinary clothes were made by the dressmaker. During the year my mother had bought suitable material for herself and me, especially at the Liberty sales, and put it away in the large chest of drawers in the spare room that faced west and in which the dressmaker would install herself and her machine, probably sleeping in the small room next door. I had little choice, though the brighter colours were for me, and often trimming was supplied by bits and pieces from foreign parts, especially Chinese or Indian embroidery. I am sure I had a white dress of Madras embroidered muslin. Unbleached linen and tussore silk were both well thought-of materials, in some way more connected with the world of good intentions. My mother's dresses almost always had lace for edgings, and this was carefully unpicked when a dress was to be discarded. I sometimes had a piece of Bucks or Valenciennes for a collar, but it was thought that I was still too rough for good lace. It was borne in on me that no lady ever wore anything but 'real' lace. Or real pearls.

I suppose I could have turned down anything I really hated, but clothes were not that important, just something that had to happen to one. I don't remember anything in the nature of a fashion book, still less being at all pleased at the prospect of being fitted, the endless measurements, with one's skirt coming nearer the ground every year, and always the long, slow turn round while the hem was pinned and measured and the fusty smell of the dressmaker herself. A drugget was put down on the floor so that the pins shouldn't escape. An uneven hem would have been really immoral. One wore a petticoat-bodice and petticoat on the top of woollen, or in summer cotton, combinations and knickers buttoned below the knee, but even so, dresses were carefully scanned in case it was possible to 'see through'.

There was an attempt, when I was around sixteen, to put me into a laced corset, an unattractive contraption of heavy white cotton, whale-boned. But I firmly said it stopped me breathing when the waistline was pulled in, so that was given up and the whole thing came down round my knees. I think Maya was a bit half-hearted about it. The waspies of the early forties shocked me, even though they were never as tight as their predecessors; it wasn't a fashion that lasted long.

I was supposed to wear a hat out of doors almost always. They were mostly plain felts or straws, except for those wretched silk caps, but one could choose a ribbon for one's boater, or have a piece of one's dress material hemmed. In winter one wore woolly caps of some kind. Again, I don't remember fashion pictures,

31

at any rate not in our house. I would never, somehow, have thought of fashions as applying to me and I don't think my classmates talked about them.

What seems in some way oddest about this is that instead of thinking what was prettiest or would suit one best, the essential was to wear the right clothes for one's station in life. The curious word 'suitable' was one which was often employed: 'dainty', 'graceful', 'elegant' and so on were for upper-class clothes, 'useful' for the lower orders, though I think 'hardwearing' would be employed for men's tweeds at all levels. Clothes accentuated class divisions and of course one was uncomfortable if one dressed out of fashion, unless that is one had deliberately broken with the range of class custom. I did that later on as a young married woman, though I was still following a fashion of some kind: the Isadora Duncan fashion, or later the Augustus John fashion, low-waisted linen in strong colours which I liked very much. But in my teens it would have been impossible. It wasn't that one wanted to wear the right clothes but one somehow ended in feeling uncomfortable if one didn't. It was too bad if fashion did not favour one's figure or colouring, but there was little one could do about it.

Today I find myself worried by the return of long skirts and the eagerness of young lovelies to hop into them. I have to remind myself that they can equally easily hop out. We couldn't, and so we fought against them, gaining a few inches of ankle revealment after 1914 when it became clear that more and more things could be done by women if once their clothes could be rationalised. I am put off Laura Ashley by the subconscious realisation that so many of her materials and dresses, including the general buttoned-up look and high necks, would have been thought highly suitable by my mother.

One nice dress, which I enjoyed, was when I was bridesmaid to Peggy Lane Poole, green with some deep pink embroidery somewhere on the bodice, a crinkly, ankle-length silk. I am sure Peggy talked my mother into a mild extravagance and I know it was suggested that the dress might have a little padding on the bust.

Maya turned this down and I felt rather insulted, both by needing to have it and then by not being allowed to. The wedding was great fun, though; we all knew one another well and there were ices. Weddings among family and friends usually meant choosing a present, a small piece of silver; we went to one of the antique shops and usually found something nice and not too dear; gradually I formed a degree of good taste in such matters and even an awareness of price.

There was one dress which I remember even better. It was for Henley, my first—and only—time there. How it started was that there was a girl called Charlotte Allen whom I loved and thought beautiful and admirable, and I was to have a dress the same as hers. It was white ribbed silk with a black velvet sash; we had black wired muslin picture hats with cherries on them; perhaps the colour repeated on the sash. But at Henley it rained and the red on the punt cushions came out and stained my white dress like blood. And then Charlotte got appendicitis and her parents were Christian Scientists, so she died, in considerable pain one would suppose, and that was the end of that. I cannot even now pass the gate to that house without a return of misery.

In my early teens there were a certain amount of children's parties, not so nannied as earlier ones in Edinburgh, but still we were under general supervision. We played party games and sometimes danced, usually things like Sir Roger, Swedish Dance and Lancers. There might even be pink and blue programmes with pencils attached by fluffy silk ties, and one knew that a lady didn't have more than two or perhaps three dances with the same partner. I went to dancing classes at the High School, in a long room with windows facing Banbury Road. I was clumsy and heavy-footed and none of the dances came naturally to me. There were free exercises to a tinkly piano, but it would have taken more than these to make me graceful. The classes seemed stupid anyhow, part of this lady thing. At parties I was quite confident most of the time, but every now and then I realised that I was too fat, a podgy little girl, that I wasn't growing any taller, and had no bosom, or at least none compared with some of my friends. I remember one such party where I crept away and up the stairs and on the top landing found a splendid rocking-horse; on it I rode, happily telling myself stories, while the dance music and the laughing went on below.

There was however one wonderful party at Sir Arthur Evans's house on Boar's Hill. He did not, I think, ever ask young ladies who had come out, preferring the genuine *parthenos*. It was the best party I had ever been at, a cotillion with favours and lots of grown-up dancing and Japanese lanterns. But in glass cases here and there were the things from Knossos, the gold and the bulls, and I dragged my partners over to see them, and the same excitement, the tension and delight, caught me again.

I don't remember what I wore at any of these parties; probably I didn't even choose it, but was told what to wear and had it buttoned for me if the buttons were behind. I had little chance of developing any taste of my own. My sixpence a week was of course worth a lot more than it would be today—there were plenty of penny commodities—but I had no regular allowance at all until I was about to be married, so that I had no notion of spending sensibly. I never went shopping; I was taken shopping. There is a big difference.

There were few babies in my young life and I avoided them. I thought younger children were on the whole silly and a nuisance. Young babies had nannies and they dribbled and smelled. I think my mother was worried about this distaste of mine. She took me once to see a friend's baby being washed and dressed. Clearly she thought this baby was very nice. I did not find it so.

IV

Books and Plays

All these years I read and read. At one point much to my annoyance I had to wear steel-rimmed reading glasses. Either they caught in my hair or they were uncomfortable round my ears. Ever since the operation on my neck gland I had an over-sensitive feeling about my neck close to the ears, an erogenous zone the other way round.

My reading was very mixed. After the Dragon School I remember no school books, only the choking dullness of any history people tried to turn me onto. I was still reading a fair number of children's books, including *Jock of the Bushveld* (predictably, several times, the scene of the beating of the Zulu) and with occasional lapses into the really sentimental. But also I was devouring Kipling and by now the science fiction Wells, and perhaps *Mr Polly*. There were bits of sociological or political slanting which I am sure had far more effect than the same thing presented straight, which I would probably not have read. In a way *Kim* had as much influence as any, not so much the imperialist, super-snob message which I accepted as a matter of course, but the idea of non-attachment, loosing oneself from the Wheel. I began to look at the amount of things that filled Cherwell. Things. Some intrinsically beautiful or valuable. Others just being there. Being things. Objects of attachment.

Now, I had a collection of little celluloid men with weighted bases so that they sprang upright. They lived on the top of my bureau; they were in different designs, a Chinaman, a Red Indian, a Scottie and so forth, bright colours, and I was constantly playing with them, almost talking to them. They pulled me back, attaching me to the Wheel. There was some kind of request for some charity or good cause. I swept them off into a cardboard box and gave them away, with pain of course, like a Creator deciding that He (She?) mustn't get too much attached to these little, silly men and women and burying them all under a tidal wave. Once, some years later, I found myself getting too much attached to a piece of modern pottery—a nice one, I think—and broke it. This probably helped me to travel light or, if I had attachments, to have them in terms of use or even as charms against danger or bad luck, which I knew to be completely ineffective, except that they fulfilled an admittedly irrational need. There was the *sgian dubh* given me by the people of Carradale which I took to London during World War Two and which helped me through air raids, in the sense that I was less frightened and because of that behaved better, more sensibly and with more regard for others. Many people used such charms, entirely realising that this was all they were. Dick, for instance, felt much safer in an air raid if he had his umbrella.

Yet perhaps the most important Kipling influence was simply style. The straight descriptions in *Kim, Rewards and Fairies*, and many other Kipling novels and stories, are written with superb clarity and colour. My own early writing is closely and even embarrassingly modelled on Kipling; one could do worse. D. H. Lawrence, splendid in some ways, was unfortunate as an early influence on some writers. No writer can immediately start with a developed, individual style.

I was at the same time reading a fair amount of rubbish. I don't count Wodehouse as rubbish, though I am not sure how well his school stories would survive. But how I looked forward to *The Captain* and the doings of Psmith every month! It was the only children's magazine we ever had in the house. Not for me *Chums* or *Beano*. A little later, at seventeen or so, I had a crush on Zane Grey, but I read *The Virginian* earlier, and Gene Stratton Porter, though I can't now remember the name of one of her books. There were baddish historical novels, Bulwer Lytton's *Last Days of Pompeii*, and Whyte Melville's *The Gladiators*, with which I was much obsessed, but not Scott, because, no doubt, I'd had him for school compulsory reading. I was much moved by a series of novels about the American Civil War, always from the side of the Old South. With all these books, and indeed with others, I tended to continue the conversations, at least those which were full of emotion, beyond the point where the author (doubtless on purpose and wisely) had stopped them. I encouraged all the pent-up passions to run out through me in 'day-dreams'. Occasionally I still do this even with my own writing, but am well aware of the kind of thing it is.

However, the popular, but actually rather bad writers had no stylistic effect on me. A writer who had more was R. L. Stevenson, in spite of *Treasure Island* and *Kidnapped* being school reading. Yet the fact that *Kidnapped* had been something one got marks on in an exam stopped me from re-reading or continuing to *Catriona* until decades later. What I liked were *The Wrong Box*, *Island Nights' Entertainments* and the *Fables*. The beautiful big edition was in the library at Cloan, lovely to read in. I made some efforts to read what was supposed to be superior fiction, partly because Jack wanted me to read whatever he specially liked. But I stuck in Conrad, Meredith and Henry James, though now I much enjoy Conrad, and am not ashamed to say how boring I find the other two. In my late teens I stuck in Dostoevsky who, later on, in my fifties, I found so fascinating. Dickens, of course, was still hopelessly a holiday task. At around sixteen I discovered Hugh Walpole and read all his books with passionate absorption, though now I can remember nothing of any of them.

Censorship continued spasmodically. I wasn't allowed to read *The New Machiavelli*, and when I peeped into it and found it wasn't science fiction, I didn't really want to. Among our ancestral books I was forbidden *The History of Highwaymen*, as well as *Tom Jones*.

There was a collected Poe at Cloan, small volumes appropriately bound in crimson cloth. I don't think it would affect me now, but then I read *The Pit and the Pendulum*, *The Masque of the Red Death* and all the rest with continuous shock and fascination. The raven Nevermore was as serious for me as it was for Gauguin. Did this climate of romantic horror vanish for ever with our own genuine horrors hitting us from every page of every newspaper? Or has science fiction taken over? But that should not be romantic.

Poe's horrors were all the worse at Cloan, since they were so close akin to those which I half expected round every turn of the spiral stair or waiting in the curtains of the four-posters. I was tautened up ready for them. At this time, too, I unwisely read James's *Ghost Stories of an Antiquary*. There would have been a case for censoring this, at least to me. I read other, lesser ghost stories, including *The Hound of the Baskervilles*, and was frightened, but James got me where it really hurt. I still dislike sleeping in a room with a second bed in case this follows the story of *Oh Whistle and I'll Come to You*. I have never written a ghost story, though I expect, out of various experiences, I could write a fairly unpleasant one. But why deliberately and for no good purpose add to the world's fears and unpleasantness?

These were much further away in those days; one only heard of terrible wars and earthquakes and fires long after the agony was past. I hardly ever read *The Times*, which of course was our newspaper, except that in Scotland there was also the *Scotsman*. I had little idea of what was going on in the world; it was not near or immediate. However, for Scots upper-class gossip, my mother depended on Aunt Christian—Mrs Fraser Tytler, born Kerr. They not only wrote to one another, lengthily and often, but tended to be so much *en rapport* that they knew when something was happening to the other. This was my mother's only concession to non-rationality, though the servants were quite encouraged to go to church.

Yet my main enthusiasm was always poetry. I read the Victorians, lots of Tennyson and Browning, though I missed out some of the longer verse dramas, Rossetti and a number of minor authors and finally Swinburne—almost all Swinburne except the very late poems. Why wasn't Swinburne censored? Well, poetry never was. Being poetry made it all right. I knew masses by heart and declaimed it, either aloud or to myself: *Dolores*, *Atalanta*, the lot. One of my favourite things was to get Miss Blockey to play the piano while I danced and declaimed. What did she play? I suspect old-fashioned waltzes to which timing much of Swinburne goes admirably. Clearly I wasn't going to act on the maxims of Dolores. Anyhow Swinburne was dead and therefore a classic. Sometimes Frances and I danced together, doing what we supposed were very daring mimes: 'The lovers whose lips would excite thee, Are serpents in hell.' How serpentinely we writhed!

But I read very little Shelley, though now I enjoy him, especially the science fiction aspect of *Prometheus Unbound*. I couldn't be doing with Wordsworth, nor yet Milton, although Jack admired him so much. I liked Coleridge, but my reading did not go much earlier, except for the ballads. My last prize from school and the only one that is still with me, was the *Oxford Book of Ballads*. I swam around in these and was not even averse to Scott's pastiche ballads, though I found his long poems boring. I think that what I looked for in poetry was magic, the light through Rouen Cathedral windows, the dead drop of the mine shaft: '*It fell about the Martinmas when nights are lang and mirk*'. Lyrics and ballads provided this fuel. I now ask myself, was I looking for the equivalent of a drug experience in altered consciousness? If so, would some of our present teenage addicts find that poetry isn't bad for getting high on? But to do this it probably has to have a very definite rhythm and evocative force. Also, I think it must be straight. So much modern poetry is ironic or deliberately held on a low note; that may be artistically admirable, but it doesn't send the reader.

In my mid-teens I got into the habit of turning over the newest poetry books at Blackwell's to see what there was. They were very amiable about letting one do this in the old days. I had at one time been puzzled by the Latin concept of the strict metrical foot and only later began to understand about stress. Once or twice I was taken up to the Poet Laureate's house on Boar's Hill; I was somewhat in awe of Bridges himself, but I think he must have dropped a sentence or two on verse construction, which was helpful. It must have been he who told me to read Hopkins, but I didn't until later. It is most improbable that there was a Hopkins among the poetry books in our house.

Although I was so put off by the set school books if they were novels, I had never minded learning poetry by heart. I knew a great deal of Shakespeare, but also *Lays of Ancient Rome, The Armada* and so on. Sometimes at school we were told to do illustrations; I always had glorious ones in my head, great allegorical figures, towers and flags, but my niggling pencil and scrawling chalks always betrayed me. Sometimes later on I tried to draw on my own, but it was no good. I expect I would have been happy to produce something like Bernard Partridge's drawings in *Punch*. We took *Punch* and I always opened it hoping to find one of Bernard Partridge's noble Britannias in the act of protecting a minority or, in justified imperial anger, punishing an offender. We also had quantities of bound back volumes from some of which I learned a bit of nineteenth-century history. These were in the revolving bookcase in the dining-room and I used to take them out and read them sitting on the end of the sofa, or even behind it, in a way which irritated any grown-up and induced them to send me off to do something useful. One of the other large sets of books in this bookcase was the complete Jowett translation of Plato; in the process of twirling the bookcase, the contents of which sometimes cascaded onto the floor, I picked up and began to read *The Republic* and was much taken with the idea of being a Guardian. This, I know, started off one of my interminable inside stories, interspersed with noble sayings in the manner of Jowett.

It is odd that I was not put off by the undoubted fact that all Plato's Guardians were male and that he said many unpleasant things about the inferiority of women. But in my inside stories I don't suppose I was ever a Greek woman. I am sure, however, that in common with only too many upper-class British, I got a lot of curious ideas from Plato. Some fitted in excellently with my mother's view of politics and the superiority of the State (in her case the Empire) over any individual, who must always be ready to sacrifice his or her self, or be sacrificed, for the Greater Good. In World War One, parents 'gave' their sons.

Now it remains that there is a human need for something, if need be, to die for. Without it, life is less interesting. But why the State? The rot spread even to the Christian martyrs whom I rather enjoyed reading about; their State was the heavenly city. And again, Plato was always full of chat about leadership. Yes, from time to time my stories enthroned me as a philosopher-king. But what did it all lead to in the twentieth century? The *Fuhrerprinzip*, the totalitarian state and the English public school. But this was something I was not to see for a long time. Perhaps I only escaped the Platonic net, so widely spread in Oxford, by being one of those inferior creatures of the wrong sex, born, not to be leaders, but perhaps with luck, like Socrates (not to be confused with his caricature in *The Republic*) to be a gadfly.

There was a curious convergence of views on the State between my mother and her disapproved-of brother-in-law, Uncle Richard, when he produced the theory of *sittlichkeit*, which she couldn't help agreeing with. To be a good citizen in the sense of active accord with the noblest ideals of one's State or loyalty-group (for instance, the British Empire) might have been the thought behind it, in reaction against the largely selfish individualist motives of the 'shopkeeper'. But when the State itself goes bad? Somehow that thought had been kept under. Thus *sittlichkeit*, product, via Hegel, of Plato, turned out to be a short, though as yet not obvious, step towards the theory of the Master Race, alone truly *sittlich*. Later on, Smuts's holism, a further stateward development, leading to the present South African situation, attracted them both. Smuts was, of course, a charmer; he quickly conned my mother into forgetting he was a Boer.

So there I was, sitting on the dining-room floor, probably twirling the bookcase with one hand and absorbing Plato. In another corner of my stocking-up was Ayton's *Lays of the Scottish Cavaliers*, illustrated. This too had a mystique which, in modern phraseology, sent me. But, oddly enough, it never led me to find out exactly what Montrose had been doing or why Argyll was the master fiend: that would have been history and *ipso facto* dull.

One day in the drawing-room Jack came in with a small red book and in a state of great excitement. It was the first Housman. He stood beside the satin-wood inlaid occasional table, which had a small book trough on it with tiny books, mostly dark brown leather from the eighteenth century, edifying works of some kind, un-read. There was a silver-handled tortoiseshell paper knife and a few other bits and pieces, probably a vase of flowers; it was usually I who did the drawing-room flowers. He began to read aloud from the small red book. Later I seized on it too and in no time we had half the poems by heart. For a while no other poet, not even Swinburne, counted or measured up to *The Shropshire Lad*.

It was Jack, also, who put me onto reading Shaw. Reading plays was fun, though not as good as acting them, but seeing them was the next best. We went regularly to the Oxford theatre; the seats were not very expensive, though we usually had stalls. I can still see the curtain with its vaguely Renaissance house party enjoying a little music. How one's eyes fixed on it for the first tremble before it went up! We all liked to be there in good time, and were very cross if other people came in late.

I suppose my first sight of the theatre was a Christmas pantomime. I have an idea it was *Jack and the Beanstalk*, with a splendid interior curtain of beans for the principal boy, Jack, to climb. This was the 'transformation scene', a bit of formal magic always included and something specially to look forward to. I think, too, that these early pantos ended with a harlequinade, with strings of sausages coming out of the clown's baggy white pants, but a little frightening because of the red-hot poker. And I have another faintly uneasy feeling about my first experience of the theatre. Can it be that I wetted my drawers?

From about twelve I was taken fairly regularly to Shakespeare, usually the Benson company. I remember *Coriolanus* best and how much I sympathised with him. There was not much artifice about these productions, but it was straight Shakespeare with the big speeches properly hammed, as I would like to have done myself. One could gloat over the words, not being distracted by clever production. In the classical dramas, everyone wore white sheets, possibly decorated with a key pattern, or purple for Caesar. For a long time I thought of the Romans and Greeks as marblish, sheeted figures of this kind, until in fact I began to write about them and had really to think what they looked like.

All the family enjoyed the theatre, but especially my father; he had few other recreations, except for croquet which he played with maddening exactitude, lying down on the grass and sighting the balls, jumping with frustration if he failed to bring off a shot. It is he whom I remember taking me, in my early teens, to Galsworthy and an occasional Shaw. Those were the days when one really listened to the dialogue! Scenery was strictly realistic, clothes much what one knew elsewhere, unless it was a historical play, in which case, again, there would be nothing unexpected nor offensive to the good taste of North Oxford. But how exciting the Galsworthy 'problem plays' were! *Justice, Strife, The Silver Box*—one followed every word. There tended to be a bit of family argument over Shaw as some plays were thought unsuitable for me. These I usually contrived to read. And, as I was always writing plays myself, it was essential that I should see as many of them as possible. I managed on the whole to convince people of this.

Gilbert and Sullivan came once a year and there was always a tremendous University rush for tickets. I always longed to go as often as possible, but the D'Oyly Carte Company was not considered as educative and edifying as Galsworthy. For some reason it was thought that *The Yeomen of the Guard* was more suitable than *Pirates* or *Mikado*, but I remember *Iolanthe*, and vaguely wondering if Uncle Richard had ever had to deal with a beautiful ward in chancery when he was Lord Chancellor. Some of my friends used to stand in the gallery queue, but I was never allowed.

But around the time I was fifteen or sixteen we had the Abbey Theatre group with Synge, Yeats and Lady Gregory. There was a superb performance of *The Playboy of the Western World* which seemed in quite a different class from anything I had ever seen. It wasn't acting; it was being. I find it difficult to remember which of the others I actually saw performed, since, in reading them, I visualised the stage so clearly. Did I see *Countess Kathleen*? I don't know. With Shaw one has such definite stage directions that it is impossible not to visualise, but it is a little surprising that I did it with all plays.

When I was fifteen or so, my brother and I started going up to London occasionally to see plays, or perhaps the cinema, but I don't think we took that seriously; it was just an amusement. With luck we got in a matinée and an evening performance. Once we were taken out to lunch at Brown's Hotel—lobsters—by Mavro, my father's young colleague, the one who was nicest to us. Once we ate a very nasty vegetarian meal at the Eustace Miles restaurant, appropriately after Shaw. That evening we went to a variety show at the Coliseum with two unforgettable things: Sarah Bernhardt, then an old woman, as Theodora—in French and the first time I realised the point of understanding it—and a Russian dancer. Could it have been Pavlova? Oh, that was magic, that was delight, staying with us all through the journey back in the midnight train from Paddington!

The plays I wrote when I was still at school never got as far as the stage, but the one I wrote at fifteen did. The dear Skipper, whose pet I always was, let us do the play during the holidays in the hall of the Dragon School on the stage where our Shakespeare plays had been performed, and the whole thing was published as a supplement to the *Draconian*. Possibly I was the first O.D. to have a play performed; it was certainly my first experience of correcting proofs.

The play was about an imaginary country, Saunes Bairos, in the Andes under a vaguely Mayan culture, about which I had picked up such items as suited me, for instance the use of quipus for messages. In the play the population was firmly kept down by a hierarchy of priests and the plot involved the birth of twins (one too many) to an important personage in the state. There was a prologue featuring two modern geneticists and several guinea pigs and then the main play with my brother as Cahu Halpa, the father. His opening lines, 'Twins, my god, twins!' was said to have lifted out of their seats and out of the hall one or two of the more respectable members of the North Oxford community. The valley of Saunes Bairos was guarded at the snow-line, and nobody until the coming of the perfect race, was let through, either way, I suppose, but at the climax of the play the girl twin (who but me?) leads a courageous band of followers, one of whom (who but Jack's friend Dick Mitchison?) watches with her the new dawn, across the snow-line to a rather uncertainly imagined freedom from the priests.

Re-reading the play, it is juvenile, but not as juvenile as all that. There is a sense of theatre, tension, and lively or occasionally poetic writing, with some charming songs, though the Kipling influence is rather too strong. But there are some curious bits in the modern prologue and epilogue, where the two geneticists are talking eugenics: '. . . things like the Mental Deficiency Bill, which is supposed to be charitable and really succeeds in being grossly unjust to the poor'—an echo from my brother perhaps? And again: 'Think what it would be for us if one merely had a rule for eugenics within the Empire! It would do more than preference or even federation.' Echoes of my mother clearly. Yes, I liked to please, and also to show how bright I was.

There was an enormous cast, largely Jack's Eton and Oxford friends and of course my class-mates—even Miss Blockey was roped in. I seem to remember writing in small parts for those who would have been 'hurt' not to be in. They are all in the large photograph taken in the corner of New College cloisters and it was 1913. There is Hartley the chief priest, whose dark and regular features fluttered my heart, killed two years later, and Gerald Boswell the snow-guard who sang my song: '. . . and all the land lies far below, Below the snow-line and the snow, The snow-line changing never,' walking up and down with his spear, making up the tune which I remember as lovely: killed too. Moss Blundell who drew brilliant cartoons of us all: killed in the same year.

War and death, suddenly coming real, hit us, only sparing half-blind Aldous Huxley, the 'old priest'.

All this meant a lot of gorgeous dressing-up, and I busily made quipus out of coloured wool. I don't remember what I wore except that it included the green Chinese necklace. I do remember with some shame being dreadfully fussy about the words and jumping on those who didn't say them right. There was also a Canadian friend, David Hossie, who got through the war without even a wound, recovered from the 1918 'flu and became a successful lawyer: he pronounced lamas—part of my local colour—with a short American 'a' which convulsed us all. I can't think how we had time for all this, but no doubt the absence of domestic chores did make a lot of time available and nobody was in quite such a hurry to cram in everything. Time's winged chariot wasn't such a hoverer, and Oxford undergraduates didn't work so hard. A nice well paid professional job would no doubt turn up for all of them in good time.

It seemed to me that acting a play at least once a year was an essential part of life. I was much taken with Maurice Hewlett's *Pan and the Young Shepherd*. But there were passages in it which my mother found 'unsuitable'. I am not at all sure what her criterion was, but she made me cut or re-write them and then send the result to Maurice Hewlett, who very properly turned down the proposal to act his mangled play with a loud bang. How did I allow myself to get into this position? I know I was uncomfortable about it, but there was this business of no lady being able to speak the banned lines, all incredibly mild. It was part of a whole stifling climate and I acquiesced. There was one terrible blame-word: *suggestive*. I remember watching the male guinea pigs agitating around the females with their very typical chittering (and these were important matings from the standpoint of experimental genetics) and quoting, 'In the Spring a young man's fancy Lightly turns to thoughts of love.' I was heavily jumped on for saying something suggestive and felt deeply ashamed for weeks.

The year when I was sixteen we did a double drama in the warm, unclouded July of 1914, using the tennis court as auditorium and acting on the slope above it. One of these was mine, *Prisoners of War*, a drama about Roman prisoners of a Sarmatian king who recognises a fellow Mithraist: something of a crib from Kipling. Jack was the Sarmatian king, Dick the Mithraist prisoner, Gervas Huxley the chief priest (I seem to have had a thing about chief priests). I, of course, was the king's daughter in a yellow dress with my hair hanging all over it and someone's fur stole on one shoulder. My brother wore an enormous wolf (goat?) skin rug. I wrote a poem about him, not very good. The Mithraic sacrament was taken in a two-handled copper pot, which I gave Dick afterwards, inscribed: *Militi Mithrae filia regis Sarmaticae d.d.* But it wasn't much good for flowers as it started leaking and it went in the fire at Carradale in 1969.

The other play was Gilbert Murray's translation of *The Frogs*. Here the chorus, led by me on one side and Frances on the other, moved round a turf altar, wreathed with yellow tree lupins, while the main drama went on at a higher level. We made a lot of minor alterations on the spot: 'Lethe, North Oxford and the rest of hell.' And we turned the little oil-can into an umbrella; I'm sure Aristophanes would have been delighted. It was all marvellous fun, waking up to another summer day of creative excitement and activity, escape into delight, though there were still those awful times when one's period was on, and one felt something might shamefully show and one wondered if one smelt, and people would get to know. Sex raising its ugly head and *hurting*. Meanwhile my mother was beginning to worry about Ulster. Needless to say she was a passionate loyalist and Carsonite: 'Ulster will fight and Ulster will be right.' I began to foresee conflict with my Liberal father, which I didn't want because I was just beginning to see another political side to things, but I needn't have worried. Something else was coming to distract Tweedledum and Tweedledee: the monstrous crow blackening the skies of Europe.

Lewis Gielgud, another old Etonian, elder brother of John and Val, came into my life then, to stay there till his death. He was Dionysos in *The Frogs* with Gervas Huxley as Xanthias, his slave, with his long legs touching the ground at each side of the small donkey; but Lewis also stage-managed my play and the choruses of *The Frogs*. He was almost professional, the real stage in his blood and we fought like cats and yelled at one another; he wanted to alter my sacred words—and I would now suppose that he was perfectly right. Also he told me that I didn't scream convincingly and again I am sure he was right; I probably squeaked. He brought his sixteen-year-old brother John into my next play, *Barley, Honey and Wine*, the last of my lost adolescence, post-war. Much later, in Paris, we wrote play after play together, modern or historical, only one of which ever got acted, and only in a very small way. They were competent, professional plays and we were always very hopeful about them, but we never managed to hit the fashion: our hue was not the wear. Only we laughed and worked and laughed as I never laughed again afterwards. So perhaps it was worth while.

V

Change

A good many changes took place between 1909 and 1914, but how aware were we? Not very. Certainly we looked at the sky. Once, when I was still a school child, a balloon floated over Oxford. I ran full pelt down Bardwell Road to tell them at school—for some reason I wasn't there at the time. It seemed an adequate excuse for everyone, masters and boys, to rush out and wave madly while the beautiful shining object wavered past. A few years later, and it was an early biplane giving a show in Port Meadow. Jack and I hurried there to watch it hedge-hopping hugely and impressively, faster surely than a train or a motor-car, the fastest things we knew. The crowd ran to look; we heard it roaring and then it was coming straight at us, or seemed to be, over the tops of the hawthorns. But neither of us could foresee ourselves casually getting into a flying machine. The first domestic planes I flew in were certainly biplanes on the smaller Highland runs, nice, friendly little things.

By 1914 London had motor-buses but they had open tops which were great fun if one could induce whatever adult one was with to climb. There were still some trams, including the splendid one that plunged underground from the Embankment to Kingsway, and in Edinburgh and Glasgow the trams were the order of the day for public transport. We still went first class on the underground, the Circle mostly, though we almost always went second on a real train. Sometimes Jack and I went third and it seemed very daring and even dangerous.

The deep freeze and even the household fridge were far in the future, so fruit and vegetables were seasonal and all the more looked forward to and enjoyed. There would be gluts of home-grown fruit, strawberries, plums, pears and so on; the green-grocers' bushel baskets were full and buzzing with flies. Prices dropped and everyone turned to and made their own jam. Tinned produce was not very good and we were always on the look-out for blown tins and the new ptomaine poisoning. I don't suppose my mother ever had any tinned meat product in the house. Cold meat was carefully put under fly-proof covers in a north-facing larder.

We had a telephone installed—the kind where one turned a handle—in the passage at the back of the dining-room, no peaceful corner for long conversations. But it certainly had not taken the place of letters; it was there mainly for my father's dealings with Government departments, or for ordering from shops. One wasn't getting its full use.

In those days games and sports were still amateur, largely happening at universities and the larger schools. Maybe there were rough games like soccer in the north, but no attention was paid to them. The immense market for sports goods had hardly begun, though a good cricket bat was thought to be an acceptable present for any boy. Winter sport was still skating, curling in Scotland, sliding, snowballing or tobogganing on tea trays. There were splendid runs at Cloan, down from the terrace walk almost into the burn. One was apt to get a bit of a bang at the bottom on some of the rocks; but that was part of the fun. As for me, I swam when-ever I could, though we did not go regularly to the sea; once we went to North Devon, but I still felt that Devon was subtly inferior to Cornwall and when I got up to my knees in a quicksand I was sure of it. Sometimes in summer I deliberately tangled with other boats on the Cherwell, in the hope that my own canoe would upset, as it occasionally did. If it had some young man in it who hoped to rescue me, that made it all the funnier, as I was usually a better swimmer even with my longish skirt and Sunday hat. I was a fairly expert paddler, Canadian style, and used to go quite a long way up, sometimes telling myself exploration stories.

The lower part of the river was getting crowded. By 1914

Timms' boat-hiring was in full swing. But we now had our own boathouse, a pleasant little building roofed with Stonesfield slates. Here we had a rowing boat, for my father still enjoyed rowing for a few years longer, a punt and two canoes, one of which I had saved up for over several years; she was called *The Ship of Fools*. There were rollers for the boats to go down and a ricketty wooden ladder off the landing-stage into the greeny-brown water, and there I swam in my so-enclosing serge bathing dress, with a towel over my shoulders afterwards in case I showed my figure.

There were water weeds then, which gently stroked one's legs in the mild current, but in winter there were always floods. These brought fertilising mud down onto the water meadows, still marked with low ridges from earlier strip cultivation, from which one could always get two hay crops year after year. I suppose the floods are now controlled and much less interesting, and perhaps there are fewer marsh flowers. I always helped with the hay, of which we had a big, square stack.

For there was also my mother's farm. The Jersey cows were heavy milkers; it was of course all hand-milking and there was no cooling of an acceptable modern kind. The milk cans were put into the shade and, for the house, poured into white enamel setting pans in the slate-shelved, north-facing small dairy. From time to time, I was conscripted to help with the milking, which took some time from these large-uddered cows, whose teats had to be properly stretched. I made up my mind then that never again would I get involved in milking. That good resolution lasted less than thirty years. The cowman had cropped fair hair and a gentle Berkshire voice; I don't think he was very bright but my mother saw to it that everything was clean and shipshape, the cows well fed, groomed and washed down. The cowshed was just below the oak tree in the field to the far left of the house. Today that oak is about the only thing I can recognise in what were once the grounds of Cherwell. Chestnuts and elms, above all poplars, are such quick growers that one has lost the familiar shape even after ten years: was it this one or perhaps that which one knew so well? Oaks change slowly. Wolfson College almost touches it.

By now I was beginning to have slightly disturbing doubts about the Imperialist Conservative background to which my mother had accustomed me. Somehow a few Ruskin students had been invited to the house; it seems likely that they were miners or miners' sons and so would be welcomed. So much of my father's work was on mine safety and for my mother, miners, like fishermen, were 'different'; the class barrier dropped for them. We went up the river for a picnic in the usual flotilla. I had a shy student in the bows of my canoe and while I paddled I began asking him questions. In a little time he was telling me his life story and I was fascinated. This was pure Galsworthy! It started making holes in quite a lot of my assumptions. Then came the Oxford meeting when Lansbury and Larkin spoke and I was much shaken. Something was happening. But I was still a young lady and I had not even come out, so it would have been inappropriate for me to air my views. I would have been shut up. I might have been laughed at. I would have been caught out, made to say something silly and—yes, feminine. For there was certainly an overtone of male superiority and reasonableness, as against female passion and irrationality, though I don't think I recognised it as such. This has had something of a hang-over; I am still fairly easily silenced in a political argument, but not convinced. Early on I learnt that one. And I knew that I was beginning to sidle over from my mother's Tory side to my father's Haldane Liberalism, though I could still feel very disloyal if I didn't support her.

It appeared, up to 1914, that one could foresee one's whole life, and this was rather daunting. One would grow up, marry, have children (not that I cared much for this idea), live a North Oxford life with a house and servants and punctual meals, and nothing would ever change. Presumably 1914 was the last year when young people thought like that. As to a career for myself, that was very vague; my mother had wanted me to be a doctor, because that was what she had wanted for herself but had not been allowed to be. But I was not much attracted. I wanted to write, but somehow that was not sufficiently serious. Science was, and I was

interested in certain aspects. But it did not seem to be enough.
I wrote a semi-ironic so-called poem about that future, and yet it
was not really *me* I wrote about; it was about imaginary grown-
upness.

In North Oxford

Soon I must plait my hair in coils
And twist it tight about my head;
Low-necked and bare-armed I shall dance
In silken stuffs of green and red.

And I shall wear My Emeralds,
And I shall wear a Ruby Ring,
With all the many coloured world
About me for my pleasuring.

But ten years hence or maybe more,
A girl no longer, I shall dress
My hair a different, grown-up way
(And in ten years I shall have less).

And I shall wear Luxurious Furs,
And lovely satins, Hats with Plumes
For Photographs in Ascot Week,
And men will come to sketch my rooms—

For I shall buy Old Masters then,
The very modern art, of course,
With fine Crown Derby from the Sales.
And I shall back my Favourite Horse.

And then a husband—what a choice!
Statesman or artist, millionaire,
Duke, novelist, American,
Romantic burglar? I don't care.

> Motors, a lovely sailing yacht,
> An aeroplane, perhaps, by then . . .

I gave out after that, I couldn't see any further; at least it scans.
Here is a letter from Andrew Lang, dated 'St Andrews, Feb. 15':
no year, of course!

> Dear Naomi,
>   I like your hexameters better than those of Mr Cotterill,
> in a translation of the Odyssey; but *all* English (and German)
> hexameters are naturally bad; as you will understand when
> you can read Homer in Greek—and the sooner the better.
> Conceive Sophocles trying to write Greek poetry in the metre
> of 'Bonny Charlie's noo awa'. It is exactly the same as anybody
> trying to write English hexameters. I did some when I was a
> boy; but not being wholly lost, *I made them rhyme*. A little
> girl died lately, about your age or younger, and her people
> found that she had written several stories. I had to read one
> of them today called 'Molly and Margaret', and I hope it will
> be published; it was so funny and like small children. If you
> never read a story of mine called 'The Monk of Fife' I would
> like to send it to you, and if it bores you, you can chuck it into
> the Cherwell, or give it to some poor child.
>   Yours very sincerely
>   A. Lang

There is a PS 'Love to the guinea pigs.'

I think this may well refer to a set of hexameters published in
the *Draconian* in 1911 by 'N. Haldane aged 13.' It appears to
be the thoughts of a ruined gambler:

> Blessed is the cool of the night when the fever of gaming is over!
> Oh, let me wander by nights thro' the streets, by the moon and
>   the starlight—
> Naught but the streets is left for a penniless beggar and outcast
> Etc., etc.

Oddly enough gambling is one of the temptations which I have never experienced, though, on the rare occasions when I have been to races or a casino, I have always won . . . though never more than five shillings!

But writing verses wasn't serious. Being a young lady was. This business of coming out involved several things: a difference in behaviour, which must no longer be silly or careless, a lengthening of skirts to ankle length and putting up one's long, maiden hair. The last was, to me, fiendishly difficult; I didn't want to be bothered with hairpins, nor did I think I looked any nicer with my hair bundled up behind. I was taken for lessons to a London hairdresser in one of the streets off Brompton Road, armed with tortoiseshell combs, one of which had to be stuck into the ends of one's hair and then wound over and over until finally the comb was pinned in at the back and one had a sizeable and heavy bun, which could be surmounted and decorated with another comb. Before long, however, I took to plaits wound round and round my head or in ear-phones. I doubt if this was a becoming style, but I simply was not thinking in those terms. It was easier and quicker, though even so they were always coming down. But silk-covered hairpins, a later invention, helped a lot. My mother still had her own hair cut short, which she had presumably done as a protest of a feminist kind some time in her twenties. But it was never suggested that I should imitate this.

By now I was regularly down for dinner at eight, and later, at sixteen, for dinner parties which on the whole I enjoyed very much. There were always a few undergraduates, and there was a lot of conversation, though I must take care to turn, halfway through dinner, that is to say at the end of the fish or *entrée* course (which we only had for real parties) to my other neighbour. I think the food must have been very dull, for I can't remember it. Chicken was still a treat, but probably tasted better than modern broilers. There was usually a choice, perhaps of roast, certainly of pudding, one of which was solid, the other frothy. In summer it would be gooseberry fool, strawberries and cream, or cherry pie. My father was sometimes bored or thinking of something utterly else which had been with him in study or laboratory. The family story has him gazing at the dish at his end of the table saying: 'Will anyone have any of this? It looks rather bad.'

But the dinner table looked nice, with crisp white damask linen and napkins folded into pleasing shapes. I had probably filled the big Sheffield plate wine coolers with suitable flowers: they looked marvellous with cow parsley and buttercups or ox-eye daisies, but good too with paeonies, which did well in our heavy-soiled garden, though they were only the ordinary ones. There was the large candelabra on a mirror stand, which, later on, at some point unaccountably disappeared. There were other candlesticks and the white candles were always new; there were the silver salt cellars and naturally the crested table silver. Fish knives were dreadfully middle-class; one ate fish with a fork. All had been polished by Miss Williamson and the current parlourmaid. The men had of course dressed for dinner; my father's stiff shirt creaked and bulged. He used to have trouble with his studs in the starched stud-holes, and he was bad at a white tie. It was essential that numbers of men and women should be even; this went on for as long as people gave formal dinner parties, but it got more and more difficult later on in the thirties as one's guests became more casual and perhaps more occupied. Whether or not Miss Blockey appeared depended on whether an extra woman was needed and if she came she would have the dullest partner. I was often quite sorry for her, though most of all when there had been an extra ticket for her at one of the 1914 Commem balls. At the last moment a cousin from Scotland turned up and poor old Blockywox was ruthlessly sacrificed, as unprotesting as Iphigeneia.

Sunday supper was less formal and always cold, often cold boiled chicken in a shiny white sauce or cold sirloin of English beef. There were more young people and it was much more fun. Nobody dressed for this, and I expect there were already some undergraduates who actually didn't own a dinner jacket! But at dinner parties, when the men were all dull black and white, the ladies were in shining silks and lace—though often with a shawl in Oxford unheated winters. They wore jewellery on their decolletées, an imposing necklace, sometimes a matching brooch and ear-rings. My generation did not have pierced ears; that was considered somewhat old-fashioned and barbaric. Most Scots ladies had a seed pearl necklace with broad, beautifully shaped leaves of mother-of-pearl, sewn scratchily with the small seed pearls. The one of my mother's necklaces which I liked best was enamel with tiny diamonds.

By this time smoking was not confined to the gentlemen or the eccentric female intellectual. Some people still considered it rather 'fast' but many ladies took an occasional cigarette, though my mother did not care for it, never smoked herself and would not have it in her sitting-room, especially my father's pipe, which, I must admit, was rather strong. Of course, I would never have been allowed to smoke, so naturally this was the only time in my life when I did take an occasional puff though I cannot say I ever really liked it. But most of my girl friends asserted themselves thus far, if no further.

Having a meal out was still a real thrill and rare. There was not much choice, at any rate in Oxford. Fuller's was best. But was the walnut cake with its thickly nutty embedding and the crisp-topped softness of the icing really as blissful as one remembers? Then there was the Cadena with the smell of coffee which I enjoyed years before I liked the taste, and the Oriental-style decor which I admired very much. Occasionally there was tea at the Randolph, very grand, and only with an occasional important visitor. In Edinburgh it was always one or another of the Princes Street shops with a view over to the gardens and the Castle if one got a window table. Cake stands were piled with dainties, scones were excellent. I doubt if synthetic cream had yet arrived and probably the main fat was real butter. Marge was still very lower-class and had not at all a nice taste or smell; it would never be bought even for cooking in most middle-class houses. I had never, of course, been inside a public house except for the inn at Sennen; one turned one's eyes away instinctively as from a public convenience.

I was in my mid-teens before I enjoyed going out to Oxford

57

parties, not that I could be asked to dinner myself, as I was not yet 'out'. But the notables were interesting, especially the Spoo, who, as Warden of New College, was the closest of the academics and occasionally even paid a call. Some of his sayings are undoubtedly made up (cherishing in one's bosom a half-warmed fish), but he certainly made some odd remarks, as to an English Jewish undergraduate, later a distinguished economist: 'I hope you will soon get on better with the European members of the College.' And he did some odd things, including, after dinner, saying to my mother that as it was rather dark on the stairs, he would give her some light, and went down switching everything off from the slippery dark oak of the Warden's lodging staircase. Dear Rosemary Spooner no doubt saved the situation. There was also his long conversation with the guy one Fifth of November. It was perhaps fortunate for my brother that his sight was bad. Jack took his turn with other scholars in reading the lesson at early Chapel, which indeed he rather enjoyed. I went along once and noticed the pyjama trousers under the surplice.

There were other senior New College dons, of whom the nicest was Joseph, the philosopher, who never managed to make the ancient philosophers palatable to the undergraduates doing Greats, but was much loved and enormously sympathetic. I remember, five years later, when I told him I was going to have a baby, as though it was the most astonishing thing in the world, how kindly he shared my wonder at this usual event. The senior Greats dons were more esteemed than scientists, historians or lawyers. There was Matheson—P. Mat.—whose lovely garden in Saville Road had enviable delphiniums, and Canon Rashdall—the Rasher—who was supposed to have said: 'I would like, just for once, to go to a Colchester oyster feast'— this in his deep, bubbly voice when talking, presumably, about hedonism. Professor Myres was about, when not archaeologising in more interesting places; many years later he sympathised with me when I changed my plough horses for a tractor, which could not be fed with the *cailleach*, the last sheaf. There was Ernest Barker who wrote a preface to my first book, *The Conquered*, to explain that it could be taken seriously as an illumination of history. Clearly a pleasant senior common room, with the unmarried members living in college, a short, moonlit walk across the quad. Among them were the younger dons, Heath, Cheeseman, Geoffrey Smith and the rest, of whom I cannot yet write without anger, when I think how they were killed in the useless trench fighting in 1915 and 1916.

And of course we lived in the world of the University characters and their wives, also formidable, especially the Smiths of Balliol. There were daughters of my own age; we met cautiously, I expect they were Liberals. There were the Lane Pooles, strong Imperialists, I think, and my remotish cousin, Robin Dundas of the House, who once marked a Greats candidate 'mud-bottom'. Naturally one expected one's friends to get Firsts or possibly 'good' Seconds.

All Oxford hospitality was in people's homes, where the wives counted, sometimes more than the husbands, but if we went to Edinburgh, we stayed at a hotel and visited cousins, including the one whose bones were always breaking and to whom my mother was devoted. I am sure poor Maya was beginning to consider a really nice Scots marriage for me, perhaps someone in the minor Tory landed aristocracy. She would have liked me to have land. Naturally she was pleased when we bought Carradale later on, but was aware that it was only the tail-end of an estate, so not quite land as it had seemed in her time. She made believe that the Cherwell fields were land in her sense and acquired some eight or ten acres more between us and the Marston Ferry road. She was now starting to sell the delicious Jersey milk and hers became the first grade A tuberculin tested herd in the south of England.

In London we sometimes stayed at Uncle Richard's house in Queen Anne's Gate, when he was not there. It was a beautiful eighteenth-century town house remodelled internally and decorated by Lutyens. Mrs Pinney, the housekeeper, was always nice to us and I enjoyed the books, collected editions in good bindings as well as the newest biographies and 'serious' novels. A good new novel was a recognised event in those days. Booksellers stocked it, had probably read it themselves and could recommend it. Or not! Reviewers had time and space to discuss one book. Sales of two or three thousand were quite good and brought in 'a modest competence'. Am I wrong to think that more depended on merit and less on packaging?

It was from Queen Anne's Gate in the summer of 1914 that I was allowed to go on one or two expeditions with Dick Mitchison. I am quite sure that by then my mother, if not my father, had been made aware that the elder of the Mitchison boys was seriously interested in the daughter of the Haldane house and that his intentions were strictly honourable. It is possible even that there had been some correspondence between the two mothers but of course I was considered much too young. I had not even properly 'come out' yet. But I think I must have been allowed the occasional daytime expedition so long as it was educational. Once, for instance, he took me to the Toynbee Hall Settlement where I think there had been a 'mission' run by New College.

South of the river was immediately different from the London I knew. But it was also vastly different from what it is now and much dirtier. There was no County Hall, no Festival Hall, not yet even an Old Vic. One was a stranger, stared at. The people who stared were another race, frightening. They wore dreadful rags of clothes. Some even had no shoes. I found myself shrinking, trying to get my breath and trying not to be so scared, but sure that Dick would protect me, if necessary by force, from the natives. I am sure, however, that I managed not to seem scared or behave in a silly 'feminine' way. We had both got so far as beginning to think that it was wrong that there should in London be people like this and something ought to be done about it. But that was as far as we had arrived and it was a very long way from revolution, or even the Fabian Society.

VI

Growing up into Science

What was my love-hate relation with science? Well, it went back some way, and there was always my father's lab in the background, though I never really understood the gas analysis apparatus, for example. But it became serious with the guinea pigs. I had started by keeping a few and gradually began to study them in a semi-scientific sense, listening to, identifying and copying their various squeaks and chitters, and seeing their relationship with one another and the whole pattern of guinea pig likes and dislikes. I even started taking notes. I certainly anthropomorphised too much, but I don't suppose anyone else has ever watched guinea pigs in this way. Scientifically they are an exploited race.

This went on for a couple of years and then Jack suggested that we should do serious genetics with them—Mendelism, as it was called after the newly discovered papers of the Abbé Mendel, on whose statue (is it still there?) I once, years later on, laid a wreath. I became quite keen and we went ahead with a whole range of two-compartment guinea pig hutches, so much nicer for them than today's wire cages in lab animal houses, built along the hedge by the side of the path that went past the tennis court and down to the boathouse. I of course did the feeding and cleaning, though somebody else must have done it during the holidays. It was an unscientific diet compared with the measured and, one would think, uninteresting, standard ration of the modern lab guinea pig, but I watched to see what they liked. They throve, reared big families and were relatively long-lived. I squeezed milk from the teats of one of my loved ones, so as to taste it, but it was rather nasty, and I understood their sex life, with its genuine likes and dislikes, so well that I thought there was nothing about sex that I didn't know. Females accepted and suckled the babies of those females whom they liked, rejecting those whose mothers they disliked. But is 'like' and 'dislike' the correct way of considering this? There are probably other reasons.

After a while I became something of an expert and was written to for advice on guinea pig habits and ailments. We got some new kinds, as we wanted to see not only how colour and brindling was inherited, but also long and short hair, and the whorls of show guinea pigs, though I never entered the show world. Occasionally we found a mutation, for instance a small extra toe, and followed that up. Perhaps the stud books we kept still exist somewhere: I named every guinea pig appropriately, many of them after the famous scientists of the day.

But by and by we began to realise that our results were not working out on expected Mendelian lines. We had in fact happened on what was then called linkage and later cross-over, but as nobody had yet got onto the chromosome structure it was very puzzling. But, luckily for me, there was little of the mathematics that seems to be necessary for modern genetics and none I couldn't manage. For a long time the physical structure of chromosomal cell division was theoretical and some of the guesses were far from correct. When Morgan's book, *The Physical Basis of Heredity*, came out, it was deeply exciting; I remember reading it in great gulps curled up on the school-room sofa and seeing how much it explained. But at first we were puzzled by some of our results; we decided to enlarge the experiments to include mice and rats; these were kept in the University animal house and complicated by the considerable ability of the mice to escape out of their cages at crucial moments in their sex life. The rats, on the other hand, bit; Frances helped with them, having vaguely scientific interests.

I never got fond of the rats, intelligent as they were, in the same way that I did with my guinea pigs. Once, going out to feed them, I heard the scream for help, ran and found Titi, whose cage I always left open so that she could forage, her hackles up, facing a weasel, while her family scuttled for shelter in the hedge—I can see them still, small brown panicked lumps among the ivy and wild violet leaves. I snatched Titi up and the weasel looked at me with wicked little eyes, humped ready to jump. Knowing they go for the neck vein I was frightened, but held Titi tightly covered in my hands, feeling her poor little heart racing, and kicked out at the weasel with my solid school-boy shoes. It went away and I put Titi down to call to her family, gather them up and get back into her hutch. One had to look out, too, for owls and hawks, especially if any of my flock were in open-topped runs on the croquet lawn grass. Occasionally we had to kill one that had been wounded, in the inner lab under a bell glass connected to the gas tap, always something traumatic for me. But I didn't mind doing PMs. If any pregnant females died or were killed it was essential to look at the colours of the unknown litter.

At the animal house I got to know some of the 'lab boys', skilled technicians some of them. They helped me later when I was doing science prelims, and for a long time it was thought on that level that I would have made a good scientist. Maybe. The first published paper I had my name on was a joint one on colour inheritance in rats, which was fairly simple. As an initial, *N.H.*, *six years old, four feet high, weighing 25·2 kilos and with rather well developed lung area*, I come, however, into one of my father's and Miss Fitzgerald's joint papers, as do my brother and various friends from the Dragon School. Later on, living in London, in Chelsea, within walking distance of the Lister Institute, I thought I could do some work on *Gammarus*, and had a shelf of labelled finger bowls full of families of these rather unattractive creatures in the bathroom. But it didn't work out. I had to give up scientific practice, and instead, write.

The guinea pig results were never clear-cut and we had so many factors to consider; besides they do not breed as fast as mice. Once we bought an apparently pink guinea pig, but the colour wore off. I would do a prowl from time to time among the cages in the market in case there was anything interesting, an extra fold on the ear, for instance. The market was always fun, though perhaps a bit dirtier in those days than it is now; I think Tyrell had most of the animals in his shop. We had our scientific eye already on the many breeds of domestic fowl, and there were vast areas of flowering plants to consider. But with the war, from 1914 onwards, there was a cutting back in the guinea pig population, both in numbers and in our interest. Later on my mother kept rabbits for eating in some of the empty hutches.

I was of course constantly in and out of my father's laboratory, but without much understanding of what the experimental work was actually about. At this period much of my father's work was in connection with mining, for the Institute of Mining Engineers. He had, indeed, worked closely with them for many years, receiving the Greenwell Medal, perhaps one of the ugliest ever to be designed, in 1904, and later becoming the President; he was still likely to be called for if there was a mine disaster, and he was director of the Colliery Owners' research laboratory at Doncaster—later transferred to Birmingham. So mining was always very close to us all. But this work, originally no doubt practical, in the sense that it was saving miners from death by breathing poisonous gases, had turned inevitably to the basic questions of the physiology of breathing and the functions of the lungs, so much more complex than they had once seemed. Breathing, both normal and under various kinds of experimental conditions, was constantly being watched and measured. As so often happens, 'pure' science was necessary in order to make practice really effective.

My father was writing one paper after another in conjunction with various people, Boycott, Damant, Butterfield, Lorrain-Smith, Gillies Priestley and others, but especially C. G. Douglas, some on such things as testing for carbon monoxide in mines, others, for instance, on the degree of absorption of oxygen by the lungs, studied in his own laboratory. But this was varied by excursions into photometry; he was still doing official work as a Gas Referee as well. He gave up University teaching in 1913. Sometimes he went over to Doncaster to test mine rescue apparatus, some of which was worse than useless, and to design

Jack at Eton and me, 1910

Engagement photographs, 1914

Off to war Dick, Jack and me, 1916

The young bride, 1916

Dick

POSTSCRIPT — FUTURE DECADES

Young mother, 1928

Portrait by Wyndham Lewis, 1935

1978 photograph by Broderick Haldane

POSTSCRIPT – FUTURE DECADES

My desk at Carradale, 1959

1987 Another book, another story.
Many books later – a signing session for EARLY IN ORCADIA
shortly before my ninetieth birthday. (Broderick Haldane)

better ones. This meant train journeys, during which he could settle down to think and work, as one cannot do nowadays, driving a car.

In 1911 he wrote six papers, five in 1912. Some are Royal Society transactions, and there is a Discussion on Vitalism in the *British Medical Journal*—for he always kept one foot in the philosophers' camp. Everything was written out in ink and the papers mounted up in piles on tables and carpet. I can't imagine that he would have been comfortable with a typewriter; he was extremely suspicious even of a slide rule. But I doubt if he ever worried much about the business side of life; that would have been taken care of in Edinburgh by the family firm of Writers to the Signet.

I might be sent in to say that somebody wanted to see him or that he had a telephone call. I would talk to Mavro or Gillies or stroke the experimental mice—or catch one if it got lost under a bench. Sometimes I did a bit of washing up, or watching what was happening in one of the large metal chambers where experiments on respiration were going on; occasionally I was left with the instruction that if the experimenter—usually my father—fell over unconscious, I was to undo the door, pull him out and do artificial respiration. But this never happened.

Work here began at a reasonable hour. My father tended to have a late, solid British breakfast, the eggs or kidneys kept hot in a silver dish, and miss lunch. At tea-time he emerged, often in term-time to a dozen or so young people, to whom he would be absentmindedly pleasant. Work went on after dinner until very late, long after my bedtime, which was still almost always around nine. Towards midnight the tray would be taken in to the study with milk and plum cake. I notice in one of his papers, in which meals were noted, the constant '12·30 glass of milk'. Beyond that, I would think that Uffer and probably one or two of the team might still be working till three in the morning. It was, I am sure, a happy time for them. It meant a great deal to my father to have his son beginning to work with him. Their first joint paper was in 1912, when Jack was only nineteen. He was reading Greats,

65

following Maths Mods; his First was almost taken for granted, so he had time for scientific discussion as well and the detailed talking over of experimental work. Aldous Huxley, who was entirely part of the household, must have been taking it all in. Later on, out comes some of it with Lord Edward Tantamount in *Point Counter Point*.

My father had perhaps built too much on becoming Professor of Physiology: to some he was the obvious choice. It had brought him out of deep depression after that earlier election when his uncle, out of deeply principled antinepotism, failed to support him, and Gotch got the Waynflete Chair (and Gotch was certainly not a great scientist) that New College gave him a Fellowship. He had a deep love and loyalty towards the College; he enjoyed the romantic aspect, the candles and the silver, and he was very fond of his younger colleagues. They, as well as the undergraduates and Rhodes scholars, came to tea now and then.

Understandably he resigned as Reader after Sherrington became Professor—and what a good teacher Sherrington was!—and there were always complications about lab space. But his connection with the Physiology Department still went on for a time. Florence Buchanan—Aunt Florence—a great physiologist in her difficult way, had to be championed; her detached retina deteriorated, though her brain remained active; today's lasers could probably have stabilised her retina and given her many more working years. University politics are always full of vicious in-fighting and presumably the fact that Oxford was particularly well padded against the conflicts which were coming up, both in less prosperous parts of Britain and in the outside world, meant that academic quarrels were very bitter and in-turned.

After his own laboratory at Cherwell was built, he finally ceased working altogether at the University Physiology Laboratory, although, for many people and especially the technicians, 'Dr Haldane's room' was still there. Some of his things, including the big balance, are still in the new building, and used; his presence remains, his papers are classics.

The one who suffered was C. G. Douglas; as a University lecturer he worked in the Physiology Laboratory. But his heart was a mile away, in the other laboratory across the Parks in North Oxford, with my father. Perhaps he was a little overshadowed —one doesn't know. But his and my father's minds worked admirably together on the respiratory regulation problems which they did so much to put into order. It left us all with an interest in breathing—I still find myself playing games with 'forced breathing'.

An increasingly familiar figure had been Yandell Henderson of Yale, full of enthusiasm, my notion of what an American should be like, perhaps the sender of my favourite American journal. It was he who had first brought Pike's Peak into the picture, I believe after a casual remark by my father at some conference that if only there was a high altitude mountain with a comfortable hotel at the top—earlier work had been done in mountain huts in conditions of considerable difficulty—he would go and investigate blood and respiration changes there. Yandell Henderson's immediate answer was Pike's Peak in Colorado.

The first expedition, in which Douglas and Barcroft took part, was an international one to the Peak of Tenerife. Here the preliminary questions and work started off, and the next year, 1910, came the expedition to Pike's Peak, with my father, Douglas, Yandell Henderson and Schneider of Colorado. This was the summit party, but they did not take Miss Fitzgerald, surely as eminent a physiologist as the rest, but—a woman. She, however, did equally valuable work, by herself, in the smaller hills. I remember her only vaguely, and as someone a little bit alarming; she outlived my father by some forty years. The Pike's Peak expedition is only in my mind because of my father's stories afterwards, especially of the visitors to Pike's Peak getting out of the carriages of the mountain railway, overwhelmed with mountain sickness. This struck both my father and me as delightfully funny, so I always enjoyed hearing him tell that one to the tea-time undergraduates.

The deep-sea diving work which had started in the Kyles of

Bute was being continued at Portsmouth with Guy Damant. Exact instructions were laid down for Admiralty divers and strictly followed. The tables are still in use and unchallenged for scientific accuracy, though diving has gone so much deeper and the free-lance divers who hire themselves out in the North Sea and elsewhere do not follow the Haldane table and consequently get bends and all too often die in great pain.

There was, then, this type of background during the years after the Dragon School when I was at home. The words were familiar, however little I really understood: alveolar air, lactic acid, the Haldane gas apparatus, the Douglas bag. There were not only the regular workers, but my old love Teddy Boycott, now a father, entirely grown-up, and then Barcroft, and the Copenhagen physiologists, the hours of talk going on in the study and the smell of pipe smoke coming out. But was that going to be my life?

VII

Oxford and Scotland

But have I any reason to think I was a budding scientist? Not really. Or a budding anything else serious or tangible? I disliked history. I was no good at languages. If I was anything, it was a good observer, not only of guinea pigs and wild plants, but also of people, and especially of people in relation to myself, a not uncommon teenage interest.

This watching of people was what I was doing with my brother, the person I loved best—though I had never formulated this. It was a deeply exciting relationship and part of it was meeting his friends, and our intellectual discussions in which I was always trying to make it into the undergraduate world. There were those wonderful teas in New College. Jack had rooms in the new buildings almost opposite the flowering cherry and in those uncrowded days an undergraduate had sitter and bedder, looked after by a scout who saw that the fire was going nicely, and we always had splendid mounds of thick buttery toast with Gentleman's Relish and then perhaps a Fuller's cake, of which I could and did eat slice after slice.

I suppose I was fairly attractive even at fifteen or sixteen, but if I was with Jack I could be unchaperoned. Elsewhere I, like the other girls, including female students, must be accompanied by a reputable female: for me it was usually my mother, to whom due deference was paid. Sometimes it was Miss Blockey, but my mother liked undergraduates and did much pro-Empire propaganda, which they were polite about, whether or not they accepted it. Any male over thirteen was potentially dangerous. One would think this must have been embarrassing for the chaperones, but it was never mentioned, so perhaps it wasn't. These social habits were taken for granted, like equally strange ones in India or Japan. I remember, rather later, there were great hunts for tactful 'chaps' who would stay in their corner whatever went on. Up to a fairly decorous point, that is! There was no necking or petting of the modern kind. But even at sixteen I wasn't really irked by chaperonage. The excitement was in the conversation between young people, spiced with clever quotations and local jokes, or witty remarks treasured.

These were still the days of the Bloods who had, it seems, dominated young University life for a long time but had only lately come to be resented actively, instead of being accepted as the kind of thing that happens in a class society. The Bullingdon Club and other Blood organisations had been behaving very badly in the early years of the century, in what would now be called a fascist way. That would be incorrect; they had no overt political philosophy, though many of their enemies held leftish views; they probably, but not necessarily, were Tory material. But they had a class arrogance which was becoming less and less tolerable in a society like Oxford, which was slowly changing into something fairly mobile class-wise. They had broken into the rooms of intellectuals, destroying books or pictures, knocking the owners about. They had torn up the manuscript—years of work— of a don they did not favour. They were forever lighting bonners in the quads into which they threw things they disapproved of. No point in going into names now; what was done was done. The College authorities were, by and large, unable or scared to control or discipline the Bloods, many of whom came from aristocratic families with quite a lot of political and social power. Some of them died heroically in the early months of the war, perhaps fulfilling themselves. That made their actions at Oxford no less detestable.

There was no sympathy in our house for the Bloods. Aristocrats they might be, but gentry they were not. My father would come out black angry at their anti-intellectualism every time the Bullingdon Club went in for one of their antics—when they

ducked someone in Mercury or smashed down the door of someone else who had sported his oak and was attempting to work.
They tended to be several against one. They were mostly English
and they admired one another. Plato might have admired them in
the same breath that he admired the Spartans.

But as I remember now there was always an undercurrent of
University gossip and giggle wherever one went. There were
endless funny stories, normally against the Proctors and their
'bull dogs', though also criticism of the Bloods for having scared
the guts out of the 'bull dogs' who had then turned aside to catch
some relatively minor offender from, say, Jesus (or Jaggers as we
would have said). My brother was an expert climber in and out of
College and tended to be somewhat boastful about it. Once, when
he had been gated, he climbed in and out every night, contemptuous
of the 'bull dogs'. Unfairly I thought, after the war when he
became a don at New College, he closed some of the easier routes,
in the interest, he said, of a fine old sport.

That was the University side. But sometimes and happily I
went for long walks with Trev Huxley; the Huxleys were so
nearly counted as kin that chaperonage was not considered necessary. We looked for birds and rare wild flowers. He tried to teach
me to differentiate bird song, but my piano lessons had not helped
me over this and I could not manage it except for the obvious,
so that I could never spot an exciting bird as well as I could a
plant. Mostly we went across the river and up towards Elsfield.
I suppose this is all now post-Nuffield suburbs, including perhaps
the damp woodlands where wild columbines grew and the usual
splendid mixture of orchis. We walked from our house by way
of the ferry, crossing our own lower meadow, often squashy
with an open field drain spectacular with golden marsh marigolds,
then over the fence and across two more water meadows, never
ploughed up but perpetually grazed or enclosed for hay. Between
them there was a fascinating mixed hedge, with a kind of path
through the middle after one had jumped the ditch; here in autumn
there were spindleberry bushes and boughs full of juicy sloes.

Then we cut down to the ferry and rang the bell; for a penny or two we were taken over, both of us pulling on the wire along with the ferryman. Then up past the inn, and on the stiled path to Old Marston with its solid village houses of golden-grey stone, on to the eastern by-road where one rarely met any traffic. Usually we turned off about the foot of Elsfield hill onto one of the many field paths, and there was endless interest and conversation, Huxley jokes and limericks. When in August 1914, Trev killed himself, it was for me and many another the end of the old life and the beginning of the personal evil and loss which we were going to experience.

What were we after, then? We were light-hearted on the whole, especially over politics. There was a strike by the Oxford tram drivers and conductors, whose wages would seem ludicrous by modern standards. A fleet of strike-breaking buses was laid on and we all went gaily into action, chanting, 'Buckell's blackleg buses!'—and trying to hamper them as far as possible. My brother caused an obstruction in Cornmarket by chanting (in a later letter to me he wrote 'singing'—but no!) the Athanasian Creed. I rather think the strikers won. But we were not deeply involved, so far, though others in the University were, including G. D. H. Cole and his friends who were already politically serious. Supporting the strikers was a pleasantly anti-Establishment gesture, not really more, and was scarcely effective against my mother, since not only did she somewhat sympathise with the strikers, but disliked Buckell, who was an arrogant townee. On the other hand there was her indignation at having to lick insurance stamps for the servants, forced onto employers by that odious Lloyd George.

All of this happened against a background of Oxford as it was then, a place of uncrowded, unhurried streets, still definitely University: handsome young men sauntering in white flannels and boaters or running in longish, flapping shorts, sometimes with College scarves and blazers or even academic dress at exam times, the women students on the whole earnest looking in their long skirts, only perhaps to be spotted in book shops, or about to play tennis. One main difference from now was the comparative absence of foreign accents. A few refugees settled during World War One, but the great influx was before and during World War Two, starting with the Jewish flight from Hitler. Oxford has always been a favourite nesting ground for au pair girls. Equally it has been a place where the elderly feel at home. Lately, on a visit to the House, I looked in at the Cathedral. It seemed to me that exactly the same congregation was drifting in, wearing much the same clothes and hats and expressions. But could it have been? Had they somehow been in cold storage since my youth? Surely I couldn't be that age myself? Would a teenager have equated them with me? I suppose so, but duck away from my logical supposition.

During my teens the cattle market was still being held and there were definitely bucolic types around with thick Oxfordshire accents, though not yet, of course, the Cowley incomers. The colleges and older buildings were much as now, perhaps even gayer with window boxes in summer, and where Banbury Road branches off there was a pretty little stone-built dame school on the right hand side, to which my brother went for a short time at around four, until his precocity was too much for them. In the triangle where Parks Road joins, which is now full of the peculiar shapes of science buildings, there was a nursery garden and a shabby little greenhouse with steps. It would, in season, have boxes of lobelias, marguerites and so on. It is clear that North Oxford front gardens were very dull compared with today. It was still privet, spotty laurel and laurestinus, with the most ordinary spring bulbs. There were pink horse chestnuts, double red hawthorn, double pink cherry, laburnum, but very little in the way of interesting *malus* or *prunus* varieties, only the standard blue *Jackmanii* clematis, only the double red paeony, little variety of iris. Nobody then would have dared to plant a magnolia, still less a camellia, although the colleges were beginning to be more advanced. But the gardening interest and industry of today were only just beginning. Both food and gardens have become much better since they have been cooked or planted by their actual owners.

Moving up to North Oxford, the entrance to Parktown was exactly the same, though the gentlemen's convenience was rather more shrouded. The Dicey's hedge was higher and wilder. On the other side there was Gee's, the smart greenhouse, that always had palms and cyclamens and hothouse grapes, which one occasionally bought for invalids, exactly the same as now. There was a post office next to it in those days, one of those nice post offices which are also small shops with a stand of post cards, which one sent to relatives in New Zealand. None of today's anti-mugging devices were necessary; small post office tills still went unrobbed, so everything was nice and open and friendly. We did a lot of shopping in North Parade and Mr Bennet still made my father's lace-up boots, working at home in his own little house which then seemed small and poor, but has probably by now been tarted up into a highly desirable middle-class residence. People had their special lasts at the bootmaker and if they acquired a corn, a model of it could be added to the last.

I suppose the river has altered rather less, though doubtless the willows are kept more in order. Are they still pollarded for use or only out of old habit? My brother rowed in College Torpids in the Lent Term, but he was a heavyweight and had to have a special oar built for him, which, even so, occasionally cracked, so it was doubtful whether the extra horse power he put into his rowing made up for the extra weight. He never got into a College eight. However, Torpids, the earlier race, also meant going into training, with fairly strict (but probably inaccurate) dieting, as well as a Spartiate abstention from this and that. But after the race all ended with a bonner and a drunk; College ale was strong. Sometimes too, it might finish up with what was known as a bit of skirt, but by no means always. There wasn't the same easy opportunity and Jack did not go in for the tobacconist's assistant type who was more or less available; in fact up to 1914 his sexual experience, like mine, was practically non-existent, except for erotic verse and guinea pig watching.

But with a certain alcoholic stimulus, what he did was to speak exclusively in blank verse of a classical, Shakespearean kind. This was well known and admired. Of course English speech goes very readily into this form, which one must be somewhat careful to avoid (note the last seven words). Note also the 'free verse' forms into which words spoken under deep stress fit themselves, for instance in *The Catonville Nine*. But during all my brother's life alcohol, even in quite small doses, seemed to release verse centres. Later it tended to be long quotes from Lucretius, Dante or, later still, the Sanskrit scriptures. Even sometimes the Bible. I myself usually, but not, I fear, always, keep this longing to spout verse inside my mouth.

Verse, yes, the running of words inside one's head, often interfering with thought or sensible planning or listening to other people. For years, and long beyond this period of my life, one of my favourite games was capping verse in its various forms: taking the last word of a line and finding another line which includes it (an easier version just takes the first letter of the last word and begins the next line with it), or simply finding a line whose author the other players cannot guess. Real highbrows can of course play this in several languages. As one gets older one tends to go back to Hymns A and M or nursery rhymes. Jack and I played this and other word or poetry games in the course of long walks at Cloan during the summer holidays in Scotland, up past the summer houses or along to where the glen flattens out into ferns and birch scrub with wild pansies and blue milkwort, perhaps even over the old hill road to Glen Devon.

We went for long walks, on which my father could still easily out-walk me. It wasn't until I was in my twenties that I found I was tending to out-walk him; but that was after his work on poison gases in World War One and his lungs were beginning to give. Almost every summer we used to have an expedition across the strath to Ben Vorlich; this had to be arranged when the Cloan car was available to take us somewhere near the foot. It was here that I was stricken with such fearful jealousy that it was like a sudden illness. The Stracheys were staying at Cloan. Amabel had a magnificent, enviable mane of red hair and appeared to me to be superbly confident, almost grown-up. And Jack asked her to be his climbing companion! Amabel tells me that actually she was feeling a bit shy and was somewhat surprised by this offer from a young man who rather scared her. Nor did they have much conversation on Ben Vorlich. Quite likely the invitation was an act of genuine good manners by Jack. Or was it perhaps that he was a little bored with me always tagging along?

I climbed with someone else and raging passion inside me. It was a horrible day. Probably I was thoroughly nasty to everyone. When I calmed down I managed to recognise that this which had come at me was the opposite of delight, was due to asserting ownership over another person and was the worst possible way of binding oneself to the Wheel. I never experienced the same emotion later on, perhaps because when I began to feel it I recognised it, tried to understand, rationalise and sublimate it. However it made me highly critical of any story or play which had sexual jealousy as its motive, including of course *Othello* and several other of the major Elizabethans. Intellectual and professional jealousy was more interesting and intelligible, perhaps sometimes justified, but usually it also led to wrong action. Or so it seemed to me.

We went on going up to my grandmother at Cloan every summer and often at New Year; things changed slowly. There were constant 'improvements' both at Cloan and Foswell. That kind of thing was not so expensive, relatively, as it is now; everything was done by the local builder and joiner. Year after year I ran out and bit off the tips of the tropaeolum flowers that shone in brilliant scarlet on the dark holly leaves of the big hedge, and sucked the honey. Year after year I gathered up the peacock feathers. In late April I picked the tiny delicate flowers of the wood sorrel, white pencilled with white, touched them with fingers and tongue, at last ate them. In summer I ate half-ripe plums and green apples, the last, late, slug-nibbled strawberries. The gong went for meals. I trailed books all over the house. I dropped my clothes on the floor; someone picked them up and washed them and they were doubtless ironed with heavy flat-irons off the stove. Bits of rhymes came into my head. Tremendous sunsets flamed over the hills on the far side of the strath; I tried to find words for them. I swung between irrational fears and sudden delights. In sparkling brightness after a shower I saw in a single raindrop hanging from a rhododendron leaf the whole thing reflected as in an eye and it threw me into a turmoil of pleasure.

Today I get great pleasure from garden flowers and especially good rhododendrons—Cloan is too high and chilly for the really classy ones!—but now it is not simple and absolute but full of expertise and questioning: how did they manage on this soil? Where did they get it and how much did it cost? This might be a *Gigha* hybrid. That has the *Loderi* scent but it looks more like a *Griffithianum* parentage. Or, more simply (but for a shrub rather than a rhododendron!): nobody's looking—if I just take a small cutting—but all this is being an elderly gardener, and in the back of her mind the thought of how many more Springs, not an adolescent overwhelmed by a particular kind of beauty, yet about to let it sweep away so as to be overwhelmed by another. The inexpert, non-intellectual pleasure of the senses: that goes.

Inside Cloan the senses had less to feed on. The pictures on the landings and corridors did not change. They tended to be monochrome reproductions of old masters; I especially disliked Saint Augustine and his Mum. In the drawing-room there were some quite pleasant water colours, but also framed photographs. King Edward, signed for Uncle Richard, in his silver mount. Later there was Einstein on the steps of Queen Anne's Gate. I found these fascinating, as also the cartoons of Uncle Richard which increasingly covered the walls between dining-room and smoking-room. But in general my aesthetic tastes were undeveloped and I found it essential that a picture should be about something or someone recognisable and interesting; I didn't start knowing what pictures are really about until many years later.

People didn't change much. Granniema in her eighties was rather more upstairs in her room but one felt her presence in the house. One was welcomed by the same housemaid who tidied up after one as before. The Foswell family, the 'Fossils', were always there, a compact bunch, perhaps sometimes resenting the way that I or other children were sent up there from Cloan, deeply aware that they were the ones who knew and understood the real, factual place, who knew where to find the birds and the fish, who were aware of exact growth and change. But they had to accept us and the young Belloc Lowndes's, for instance, or the young Inges. I felt that Elsie, my senior, was the completely competent and admirable one: 'One of the horses bolted for a mile with Archie but Elsie managed to get beside and stop him.' Or again: 'Elsie is an expert motorist now and she drove us to Dunblane the other day.' My brother did some riding on a horse called Sir Edward but I never felt I wanted to ride after my broken leg.

We went on longer walks every year, especially over to Glen Devon by the hill road. One of my letters goes: 'We walked over to the Scott Moncrieffs on Wednesday across the hills. It was awfully jolly particularly coming back in the dark with an inadequate lantern which went out half way. The road was frightfully bad—most of the way merely a channel for a small burn but we waded through the water where we could see it because there might be all sorts of pitfalls which we could not see on the dry road while the water was merely wet.' There was Craig Rossie and the burn below it. 'We went to the Black Swelch one day. It was looking splendid, the brown flood water gurgling up against the rocks and banging the stones about.'

Whenever I was at Cloan without my mother I duly wrote to her almost every day. By this time my handwriting had become (unfortunately) much what it is now. There are longish letters of description written on Cloan paper, which my mother kept, just as I have been unable not to keep letters from my own children. 'We thought the big spruce in front of the house was coming down on Tuesday night and went to the door to watch it fall. It was rocking and straining like anything but it did not go. The lower part of the high wood and most of the low wood is absolutely "squishé" and they are cutting up the wood.' This was in New Year, 1912, when Jack and I were both there. I certainly remember that chaos of uprooted and broken spruces blocking the winding paths—or do I remember one of the several other times this happened?

Clearly my mother had written a fussy letter, for I write: 'My hair is all right and Burser [she must have been the then head housemaid] brushes it almost always and ties it in the evening.' Then at the end, 'I think there is going to be a fancy dress dance in the barn on the 3rd. I think I will see if I can manufacture a hoop and wear Granniema's old dress.' I don't remember if I did but I do remember Granniema's old dress with its marvellously narrow waist which later I inherited and lent to a daughter—and never saw again. Fancy dress was always a delightful thing in those days: much less necessary now when everything can be fancy. Then it was one's only chance to wear—just possibly!— trousers, doubtless with a baggy blouse decently covering the flies.

A few days later my mother had another letter from me: 'Can we have our stockings the night we come back? I have a Venus of Milo two inches high and did you remember the bullseyes? They are in the top drawer of the glass top cupboard in the sitting-room.' Yes, there was the revolting little Venus of Milo in white ceramic which both my brother and I liked so much. It was, like the Christmas stockings, a bit of non-grown-upness.

Every year there were August shoots at Cloan and Foswell. My brother took a gun and was a reasonably good shot. But, like many another, he never shot again for pleasure after the 1914 war. I was once taken into one of the butts, but was so upset by the slaughter of the grouse (although I helped to eat them later) that I wasn't taken again. Picnics happened at the edge of the moor above Foswell, all females hatted against the sun, the men large in tweeds, keepers and gillies discreetly eating, and doubtless drinking, in the background, and an exquisite tiny burn over-hung by miniature cliffs over which grass of Parnassus and bell heather hung from moss beds. But for the Foswells, a burn, even a small one, was a hiding place for trout. Archie, three years younger than me, would go down and guddle trout if Uncle Richard had some specially important guest and none had been caught with rod and line. One can see in his books the same passionate feeling as mine for certain aspects of natural beauty. Yet it was half a century before we could talk about it with one another. Nothing is better eating than a grilled brown trout. But I was beginning to have vaguely humanitarian leanings about blood sports. That was in the air, at least for ladies.

By now I was beginning to listen to the grown-up conversations at Cloan, though unhappily many of them ended in the library, which was also the smoking-room and gentlemen's ground after meals, even if I had been curled up reading there all morning. Sometimes I had to trust Jack to tell me the end of stories, like Uncle Richard's legal one about the lady who was domiciled in Jersey and the St Bernard dog. I was already beginning to pride myself on never being shocked, though sometimes I was.

Although this was the full period of suffragette militancy, some of it, I would have thought, very much up my street, it did not affect me at all, and this must have meant that I didn't hear it talked about. With the dullness of newspapers and of course no radio, one could easily miss what was going on. Yet both my mother and Aunt Bay were keen feminists and certainly believed that the vote was important. But both were anti-militant, deeply shocked by behaviour which they considered both unwomanly and unladylike. Aunt Bay had been immensely active in public works, a member of various royal commissions, a trustee of the Carnegie United Kingdom Trust, and so on; she was to be made the first woman JP in Scotland. But I doubt if the Pankhursts would have been received either at Cherwell or Cloan.

I was becoming more interested in our Perthshire neighbours, though the Haldanes of Cloan had cut themselves off to some extent by supporting the Free Church, the people's church. However our cousin, Bishop Chinnery Haldane, was also a splendid eccentric, much loved in his vastly scattered Argyll diocese on which he spent all his salary, where he walked across country, swimming lochs (or so the story goes) and walking into any cottage at night for hospitality, where (again the tale is) he took the peculiar action of opening the windows. Long after, in the sixties, when I stood as Labour candidate for Kinlochleven in the County Council elections, I was billed as the Bishop's niece, and many a good Labour and Church of Scotland voter had his photograph in the best room.

By now I was expected to go to kirk on a Sunday from time to time, walking of course. Afterwards we had singed sheep's head in barley and Uncle Richard would tease me by picking out an eye and offering it. But with luck one could get cold beef instead. There was one Sabbath when I was so cruelly affected by giggles which had to be suppressed that I ached for the rest of the day. Earlier, one of the party had torn a hole in his trousers—fairly high up—the text was new cloth on old garments. Of such material are giggles made; I was no more immune than any other teenager.

At Cloan we had hothouse grapes for dessert, of which one was allowed a small branch, usually cut by the butler. Here again, everyone dressed for dinner, though Uncle Richard often wore a velvet smoking jacket, the height, I thought, of almost decadent luxury. The nicest things to eat were apt to be in short supply. I could never get enough of the broad beans which had always, of course, been skinned by the kitchen maid. As another matter of course we always had excellent oat cakes and there was comb honey for tea, with hot scones, smaller and crustier than our Oxford ones. Any house to which one went for tea would certainly have hot scones, muffins, crumpets or tea-cakes in a covered china or silver dish. But crumpets were always 'bought'. At Cloan Uncle Richard sometimes had separate little snacks of red herring or German delicacies. Once or twice during the holidays I would go down to Auchterarder with Aunt Bay, to Eadie the baker, for shortbread and their big tea biscuits which were particularly good. We still visited the sick and old, but no longer, I think, went to the Poor House, which by then may well have been much improved.

There was more machinery now on the farms and fewer horses, though the yard was still pleasantly full of horse noises at lowsing time. But I think already there was a steam threshing mill going round. Aunt Bay was pushing the garden out, making new little fountains, planting more apple trees and yew hedges by the dogs' cemetery, and the fine sweeping border just before the start of the upper walk along the glen. Foswell was somewhat rebuilt, becoming the charming house it is now.

I took little interest in the farming or the forestry, though it was always interesting to see a side of the glen clear-felled and pouring up leaves and flowers into the new sunlight between the resin-oozing stumps. The wild roses were different from the Oxford and Berkshire ones, though Bentham and Hooker did not really distinguish them; the ripe hips tasted slightly different, too. We hunted for blaeberries, but seldom found enough to bring proudly back. But always the things I really wanted were the walks with Jack, the throwing out of a feeler for the poetry game and between questions letting the words and phrases run in colour over one's inner background.

VIII

Class and Prejudice

It is difficult to reconstruct the standards and fine distinctions of the society in which I grew up. One was supposed to know them all in some subconscious way. Occasional echoes flit across my mind still. It was clear to me for instance that my mother felt that there were sometimes guests at Cloan who were not what she herself approved of, and this meant that her in-laws were either insensitive or not themselves quite her own social class—I fear the latter, always excepting Granniema. Or was it simply that they were Liberals, which in itself meant lower standards? But it was very puzzling for me. Maya had a great covering word: 'undesirable'. This might mean either a wrong social class or bad habits in our own (or higher?—no, we did not admit that, except for Royalty who were part of the Empire): things like drinking or fornication or showing off. Or being foreigners. But this wasn't clear. Danes, for instance, were quite all right. So were Austrians. But Germans were certainly among the undesirables, and there was a certain Germanic bias among the Haldanes. My father had few French colleagues and on the rare occasions when he met them, he tended to address them as '*Ach, mein liebe Kollege*!' I think they might have been suspected of flirtatiousness. As for Americans, they also were rather suspect, except for my Keatinge cousins—on my mother's side! But I myself saw them in the witty and memorable terms of some American magazine—was it perhaps the first years of *Vanity Fair*?—which for a year or two floated into the house, perhaps a gift. I always seized this, if possible, to have a first read, especially if the issue appeared likely to be disapproved of!

But what about Jews? Now, Maya had sufficient Jewish ancestry to have a somewhat ambivalent attitude. And my godfather, Professor Alexander of Manchester, was a Jew (and of course I was an unbaptised bairn, so it was an oddish relationship, though a very satisfactory one) and he looked like an Old Testament prophet with his great brown beard and soft brown eyes. I was increasingly fond of him as I grew up and talked to him a lot about my literary ambitions, which he took seriously. By now I was going in for competitions in the pale green Saturday *Westminster*. Uncle Willie had given me a typewriter for my sixteenth birthday: a good little portable Corona which lasted me for years. In those days one got free lessons and I went to Hunt's in the Broad for them, but, though I have typed fairly fast for many years, I never use my fingers sufficiently and if I don't think I can see the keyboard, I don't touch-type properly. My father immediately asked me to type his papers, but was worried when I dropped a line, as one so easily does with copy typing; he felt I was not attending properly to the sense, nor was I. But how much better my own poems looked in type! I sent them sometimes to my godfather, who might afterwards discuss Beauty with me, to our mutual advantage. It was clear that being a Jew—that kind of Jew—was a proud and splendid thing. But many, alas, were not like him, as was made clear.

There was a friend or acquaintance of Jack's, most definitely a Jew and looking it. He was one of our frequent visitors for the parties where we played Nebuchadnezzar, and had acted in *Saunes Bairos*. Yes, there he is in the photograph. He was one of the 'natives'. I suspect that Maya thought he might be buzzing round me, though I rather doubt that this was so. At any rate she told me not to pick him if we were picking sides. I was often the picker, since the host and hostess were more likely to know everyone's names or nicknames—besides, I liked doing it! That evening the sides were picked, the known best actors and prettiest girls went first, then there was a smaller pool and at last, at the end, my pick and poor Clausen standing there—and was I to disobey Maya's explicit instructions? I certainly didn't dislike him, but the prohibition had been given with great seriousness which I had not questioned. I still remember his darkish, injured face, his eyes dropped to the floor, suffering as Jews have suffered for a long time. There was some kind of rush, joke, compromise, diplomatic lying, I don't know now. I was confused, felt awful, not so much for him but for myself having been put into this position by some sort of net I didn't understand but which had caught us both, Clausen and me. Yet I didn't protest, I was too embarrassed to say anything further to my mother; there must have been some reason which I didn't grasp, so it was probably my fault. Occasionally, if I had lied my way out of a situation, I would have a word of praise for my social sense; this kind of lying was quite all right, and the parallel suppressions of truth. Nor do I know whether this poor young man came to any more Neb parties—this may well have been one of the last before, so to speak, the ceiling came down: before August 1914. Nor do I know if he was still there when we started picking up the pieces in 1918.

Anti-Semitism as such would definitely not have been approved. As far as colour went, Indian 'natives' were approved if in the Army or even as students if sufficiently high caste, polite and well connected. Maoris were definitely all right, perhaps because of their enthusiastic acceptance by Rob Makgill, our much loved cousin, chief MO of Auckland. Perhaps also Stevenson's poems and stories of Polynesia helped, though I doubt if I had ever seen anyone from those still delectable islands. But I am almost sure I never met any African socially, though as a child I had stared at the inhabitants of 'African villages' at shows. Chinese and Levantines were the picture-book villains, but the brave little Japs, who had so valiantly defeated the big Russians, were still admired.

As to religious barriers, we knew a few Roman Catholic families, but I think my mother was always slightly suspicious of those who gave allegiance to the 'Bishop of Rome'. And there was always a slight background of walling-up nuns, and, of course, of the lower-class Irish who were distinctly undesirable, even as servants. Our maids would normally attend some religious service on their Sundays off: Chapel was very suitable, but they might also be C of E. My mother would have been careful about food, not to break any known religious rules, either for Jews, Moslems or such Brahmins or Buddhists as might have been invited. This was standard social manners. I rather doubt whether these various fine lines and distinctions meant much to my father, though he was certainly a fairly stern moralist, taking a much more conventional attitude on such things than one might have expected.

But there was another strange race: men. I am not sure what, if any, explicit sex instruction any of us had. The boys who were leaving the Dragon School had an admonishment from the Skipper, which I tried vainly to overhear by hanging about under a window, from which I was promptly dislodged. I think it was on the general cold-baths-to-avoid-temptation, and keep-your-hands-out-of-your pockets, line. But girls? It seems odd if Frances and I never discussed this, yet, if so, I can't remember. Perhaps here there is a real memory blank, a depth of embarrassment, into the bottom of which my fishing memory cannot reach, just as I have utterly forgotten the probably erotic stories I told myself. I doubt whether any of the information we got was very inaccurate, certainly not deliberately so. It was the continuous slanting.

For instance, my mother told me that if anyone proposed marriage (no other proposal would conceivably have been a possibility!) I must ask whether he had ever had anything to do with another woman and if he had I must refuse him. This was straight feminism of the period, an attack on the double standard for men and women, which was still, of course, socially accepted. I wish I could remember the wording: 'slept with' perhaps? Or simply 'had a mistress'? One knew that from the history books.

It was asking for trouble, especially on the assumption that the man was normally at least five years older than the girl he married. If he was still a virgin nearer thirty than twenty, then there was likely to be something wrong. There was at this time no respectable sex instruction or advice book for either sex. My poor Dick, just before our marriage, seems to have asked a few questions of the regimental doctor, who said in a hearty and reassuring way that he would get to know soon enough. Might things have gone better if he had acquired some earlier experience? Perhaps. My mother was clearly longing to have a cosy last-minute chat with me, but I brushed her off, convinced that anyone who knew as much as I did about guinea pigs had no need of further knowledge. The notions of either sex about the expectations and needs of the other, whether in courting or in intercourse, were minimal. There was only the social assumption, reinforced to some extent by religious or educational exhortation, that the young man and young woman 'kept themselves' for their future spouse. Is it better, if you are dying in the agony of modern warfare, to regret what you haven't had or, perhaps, what you have? There were plenty of virgin soldiers in 1914. There was also a generation of women now past retiring age who lost their men for whom they had kept themselves, and never replaced them. They were historically important in the development of education, health, politics, the arts and sciences. In the next war the sexes died more evenly.

Over this business of parallel virginity, I jumped at the feminism and the implicit possibility of getting the better of a man, but did not in the least grasp the dangers of sexual ignorance. But I did grasp that for a man to 'have a mistress' was a nasty, continental thing—look at all those French kings!—and in Britain only practised by the *nouveaux riches*, themselves appropriately described in French.

Some of the rules were quite simple. I knew, for instance, by the time I was sixteen that one must not get into, or be seen in, a hansom cab alone with a man, unless one's brother. Hansoms were delightful, hopping up into such a good position for the view, the closing of the clever doors, the quick clopping of the hoofs; one always hoped to be allowed one at a London station. It was only if we had a lot of luggage or were in a family party that we had to take a growler—the smelly old four-wheeler. But the runners, who in my very young days used to run alongside to help with the luggage in return for a small tip were, thank goodness, extinct. Or did they still do it in the bad bits of the industrial belt, out of sight of London and Oxford?

There were other rules about possible danger spots, such as hansoms. Being alone was always perilous in the imaginary jungle. I suppose the mothers of the period all fussed about their virgin daughters, possessors of so desirable a property. Hence the chaperones, the rules, the exhortations. Hence trouble for males suspected of interest, unless they were 'desirable' and their intentions were honourable, in which case they would delicately consult their prospective parents-in-law. One was told vaguely of certain loathly but un-named diseases which could be picked up, one was told, from used towels or glasses and especially lavatory seats. Hence anyone visiting 'the continent' took a supply of paper lavatory seat covers. Did visitors from those parts do the same for England?

The virgin daughters tried to escape, but not too far. We were all somewhat scared; there was too much we didn't know. But our plans for the future always included more freedom. I was now vaguely thinking of architecture as a profession; I often used to scribble plans of houses, none, I think, of any merit, and I never could draw the outsides to look the way I wanted them to. However it was not yet possible for a girl student to become an architect in England, though it was in Scandinavia; so that was that. But what with guinea pigs, acting, reading, collecting wild flowers and day-dreaming, life was fairly full.

After a certain amount of parental agitation, it was decided that I could be allowed to 'come out', temporarily as I was firmly made to understand, in June 1914. It would be my brother's last Commem; my allowance was to be two Commem balls. In preparation for this there were several weeks of ball-room dancing classes at the Randolph. My partners were mostly in their last year at Oxford, or possibly in their second year. I suppose mixed ball-room dancing classes were something of an innovation—or weren't they? Were there Edinburgh dancing classes in the Assembly Rooms for bouncing Highland girls in for the season?

88

Mine were indeed a different matter from the old High School classes. What I enjoyed were the patterned dances with intricate steps, especially tangoing with Lewis. It was all building up towards the real thing. Jack and I did mostly heavy waltzes with little reversing, but seeing which of us could whirl longest without getting giddy. There were also delightful fast polkas. These classes were, naturally, ringed with chaperones; sometimes they ended in tea but often our partners had to rush back to College and work.

For the real thing I had a long white dress, silk georgette, I expect, with a fairly low neck, short sleeves and, to go with it, long white, pearl-buttoned kid gloves which took ages to get on. I wore it also for my first Old Dragon dinner, where I was the only female, among white-tied or black-tied white-fronted males. I was given a gold chain with a little opal drop in a blue enamel setting, my first 'real' jewellery, in preparation.

The real thing came, the carefully organised Commem parties, the instruction about behaviour, the photographs in the sleepy, bleary early morning. Not too much claret cup, come back between partners. See that you 'go into private life'—that was then the phrase—in good time, as there will be a queue. Above all, not too many dances with the same partner. But Mitch—was he yet Dick to me?—wandered down with me in my white dress to the empty High. A single motorbike came and went, passing Univ and Queen's and I saw for the first time, the shape, the exact, beautiful curve of the High, normally blotted by two-way traffic, but suddenly clear. We both saw it.

We girls were always rather thrilled at the news of an engagement. On the whole in our class, marriage was somewhat later than now, when the husband could be expected to provide for his wife in the manner to which she was accustomed. In the respectable or rising working class, it was often considerably later. Couples walked out for years on their half day off. And walking was probably about all they managed to do. Any of us in Miss Blockey's classroom would have reacted violently against being kissed, unless possibly a light and respectful touch on the brow. A flirtation did

89

not necessarily involve any contact. There were no love scenes in my plays and they didn't even come in much in Nebs or charades, where we tended to have battles, murders or incidents where our fancies were free to embroider ('Alexander the coppersmith has wrought me much evil') or which could be used to puzzle an audience ('Is it M for Marat or A for Agamemnon in the hip bath, vigorously soaping himself?') or needed great ingenuity (Lord Burleigh 'walking up and pacing down', Enoch Arden's funeral, Cerberus with his three heads, Canute with the waves coming in). Today C (or K) for Circe would be seducing O (or U) for Odysseus; but then she was turning the crew into realistically grunting swine.

We usually cleared up the acting box ourselves, but otherwise tidying and washing-up was just left. In the morning it was done. One was unfamiliar with the process. Dusters, soap, soda? These belonged to another world. A trusted maid informed my mother of what was needed; no doubt she checked occasionally. There were locked store cupboards, as well as a strong-room and cellar. Once I was taken to a country house where there was a genuine still-room in which essences were made, interesting drinks and bunches of dried herbs, and there was an impressive and beautifully labelled and arranged array of jam, jelly, chutney and so forth. But this was not at all my mother's line; the early twentieth-century feminists had thrown all that off, though we did make a fair amount of jam. However jam-making was the cook's department, although the family did the picking, whether of wild or garden fruit, and servants' work ranked low. A kitchen maid cut her hand, which I did up with iodine, lint and bandages. Shortly afterwards I was discovered to have nits in my hair; probably the kitchen maid was given notice! Lice were very lower class; if anyone caught them it was extremely shameful, that is to say until World War One, when any kilted soldier, officer or private, coming back on leave, would almost certainly have to have a very hot iron run along the seams of his kilt.

These fine shades of class distinction are rather hard to get into perspective, and most of all my own acceptance of them. But there they were, and are still in societies which have sufficient spare time and energy to bother about them, that is to say in all the countries we know though they change and shift with the years! Class divisions today may be along lines of money or caste, party or religion. Whatever division it is, most people in the country concerned accept it as natural and obvious. I tend to feel divisions most clearly today along education lines, by which I don't mean qualifications, but the intellectual freedom and wide-ranging sets of knowledge which an educated person should have. And yet—and yet—there are other values, honour and courage and generosity, which used to be thought of as the virtues of gentle birth, but which are, as we should know by now, not the prerogative of any class or race.

Did I ever become educated? If so, only accidentally and occasionally, with a few questions filled in during odd times in the lab, or perhaps talking with distinguished guests. I suppose it was in late 1913 or early 1914 that I sat 'Locals' in some Oxford public building. I'm not sure what they corresponded to and have an idea that there were Junior and Senior, the latter being equivalent to university entrance. The standard, especially perhaps in science, was clearly much lower than today. I don't recollect being worried by these exams or even doing any hard work, in fact all I remember is a very easy Botany paper, with a specimen flower to dissect and label. It had two small green caterpillars inside it, which I made race across my desk.

IX

Inside Naomi Haldane

And what about the ghosts and devils or whatever they were? The appearances that beset me if I wasn't careful? Well, they were still around. And are, though not so obtrusively, and as one grows older one finds means of making them work for one, as in a number of episodes in *We Have Been Warned* and *The Bull Calves*. By fourteen I was no longer worried about treading on the lines between paving stones. Finials on the ends of North Oxford tile ridges ceased to look at me. But I was still very conscious of good and bad in houses and in furniture, especially mirrors. Our expeditions into curiosity shops in search of wedding presents might bring one suddenly face to face with something which was clearly hostile, a twister of the straight look. I noticed much the same, not many years back, in the Soane Museum, which I suppose I ought to re-visit. But probably won't.

I was also beginning, in my reading, to come across passages in which it was clear that the authors were describing and had experienced, my kind of thing: fairly often in Kipling short stories, occasionally in Wells, Eden Philpott or Buchan. The last time I remember being struck in the same kind of way was in the last chapter of *The Teachings of Don Juan*, a book which had interested me very much. I read this at Mochudi in Botswana, in 1972, by candlelight certainly, but in my friendly white-washed rondavel where I could normally feel nothing but goodness and safety. At the end of the book I took a tablet of librium, but had the father and mother of a nightmare, one of the old kind. Nor am I the only one to be affected by this book. I am only thankful it didn't come my way when I was a lot younger.

The older parts of Cloan were still frightening and there were bad patches even in the glen. Does one ever completely grow out of such things? Of course not. They are as much part of oneself as one's bones. The best one can do, perhaps, is to have convincing dreams in which one traverses the black spots but the expected evil does not emerge. Occasionally my father comes into such dreams as the area of safety, occasionally as the exorciser or perhaps the explainer who makes it quite clear that as a matter of fact and once one grasps the pattern of what it is all about, everything is perfectly all right. In these dreams I am often aware that my father is, actually, dead, but that seems to make it all the more probable that he can help. There is nothing to be afraid of. In these reassuring dreams it is always my father, never my mother, once the childhood dispenser of safety and reassurance, the one on whom one had become dependent. It seems hard that poor Maya, who always longed to protect me, should not be able to do so! It is also curious that it is my father, who in life could not realise my frantic horror of bogles, nor how the family teasing only drove me into deeper terrors, has now become my dream understander and sympathiser. To each his own unconscious.

The nightmares were bad during my teens, I would think once a week at least in the worst patches, and not helped by the economically low-powered electric lights which one must always be sure to turn off at the landings. But how well was I? Or any of us? It was taken for granted that one would from time to time during the winter months have a bad cold, an earache or a cough that went on and on. These were depressing, to say the least. So was the sense of guilt if one's bowels were not regular, especially if one had lied slightly about them. One took tonics, though at least no longer cod liver oil which was perhaps out of fashion, and inhaled Friar's Balsam. Later, in the thirties, when I used to get these winter coughs, heroin lozenges got rid of them, nor do I remember ever getting addicted—they were rather nasty. But cough lozenges were part of winter life, from the chemist next to Gee's, formamints said to contain formalin and if so surely rather bad for one, and of course the delicious blackcurrant Allen and Hanbury's, for which it was well worth simulating a cough. At some point some kind Australian sent my mother a box of eucalyptus lozenges. As a British Empire product these were specially welcomed and after that she often got whole packages of them; I liked them myself and even found them fairly effective. The routine yearly visits to the dentist were rather fun than not, for I had a good dental inheritance and had also been breast-fed. Of course no dentist was a gentleman and one could never meet one socially.

But, to return to the nightmares, there was something very peculiar and alarming about them, or rather about a condition which was not sleep or dreaming, since I was often perfectly conscious of the external world and sometimes even had my eyes open, though this was difficult, as my eyelids stiffened. In this state I was held, unable to move, while something rushed by or through me—through, it seemed when I could manage to concentrate, the base of my skull—apparently taking with it some part of my thinking or will. This was sometimes preceded by a tension, not quite pain, but a feeling of alarm and distress, equally in the base of the skull. Whether this had any connection with my early concussion, I don't know. But it seems possible that it was a very mild form of *petit mal*, something which probably affects far more people, especially children, than one might suppose. The condition still very occasionally occurs, but is not alarming as it used to be. One knows it will pass: 'they' will let go, not really being as powerful as all that; one will soon return to normal.

No doubt part of this general ill health was due to the remarkably unheated state of British houses. The copper and brass hearth around the drawing-room fire was nice to sit on, but one couldn't do that all the time. Draughts breathed round one's ears. And most grates had slow combustion devices which were economical both of fuel and heat. It was all coal at Oxford and a coal cellar holding perhaps five tons from which the polished coal scuttles were brought. When it was used up one rang for more and still there was always an under housemaid to bring it. Sometimes I or Jack brought in a log of wood but it was usually elm or willow, not much good for burning. At least at Cloan one could gather fir cones. But there again, the usual solution was to ring for more coal. There were the new electric bells, which were not as decorative as the old china bell handles, but doubtless as unwelcome in the kitchen, where it was clear which room had been ringing.

I doubt whether there were any electric fires yet. But there were hot water bottles in plenty. In the inner laboratory there was a gas fire, another in the main bathroom. I expect it had been installed for Granny, perhaps for her maid to heat something—it had a gas ring. But it was seldom lighted; we were all chary about gas. Indeed for me the word had already a sinister connotation to be brought into sharp focus with the Battle of Ypres.

Yet, although conditions of ill health probably made a good breeding ground for nightmares and obsessions, it was kept bottled up, under considerable pressure. When the intellect was involved, it did not show, nor during the happiness of communal activity—conversation, playing games, acting. Nothing could touch me during the times of aesthetic satisfaction. Only, the head would lift, suddenly. I could not have spoken to anyone about the ghosts. Nor, as yet, could I use them as raw material for writing. That would have been too like touching them or being touched by them. They could have revenged themselves. And yet the first time I was to use them, in a verse drama, *The Mirror and the Clock*, was only a few years on, might have been already incubating. But it would have been risky still to put them onto paper; instead I wrote endless bits of romantic verse, but at least it always scanned:

> Deep in the north, a silver flame,
> The pole star pointing whence we came.

It was impossible to speak of my under-life to anyone who would treat the whole affair on a rational basis. Indeed this is only too clearly what happens often enough to mental patients. They must be met half-way with understanding, as I am sure happens when there is a combination of good psychiatry with enough time. One can't be rushed when pulling out these thorns.

My brother had the irrational streak, but he would probably have thought it inappropriate to share it with me. I could not speak to him, still less to parents or teachers. It would never have entered my mind to speak to a doctor. I could not have mentioned such things to my classmates, who would either have laughed or thought less highly of me as a competitor or leader. I told Andrew Lang of the nice bits of the irrational world and may perhaps have mentioned that not all the appearances were pleasurable, but if so he did not notice but encouraged me to see fairies; this I did from time to time, the last encounter being on the way back from the 1937 Labour Party Conference at Brighton—we had stopped to eat sandwiches and talk about George Lansbury. I happened to notice a hobyah type of fairy just going away.

The first attack on the powers of evil came suddenly and without preparation. I was sixteen. Jack's Eton friend, Mitch, was coming on an evening picnic up the river; when the flotilla set out, he was in my canoe and we were sufficiently alone on the green-shadowed brown of the slow water. I don't remember how it started, but suddenly I was telling him everything about the clock and the chair, the claw-legged mirror, the nightmares, the deep currents of fear and propitiation, and he was responding, not with disbelief or rationalisation, but with understanding. With love, doubtless, though I did not think of it in that word. What I experienced was an extraordinary sense of relief. I had spoken. They had not got back at me, were not able to. I had touched them and no evil current had passed; another hand was holding mine. What I did not realise was that, in partial—at least—breaking of a relationship between myself and my nightmares, I had inevitably started an equally deep counter-relationship between myself and Mitch, and that this relationship would key in with Rouen Cathedral, the tension and the delight.

But before that, in my mid-teens, when it would have been normal, why did I never become religious in any formal sense? Might not that have been effective anti-nightmare stuff? Well,

I suppose I was just not that kind of person. Perhaps magic and religion don't entirely mix; I have never quite appreciated what, to others, seems a clear boundary line. I certainly made some attempts to acquire a rational Haldane-type *weltanschaung*. I began trying to read Hegel. That sentence, however, might have been written about any decade of my life up to the sixties when instead it might have changed to: I stopped trying to read Hegel. But he did seem to be part of the family tradition. There was enjoyable old Plato, with the settings of the dialogues, but I was uninterested in the genuine philosophy. I pushed myself, or was pushed, through Berkeley and even parts of Hume, though now I think of Hume, not as a philosopher, but as one of the Edinburgh eccentrics. But Christianity, as exemplified either in New College chapel or in either of the Auchterarder Free Churches, had no impact. One just couldn't take things like the Creed seriously, as they stood. Later I was more inclined to allow for the historical context, to admit that, in a sense, there might be validity in some of the statements. If by any chance I now find myself at a Church of England service, I tend to repeat the General Confession. One may as well keep oneself reminded of the things one has done or left undone.

But other religions, or hierarchies, were more attractive, although what one felt was not belief, whatever that is. In different adolescent moods, Apollo, Artemis, Dionysos, or even the grey-eyed Athene, found a temporary votary. I still thought highly of the Norse pantheon, fed by versions of sagas. And I was beginning to involve myself with the Celts, first through *Celtic Fairy Tales*, then through Lady Gregory's *Gods and Fighting Men*. And there was a book about Isis and Osiris which I much enjoyed. At Cloan I varied my old gardens for fairies by building altars to unknown gods and making offerings of flowers and berries and small scarlet toadstools, sometimes in a pleasingly pre-Constance Spry manner.

Then of course there were all those fascinating Swinburnian deities, Cotytto, Astarte and Astaroth—'in Lampsacus fervent with faces, in Aphaca red from thy reign,' which places I even looked up in Murray's classical maps. But when, with the aid of the *Encyclopaedia Britannica*, one tried to find out a bit more about these deities, they turned out to be rather horrid. I suppose I read all Gilbert Murray's translations of Greek plays, and was of course much interested in the Furies whom I recognised; and there was the occasional Greek play in the Summer Term. It was Jack's friend, Mitch again, who tried to lure me into learning Greek with a charming little book: *Lalage ou le Grec sans Larmes*, but that didn't take. He did however give me a lovely edition of Leconte de l'Isle, whose high-tragedy Norse mythology appealed to me enormously. My own stories at the time were full of heroic deaths, since this was not the hideously common thing it was to become not so far ahead. The book was exquisitely bound in red morocco with my initials on it in a small gold motif. We went together to the binder's workshop in Long Wall Street, up a flight of wooden steps, close under the old City wall, the other side from New College garden.

But the religion that really got a grip on me was Mithraism. One attractive aspect of this was that I always imagined myself a man, a friend no doubt of Pertinax and Parnesius in Kipling's version of the Wall, or else one of the equally Kiplingish Winged Hats, in which case the Norse side of things could slide in happily. I read Mithraism up in some detail when I was writing *Prisoners of War*; the reference books included Cumont's *Mystères de Mithra*; at least I was able to read French easily by now. There was a Buchan story too that gripped me. Then came those July plays and the wreathed altar and my hair bunched up into what was supposed to be a Greek fillet. And Mitch (but now, surely, he was Dick) wrote:

> The gods, O faithful mystic, are not dead.
> They wheel and murmur through the summer night,
> And shaping dimly round thy lifted head
> They come once more into the waning light
> And lead again such dances as they led
> Through Thessaly, in swift enraptured flight.
> The Gods, O faithful mystic, are not dead.'

Oh many were they, far and wide their praises
Once sounded. Last of all, from tower to tower,
Even far Solway saw the upturned faces
Turned towards Mithras at the evening hour.
Where now, save on this hill, are their high places,
Where now, save here, are heard the words of power?
The Gods, O faithful mystic, are not dead.

After that the probable next step should have been clear to me.
But was not. Yet I had already written a poem myself about the
New College Commem ball, which should have informed me about
myself and my dance partner, with whom I was sitting out.
Again it did not. But it is an almost grown-up poem.

Sitting Out

The Chinese lanterns in broad day
Like orange ghosts show faint and strange,
We feel the throb of dancing feet,
The distant music's halt and change;

I thought I heard,—did you not hear?—
Piercing the golden violins,
A foreman's whistle, sharp and clear:
They go to work; did you not hear?

The dancers stream across the grass,
The morning wind lifts up their hair;
The music deadens heart and brain,
They do not know, they would not care.

Surely you heard, as we sat here—
It pierced right through the violins—
That foreman's whistle, shrill and clear?
They go to work; and we sit here.

99

We should not come outside and flaunt
Bare necks and shoulders to the sun,
Our dresses look so hot and crushed,
We should have gone when night was done.

A moment since—too near, too near—
It pierced the singing violins,
That foreman's whistle, fierce and clear!
They go to work; with us so near.

X

The Sky Falls

In early August there was the Curragh incident. My mother thought all the time about Ulster; nothing else seemed to matter. Then in three days we were at war. A letter from one of the cousins in California to my mother: 'You wrote two days before it came and your fears were all of the Ulster troubles and then it came in a moment.'

We would win, of course—we always did, didn't we? It was wonderfully exciting; one wanted to rush around all the time. For some reason we rushed to London and at my uncle's Queen Anne's Gate house I saw Sir Edward Grey, the Foreign Secretary, looking desperately anxious and worried. Wasn't it all going right? It must be! Yet this was the first tiny doubt, a white-faced, middle-aged man slowly shutting a door behind him, not noticing a girl on the stair. Everything was disorganised. Our friends were hurrying into khaki; many of the young men had been in OTC's and now the way was open to real war—if only they could get out soon before it was all over. It couldn't last until 1915! If anyone seemed to hesitate, the girls—the older people as well—were ready to push them into glory. Dick, who had left Oxford after his expected First in Greats, was reading for the Bar and had joined the Inns of Court OTC, a mounted body—he liked riding—and from there was sent as a Second Lieutenant to the Queen's Bays and a more severe riding school. Bey Gillespie, who had shared the London flat, went off too, both of them leaving everything just as it was—surely they'd be back soon! If only the war didn't end without giving them a chance! So it seemed at first. My brother had of course gone to the family regiment, the Black Watch, with his cousins.

Glory. Yes, it did honestly seem like that to me at sixteen. I was upset because I was 'out of the fun', as I might have put it. Or my mother might have, at first. We had Red Cross first aid and home nursing classes at Cherwell taught by a couple of nurses. At last I learnt how to make a bed. Frances and I bandaged one another, those splendid elaborate bandages that in practice one never used (except perhaps the capeline to keep a dressing on a very scabby head!) We found it rather exciting to see one another relatively unclothed. There were the songs: *Mademoiselle from Armentières*: *Tipperary* of course. Bernard Partridge drawing villainous Kaisers in *Punch*. Gallant little Belgium, the horror stories—babies tossed on bayonets, rapes spoken of in horrified whispers; eagerly we believed it all. The thing which really upset our household was the wrecking of pithead machinery at a working Belgian colliery, including of course the cage and ventilation. Yet most of it seems very mild compared with what we are used to now in any war and speak about aloud, see on television and then forget.

Then the casualties began. Inexplicably we were not winning and our friends began to be killed: really killed so that we would never see them again. Then it was clear the war was not going to be over by Christmas and all the men in training were threatened. We began to be afraid. Jack with the Third Battalion of the Black Watch up at Nigg was fairly immediately threatened as casualties came in from the First and Second Battalions. Pat, our first cousin, also in the Black Watch, was killed. Graeme, his brother, was in the Navy, off having adventures in the Mediterranean. Elsie became a nurse.

Meanwhile I had been asked down to Frolbury Manor, to stay with the Mitchisons. I did not at all realise that the respective mothers (at least) had spoken to one another or that I had been invited for a purpose. I think this was the first rail journey I had done quite by myself. Perhaps I was met at Paddington and driven down to Surrey; they had a big comfortable car with a chauffeur and carriage rugs. Probably I wouldn't have managed a change of stations in London. Everybody was very nice to me, nice to me myself, not just to the family. Yes, I was counted as a real person! I was fascinated with the comparative luxe of the house—the furnishings, the food, the china, my future mother-in-law's French maid, the fact that a bathroom opened out of my bedroom, a bathroom all bright and gleaming, better than Cloan, with stuff in bottles that I sniffed but didn't risk. Then Mitch—who now must be Dick—turned up in an incredibly smart cavalry uniform. I am inclined to think now that I might have said yes to the first man (I beg your pardon: officer) in uniform who asked me to marry him in August 1914. It would have been 'war work'; it would have been involvement in the great excitement. Anyway, it was Dick who did ask me.

I was extremely worried almost immediately afterwards at what I had done. I think this is, or was, fairly normal for a quite young girl who has accepted almost without thinking. And at that period an engagement was not something one could honourably get out of. Marriage—what was it really? Something gone for ever, all one's life changed. I had swapped the slight measure of freedom I was beginning to experience for—what? I felt that yet another set of grown-ups was going to own me. Even the shining bathroom was no longer fun. For the first time in my life I couldn't sleep.

I rushed back to Oxford so as to be in time for the first aid and home nursing exam, though this must have seemed a bit odd to the Mitchisons who wanted me to stay on. I took a cab from the station, dashed in, said to Maya, 'I'm engaged to Dick. Where's the exam going on?' and left her sitting in an understandably emotional state on the hall settee, vainly trying to ask questions. So that was that. I got my Red Cross certificate all right but I gave one wrong answer in the oral exam—peritonitis for peritoneum—why remember that for sixty years? I was told I mustn't say anything, even to Frances (whom I had already told, so there was a first bit of guilt complex) until there had been further consultations. It must have been soon after that Dick came to see my father, vainly trying to interest him in the financial details which his parents had told him to explain. Finally, asked about his interests, he said he was now reading the *Encyclopaedia Britannica*. 'Yes,' said my father, 'but do you understand it?' Poor Dick.

Jack seemed pleased when he heard. It was a deep and lifelong friendship not interrupted later on by little things like Dick being in the Labour Party and Jack in the Communist Party: of course Jack would come and speak for him! It was not interrupted by Jack's bitter quarrels with me; they went on swapping jokes and stories and information whenever they saw one another. Almost half a century after 1914 they were joking about one another's false teeth.

Nigg, where the Third Battalion had their camp, was a strange gaunt place. We stayed at a small farm with a most charming Highland family. Jack was now deep in this new life, intent on doing it as well as possible. Here he succeeded. A year or two later privates joining up in the Black Watch heard of Jock Haldane already as a story, a myth figure, a killer silently getting to the enormously dangerous but only correct spot from which to lob his bombs, often his own make, into the enemy trench and watch the shower of corpses. But he was also an officer to be completely trusted; his fatherly care of his men had taken them safe through utmost perils.

All the young men whom we had known in the old days developed an immense conscientiousness, perhaps some aspect of a shield against the kind of war which they were now beginning to be aware must be faced, however excitedly they had gone in at the start. Perhaps too something to set them apart from the civilian world where 'business as usual' was still going on. That was to become increasingly shocking to those with other standards and who were not profiting by it. Dick learnt an immense amount about the possible diseases of horses. The Queen's Bays were still practising cavalry charges. He was becoming aware that this was silly and wanted to change, but that was not easy.

I went down to Frolbury fairly often after this, at weekends.

Surrey was not yet a stockbroker's paradise, but partly at least a refuge for the intelligentsia, sometimes with cottages in genuine villages inhabited in the main by genuine villagers. It was a new botanical area for me, the sparse heathlands of dry Surrey, the smell of pines rather different from that in Scotland. We went walking in the woods, first in full summer then turning to autumn, winter with crunching beech leaves and at last spring. We met various interesting people, mostly left-wingers of some kind, including Amber Reeves, heroine of a much publicised affair with H. G. Wells. This shocked my mother deeply and I believe she protested about her innocent daughter meeting a 'loose woman', someone about whom there had been a major scandal. I doubt if it shocked Dick's mother; she, I am sure, was much more shocked by my lack of fashion sense—or even presentable clothes —and my social ungrown-upness as it appeared in her milieu, terrifying Aunt Kate and gentle Aunt Helen. I in turn found her sisters alarming and disapproving. She gave me a black velvet suit, a creamy *crêpe-de-chine* blouse with round blobs of buttons and a hat with a black cockade on the side. I didn't mind dressing up, but nobody was going to get me out of my clodhopping 'sensible' shoes into high heels, nor would I take any extra trouble over doing my hair in a more attractive way. I must have been singularly irritating.

Frolbury Manor was a largish modern country house, the main rooms looking south and opening on to a broad stone terrace with geraniums in tubs and garden chairs. Inside there was a big hall with sofas and rugs, overhung by a gallery. I doubt if it had any right to call itself a manor but it had a large garden, terraced down to a couple of paddocks with a stream winding through them and a small wood where we tried to make a swimming pool. There must have been several gardeners as well as a very complete household staff, and the big light drawing-room with its valuable furniture, pictures and china had always two or three banks of greenhouse flowers, brought in and arranged by the gardeners; I was much impressed, especially by the schizanthus which I had never met before. In one corner was a rather horrid large white Dresden china monkey, which later on always wore a captured *pickelhaube*; perhaps Willie put it there as a joke and nobody had the heart to to take it off. There were also splendid greenhouse carnations which were new to me, and gorgeous to put in one's hair, real dressing-up material, heavily clove-scented. At this point I had myself never used perfume or for that matter any other beauty aids. I would have found it shocking to do so. There was a billiards-room at Frolbury where Dick and I were supposed to conduct our courtship. As to that I was still unsure of anything. I couldn't explain that there were words and touches I didn't want. It had been somewhat of a shock to find that someone whom I had considered as another brother, somebody who had understood about the nightmares and not laughed, had suddenly turned into something else. Perhaps if it had been possible to take the whole thing at a slower tempo I would have been able to respond. But there was a war on and nothing could wait.

Dick did not get to France until the early summer of 1915. I went quite often to Frolbury and must have written to Granniema about it, when sending her a pin-cushion for her birthday— it is difficult to think of suitable presents for a ninety-year-old grandmother. She writes on April 10 1915, 'I do not exactly know the country, but I know something of the adjoining country, having seen a considerable part of it while driving in different directions. It is a very attractive part of England, and abounded with wild flowers, especially white violets to which I am much attached!'

I must have found and sent her some, no doubt well packed with moss, for the next letter, on April 19, says: 'I was very much pleased with the white violets. I am very partial to them and they remind me of Hampshire and Surrey and pleasant days there. I have some white Devonshire violets, but they are different and also some from Innerpeffray, but they are not in flower yet. They are in my garden and have a character of their own; I think they must have been there when the old Abbey was in use.' She writes too of Pat and of Jack, and of Graeme guarding convoys between Egypt and Asia Minor in the *Doris*. The wild flowers down south must have been a fortnight ahead of the Ochills, and with these subtle differences which, to the close looker, as Granniema and I both have been, are half the fun.

But, to go back to 1915, there is plenty more I remember about these months before Dick went off to France to join the Queen's Bays there, but it is not relevant. However, to show the completely different ambience of the times, here are two episodes from one of his 1915 leaves. Dick really enjoyed taking me out to meals; I was young and greedy with the digestion of an ostrich. To eat as many Fuller's cream cakes as I really wanted was heaven! But once he took me out to lunch at Simpson's. It was the first time I had ever had lunch in that kind of restaurant and I enjoyed it immensely. But our respective mothers got together and spoke to us very seriously indeed about how Dick's actions might have 'compromised' me. We were both very angry and upset; I wrote a bad and furious poem, but what was the use against grown-ups? Then, one leave, Dick was to come up with me to Cloan, meet Granniema and the family who all liked him—but we were not allowed to have sleepers (even first class, obligatory for him as an officer) on the same train. Again this would 'compromise' me. Remember we were formally engaged with an announcement in *The Times*. Nor was I at seventeen all that much of a shrinking violet. Anyhow that was the parental attitude, presumably that of millions of other upper-middle-class parents.

Twice in late 1914 my parents and I went up to Nigg by the Highland Line beyond Perth. Jack and I swam in the October North Sea, I decently turning my back and putting on a swimsuit. Did he? In those days no kilted regiment wore anything below the kilt except possibly for regimental full dress. I remember the rocks and the waves and later in the evening watching the full moon racing among the clouds, trying to take omens, for him of course. Apart from this I never swam for pleasure during the whole war. I wanted to of course in summer, but it seemed—well, I might have said unpatriotic, but it was even more irrational than that: if I could make a sacrifice perhaps the wrath would be averted from someone 'out there'. We went as a family to

Southampton to see Jack off with the Third Battalion, my parents putting on brave faces, I in terror that this was a final goodbye. It must have been very trying for him.

I remember with such embarrassment and distaste that my memory shies away, how my mother seemed determined to share all emotional passages with me. It was as though Dick's presence stirred her in a way that it did not stir me. He was certainly very fond of her and always very nice to her, but that was not at all the same thing. It was all mixed up with the war tension, the fact that now her God was threatened, the Empire itself, and these young men were the priests and/or the sacrifice. Curious how the sacrifice idea went deep in the family. Was it the Jewish streak from my mother's mother's side? It was quite different from the parallel but sensible idea that one must be prepared to take all risks, including that of one's life, for objectives that appear morally and intellectually sufficiently important. I also remember very clearly being told that the period of her engagement was the happiest time in a girl's life. This seemed to me to bode ill for marriage.

Then there was the problem of an engagement ring. Dick gave me a family ring, Australian gold in small knobs run together into a circle. It was a little too big for me and one day I had taken my mother's invalid cousin Archie up the river punting. Wet from the punt pole, the ring slipped off my finger. I dived for it without even taking my shoes off, grovelled in the mud bottom of the Cherwell, but failed to get it. Dick was immensely sweet and comforting about it, I mustn't take it as an omen—what other ring would I like? I didn't like to say that what I really wanted was a star sapphire, just by itself, no diamonds. I did mutter something about blue stones. His mother went to an antique shop in Brighton and sent several rings for me to choose. The only blue one was turquoise which I didn't like. I chose one with small emeralds and diamonds, which I never liked as much as the gold one; Dick and I agreed to sell it later on to buy something for the house. But his parents also gave me a double string of small pearls, with a diamond and emerald clasp which later I turned into something else. It was an almost overwhelming present. My future mother-in-law wore coloured pearls, pink and grey, large, and I would think very valuable. But I never quite saw the point of them.

The only other one of the family whom I was really fond of was Dick's younger brother Willie. He had volunteered as a despatch rider; he was a dear, gay and affectionate, with a certain talent for drawing. He got a Blighty early on and a few months in hospital and on leave, but unfortunately it was too mild a wound. He was killed in 1916. I don't think his parents ever really recovered.

XI

The Impact

Oxford in wartime still managed a certain amount of gaiety. But the colleges were emptying; Aldous Huxley came and stayed with us, which was nice. Now that Miss Blockey was away he played for my dancing and he asked me what being in love was like. But I, not being 'in love', did not answer satisfactorily. At first he was badly depressed though not speaking much about Trev, but gradually he began to unshell. There were things happening, a few poets left, the university co-op shop which we took turns to staff—this was great fun, almost like acting. I loved being behind the counter. That, rather than the political side of the co-operative movement, was the attraction. In the room above I experienced my first grown-up style committees. There was a co-operative dressmaker who made Earp, one of our poets, some pyjamas out of a piece of Liberty silk he had bought; they had the word 'Liberty' on the selvedge and this was incorporated in the trouser legs. How we laughed!

I was beginning cautiously to investigate politics, or rather to see the man who interested Agnes Murray so much, for I loved Agnes, Gilbert Murray's beautiful daughter—our families were by now on friendly terms—and she admired G. D. H. Cole, the dark and flashing Magdalen revolutionary. Or so he appeared to young sillies like me. I doubt if he ever spoke to me at this time, but that didn't matter. I was allowed to go, so long as the meetings did not go on too late. I went to several where guild socialism was discussed; I didn't understand, but liked the taste of it all.

Meanwhile I managed to absorb a fair amount of learning; for me lectures had a certain interest but dissection had much more, especially the elegant inside of a pithed frog. Worms were all right but the crayfish tended to disintegrate and the dogfish were foul. The rabbit was interesting but I didn't care for its dead face. Guessing slides was fun too and the lab technicians, I think, went out of their way to help Dr Haldane's young daughter. It was no part of that year's course, but I also went to some more advanced lectures on genetics. But I never got on well with physics and chemistry; one of the lecturers tried to kiss me, which I didn't like at all, yet probably giggled while dodging, which only led him on. One simply couldn't help this giggling and it often had quite unintended results.

I was what was then called a Home Student, though now we are St Anne's and have a very attractive College of our own and a high academic standard. But at that date there was a rather limited academic supervision. I remember nothing in the nature of a tutorial system. There was just tea with the Principal in one of those monumental houses in Parks Road. It was perhaps rather unfortunate that she was more interested in educating her girls than in getting them degrees. Perhaps those of us with academic homes were supposed to be looked after already. Women's higher education was still rather new and unorganised. I doubt whether Somerville, where I would have liked to go, would have taken a sixteen-year-old, as I was at the beginning of the academic year in autumn 1914. Somerville and Lady Margaret Hall were the only women's colleges which had really made strong and permanent growth by that time, though the others were beginning, sometimes in rather temporary buildings.

We did botany in spring in the old botany labs facing out across the botanical gardens, a lovely place. I learnt to cut sections of plant material with an old cut-throat razor that my father had given me; I learnt to stain and the elements of microscopy. It was more than half a century afterwards that I used again the techniques I learned then, at Mochudi with the microscope I brought to the school; they were still in my head and fingers. Professor Vines was our lecturer and I remember that the life cycle of ferns had just been discovered; I don't think we got as far as fungi or lichens. But plant cells are large and beautiful and convincing, stomata are easy to see; botanical drawing is a pleasure; and we could take our lunchtime sandwiches out into the gardens or down on the close-mown green grass by the river.

It was only when men came back on leave or wounded that we imagined at all accurately what the fighting was really like—so far from Oxford and ourselves. But could we really imagine it as it was? No. In the papers news was edited and censored; it always is in wartime but we were not yet used to automatic disbelief of the kind that is usual now. We kept on thinking that it must be over soon. Then came the first gas attacks, my father hurrying out to headquarters in France where Jack joined him, the post mortem on the Canadian officer, the certainty that it was chlorine, the experiments to get an efficient gas mask, then coming back across the Channel to find Kitchener appealing to the women of England to make a totally useless mask which would only betray the men it went to. My father describes this at length in his own papers and one gets a sense of his anger and frustration. But his own lab was mobilised; all the men who were still there were completely involved in the struggle to make a cheap and efficient gas mask. The house reeked of chlorine, the noise of coughing and retching was continuous from the study and beyond. Everything that would make into a mask was seized on—stockings, vests, Aldous' woolly scarf, my knitted cap. They got it right in the end and then there was violent telephoning to the War Office. Aldous did most of the necessary type-writing. I remember my father, cut off, shouting at the operator: 'Damn you, I'm the Lord Chancellor!'

More wrong gas masks, but at last the right ones getting made and going out, though exasperatingly slowly. The women of England ones never left London; that had simply been a ploy to ease civilian tension and fear. But I had been sent round to stop our neighbours making them, urging them to wait till the right design came out—every mother wanted to send a gas mask to her own boy. I felt even then that some of the neighbours were suspicious and probably felt that these Haldanes were pro-

German after all. Later my father was not put on to the committee on gas warfare, just because his brother had been attacked by the Harmsworth Press for a few remarks about German philosophy and for having been at a German university. That may well have resulted in a few extra deaths of men in the British Army.

If my brother had not been sent for to headquarters to work on the gas he would almost certainly have been in the fatal charge at Richebourg L'Avoué where most of the officers of the Third Battalion of the Black Watch were killed. He got to the front in time to see it happening far off, was himself wounded behind the front line by a shellburst, then picked up and taken to a field dressing station by the Prince of Wales, who was trying, as he always did, to get as near as possible to the real fighting and danger. Jack came home with a useful Blighty which kept him with us for weeks. How marvellous to have him back! What fun we had! But the caked dirt and lice on his kilt, that was something real too.

By that time I had managed to make various other girl friends, mostly my fellow Home Students. Some were Catholics staying at their hostel, Cherwell Edge. Was it then I got to know Liz Belloc, whose life so twined with mine later on? How nice it was for everyone when they had a young man to go around with again, especially perhaps one who had been wounded and was therefore approved of by the authorities. Many of my fellow Home Students were the daughters of Oxford parents. We were kept within the family bounds. I still of course had to be home for dinner and in bed at 'a reasonable hour', probably ten. I still slept in my mother's room. I was still afraid of the hall clock and dodged the clawed mirror.

Smoking was, of course, as immoral as reading forbidden books. I did however do both, but I really rather disliked smoking, just as I found *Madame Bovary* vastly dull, not worth struggling through in French. So, having made my point, to myself and, doubtless, to Frances and Aldous, I didn't persevere. Not liking tobacco smoke was a great nuisance later on in the twenties when any party, and above all any meeting, was thick and stinging with smoke from the addicts.

We Home Students had a common room in Ship Street whose amenities I enjoyed enormously. I could feel, once I was inside, that I had really got away from home. We could have coffee—by that time I had begun to like it—and buns or cakes which were still plentiful in 1915. There was a decent little loo where, in 1916, I had one of these very early miscarriages which are so usual; I told nobody. I must have had a slightly larger allowance by that time, but still can't have done any serious shopping unless possibly for a pencil or for yet another packet of hair pins. We weren't allowed to have men in—but a wounded officer on leave and a Haldane at that—well, when he dived under the sofa, whichever female don it was who came in pretended not to see. To conform with the rules, Helen Simpson, a keen rider, attached a lump of sugar to the end of her riding crop and dangled it out of the window for Jack to jump for. I expect we were scolded, but not hard. Much was allowed to Our Boys.

Aldous meanwhile had discovered Garsington, the house where Lady Ottoline Morrell held court and was hostess to so many distinguished or promising officers. How exciting it sounded! But alas, I was never allowed to go there. Frances did; she was less firmly kept in bounds than I was. Her grandfather was dead, so they were no longer in Wadham; they had a house halfway up Boar's Hill with a big garden where she and I used to play—and I have a feeling that we were still playing make-believe games. But I think she felt shy at Garsington; like so many highbrow paradises then and since it was more a place for young men than young women. I resented being kept out of it even if it harboured people of doubtful morals and conscientious objectors, surely the lowest of the low.

It was part of a world of minor arts which seemed marvellous at the time just because they were a break from the first decade of the century. There were also numbers of japes and harmless practical jokes. Aldous writes to me about one of them:

'Next Sat there is to be a conciliabule at the Co-op of Patricians—or members of a non-existent St Patrick's Club. There will be tea where you'll meet Robin ffaussett, Grattan Esmonde, myself and the Inimitable Miss Cox—together with others—including supers such as parsons, buffons, old ladies to act as chaperones. It will be funny, so come. You can be one of the non-Irish members like myself—the joke being that the tame parson thinks it's a serious meeting for the spread of Urse and Keltic Kultur! . . . I am frightfully busy, having to write an essay and a vast literary paper by Monday and Tuesday respectively—neither of which I've touched so far. But—will you come to tea on Wed—not unaccompanied by your mother, if she'd care to . . .'

I don't think I can have managed to get to this, for how could I have forgotten something which was such fun? And mild enough compared with today's more bloodthirsty and violent jokes.

He writes again about my wedding:

'How admirable! I shall be on the spot all right, I think. Pity it's not to be ecclesiastical—I would have made such an excellent Page. Meanwhile what in the nature of a wedding present do you want? Unless you tell me I shall get something jolly like a set of real old Victorian antimacassars. I saw Gervas yesterday in quite good form.'

And a PS 'Did Frances get through her exams?'

And finally as the wedding day came nearer:

'Should you care to commit your last indiscretion before you become a British Expeditionary Force Matron by coming to tea on Wednesday? I am asking Frances to come. I trust the IMPURE PURPLE picture may by then have arrived.'

What he finally gave me was a somewhat Art Nouveau print of a veiled figure, yes, purplish. I was delighted with it then but in some of our moves or other troubles it disappeared.

These are cheerful letters and his gaiety and affection show even in the handwriting which is not that of a depressed or anxious person. It doesn't hurt to re-read them as it hurts to read the letters of those who were going to be killed. Aldous lived and left a life's work clearly stated at the end. In the gaps between slaughters we were being teenagers with our own delights and problems, our embarrassments and importances and giggles and glimpses of overwhelming beauty and excitement.

In the middle of all this I managed to get through science prelims. It was hot June weather and the slides dried up. The crayfish were disintegrating so that it hardly mattered where one stuck in the green gland flag label. I had been reading around a bit and brought in some remarks out of an early Julian Huxley, perhaps his first, at some point in my written paper. I thought, and rightly, that the examiner would not have read this book and would not have recognised the quotations as being anything except my own intelligence. The viva was all right except that when the examiner took a dog's skull out of a paper bag I was nearly overwhelmed with giggles because it looked as if it was going to be sandwiches. However, I kept my cool and remembered the foramina. I got through. I sometimes wonder if this was not because the examiners didn't have the face to turn down a young Haldane.

XII

The Letters

In come all the ghosts, including my own. But I got by and went on into another life with other values and a different set of words. So did Dick. So did Jack. But so many of the rest—no. And here are the letters, anything from privates to major-generals. Most are very young officers recently commissioned and apparently, in spite of their higher and expensive education, swallowing whole in the autumn of 1914 what was a very primitive form of patriotism, fuelled by newspaper propaganda, and using the kind of phrases which today make one shudder, since one has become aware of the realities and motives underneath them. It was as though these curiously innocent young men were utterly uncritical of anything their elders told them. Criticism—disbelief of any kind—was unpatriotic. This makes for a terrible embarrassment and sadness, re-reading these letters, which are all round me where I have undone the bundles or looked into the heavy manila envelopes that wait for me like hungry bivalves in a coral reef. Rupert Brooke said it for us; his war poems are hard to take now although then they were just what we thought we wanted. I find myself overwhelmed by pity and anger. It is particularly hard to find Dick, with his normally incisive mind, using these dreadful phrases, though perhaps rather more in letters to my mother than me. After all, mothers-in-law must be placated and perhaps he thought me too young for these big ideas of country and sacrifice.

The letters to my mother are sometimes from older people, using the set phrases which all the same came naturally. 'We Canadian mothers are so proud of our sons being permitted to take part in the great struggle of our Mother Country.' Or again from an old soldier to whom my mother had given money and a pair of old boots so that he could walk back to his regiment: 'Now i shall have a Chance to go out to the Front and do my Duty once again for my Country and help my chums out their.'

The letters are flimsy, often written in pencil with the red stamp giving no date or place and the corner saying 'Passed by Censor'. This letter written in the summer of 1914 was from someone to whom my mother had clearly sent a parcel. We were always doing them up and sending them off. He says, 'The iodine tincture was a particularly happy thought for my own had been lost.' It looks as though people had to make up their own first aid packets. It goes on:

'You will be glad to know we had a lively time the first night we spent in the trenches. The Germans entertained us to everything but gas. We had been sent in for instruction and were attached to an infantry battalion. We had such a doing we never expected to see the morning. In the company to which I was attached one officer was killed, one wounded, so it fell to my duty to take over two platoons and my own troop and to reorganise the defence.

'The OC of the company was kind enough to thank me for my assistance and man enough to say he did not know what he would have done without the extra men.

'I can't tell you how proud I am of my troop. It may sound extravagant but I love them all for every man was a fighter. The apparent wash-out is one of the surprises: my weediest trooper, when hit, had his wound bound up and stuck to the parapet till dawn, refusing to quit his post while there was any danger.'

There are letters of pure grief. This from Dick in October 1915, from Flanders. The evening before

'We'd had the Maire and the schoolmaster to dinner and I got so utterly exhausted talking French to them . . . Nou, isn't it

cruel about Heath? I heard from your Mother yesterday. Chug*
and then Gillie and then that wonderful little man, one after
another. There's no use in whining about it—but it did hurt,
didn't it? And does still—half the magic gone out of things.
And I do remember so many, many times spent with him.
He'll be the most mourned of them all; he did so much for
everyone. They're all such empty words for something so rare
that's gone—it's horrible to write about it. Writing about it calls
up all the times I've been up there, in that room, and all the
things we did and said.'

He goes on: 'Our winter billets will be just S.W. of —' And here
the censor has scratched out a name in purple pencil which spreads
more or less over the whole letter. Like tears. Does one wonder
that the first years of peace after that war were singularly desolate
for the young survivors?

And now here is one from Major-General Egerton in command
of the 52nd Lowland Division, written from Gallipoli in August
1915. I quote this fairly fully as it seems to be a bit of history.

'From the English papers it is clear that you know nothing
and hear very little and are told very little of what goes on
here. Possibly, indeed probably, it is necessary for Army reasons.
All I can say is that when I think of Winston's statement "that
we are only separated by a few miles from the greatest victory
the world has ever seen" I wish I had him out here.

'We can hold our own here, we can occasionally bite a small
piece out of the granite wall in front, losing a number of teeth
in the process, but until the great force operating in the north
succeeds in getting *across* the peninsula on the other side of
Achi Baba it is and must be stalemate.

'They have had very heavy fighting and I dare not mention
their losses, though no doubt those of the Turks have been
gigantic. Some day you will know that for the number engaged
this is far the bloodiest fighting of the whole war. . .

* Cheeseman, one of the young New College dons.

'My poor S. rifle and K. Scots Brigade* lost seventy officers and 1,300 men on the 28th June. You ask whether I have had a chance of using my division myself. Why, yes. On the 12th and 13th July the 52nd Division entirely alone, except of course for corps artillery, fought a very hard and trying engagement and took a very large group of Turkish trenches, *all* they were ordered to take except one small piece, and *held* all they gained, which everybody has not done. I can tell you—I confess the good God was very merciful and the Turks made no real counter-attack as we were so done and exhausted that we should certainly have lost some of the ground gained. The division lost a hundred officers and 2,800 men. The only recognition we have received was a telegram in *The Times* of 16th July saying "Part of the forces under my command attacked and captured, etc. etc."—not one word about the 52nd Division —and then to put the lid on was a statement that the RN Division was sent in to recover a trench that was lost. They were sent in late on the afternoon of the 13th to attempt to take the one trench that we had *not* captured. They never got near it, never retook anything, lost thirty officers and their attack was a complete failure. So is history in the newspapers written.

'I am getting old now and impervious and indifferent but the younger men feel and resent these mistakes. My division, as you will gather, has received a severe shaking which would try any of the best troops in the world. In France troops undergoing such a shock get a period of rest out of danger and receive reinforcements and refit. Here this is not possible as nowhere are you out of fire, and digging and fatigue work are continuous, and though I have received a lot of young officers from Scotland not one man has been sent me and new blood is most sorely needed.

'With one or two exceptions the division has pulled round well and we are again in the trenches, and have quite got the ascendancy over the Turk as regards bombing and sniping. Such experiences however must have their mark on second line

* Presumably the Scottish Rifles and King's Scottish Borderers.

troops. The Turk I think is a very clean fighter, recognises the red cross—and we hear today that eleven men of mine, missing on the 12th, as being in Constantinople all wounded and being well treated. Missing as a rule has meant dead.

'In my opinion the men who have done best here have been the City battalions, Glasgow keelies and Edinburgh clerks and Leith dockers. Miners too fight well. The Border and South of Scotland agriculturalist is good in parts but not up to the others. Give me the Glasgow corner boy with good officers.

'They are making preparations for a winter campaign here and are getting out designs for huts. The prospect is not pleasant—at present we are troglodytes, but the first rain, and it is not far distant, will drive us from our burrows. Oh, that Winston and his swollen-headed attack on the 17th March with ships alone! We should be in Constantinople now if we had attacked then with an adequate land force—such a force as we have now, not two divisions as they attempted it a month later.

'The health of the troops, *considering*, is not bad but diarrhoea is very prevalent and we have a great many off duty with it. Practically every shrapnel wound becomes septic but we have had only three or four cases of the invariably fatal "gas gangrene". There is enteric, but very little. The troops are well fed and get rice and dried fruit and raisins. The hospital arrangements here are good and the evacuation of the wounded very speedy. At first I fancy it was awful—one ship arrived at Alexandria with 400 wounded on board and one vet in charge! When I was at Alexandria in early June it was one vast lazaretto, so was Cairo.

'The last fortnight's fighting here (on 6th and 7th August) and to the north must have put a tremendous strain on the RAMC. I know the number of wounded that have passed into and through Mudros since the 8th but I must not mention it. . . . Please send any parcels or any goodies. All are welcome, even if one can't eat them oneself—as is my case at present. Half our parcels and packages however are stolen and looted— it is infamous—a parcel by *post* often takes six weeks from

England and if it bears the imprint of some purveyor of tobacco or groceries like Fortnum & Mason it often never arrives. By post, mind—not parcels by ships. They are nearly always looted. We want HE and shells however more than we want parcels' . . .

But the letters to me change during 1915; the dew of that early patriotism has dried away. I quote a 1915 letter from another Old Etonian. It begins by thanking me for a letter and shortbread,

'. . . both of which were extraordinarily acceptable in this almost uniquely loathsome part of the globe. I always said war was a mug's game and now I know it. I cannot conceive of any object, material or ideal, which would justify any sane man in undergoing such a combination of extreme danger and extreme physical discomfort. The regiment went into action about three weeks ago, leaving myself and four other officers in reserve at Lemnos, at which we (in our ignorance) groused. It was completely cut to pieces and when we arrived a week later we found that of the 360 men and ten officers 170 men and two officers remained. We found them in what was euphemistically called a rest camp which consisted of a large number of holes, some few hundred yards behind the trenches. During the two days after we arrived twenty-five men and four officers were laid out by shrapnel—one being killed horribly in the hole next to mine—and I came to the conclusion that my idea of a rest camp and the General's (who has now completely disappeared into the ground and is thought by this time to be somewhere near Athens) did not tally. . . I had some extraordinarily unpleasant escapes, one shell exploding on my seat in the officers mess about one minute before my occupation of it . . . I have a vast deal to say still on the subject of war but the flies make letter writing impossible and as I shall indubitably be killed before returning to England you will probably never hear it; which is a pity as it will probably aggravate you intensely.'

But was he killed in the end and if so, where? When do we meet again? Ned Grove, are you there?

Another letter from my friend Millicent at St Hilda's.

'We have just had very bad news. My dear brother Philip has been killed at the front . . . Nothing can make up for his loss, he was the dearest brother one could have. I know you will understand if I put off our tea party for the present . . .'

So it went on and there is one letter after another from Lewis Gielgud and quite a few from Aldous and Frances. There was this group: Aldous, Lewis, Gervas, Frances and me, always trying to get together and writing one another either long letters about everything or cheerful short scribbles, as so many of mine from Aldous are. Today we would have telephoned to one another, perhaps keeping in touch almost every day. But then it was letters and because of that something remains. Today's young groups will disperse as ours did and later on there will be nothing to remind them of the fun and worries and fears and plans and good ideas which they had. But there will be fewer ghosts, fewer letters to trap and bite their older selves, armoured by experience and yet still vulnerable.

XIII

St Thomas's Hospital

In 1915, with Dick away I became more and more impatient
with Oxford and my own non-involvement. Girls I knew had gone
to do 'war work'; one or two were even in munitions factories.
And at least I had passed first aid and home nursing examinations
and what was more Sister Morag Macmillan had chosen me as the
one to whom she could teach massage, feeling the hands of half a
dozen girls and rejecting them before taking me on. Whether she
knew I had some capacity as a healer which might be brought out
is something else again; had she sensed that she would wisely have
said nothing about it.

I nagged and nagged and finally went off to be a VAD nurse
at St Thomas's along with May Douie, an Oxford friend whom I
did not know very well. We stayed with the Hale Whites in Wimpole Street; he was one of the most distinguished and sympathetic
doctors of the period. Both were great friends of my parents and
related to the Douies. The Voluntary Aid Detachments of auxiliary
nurses had some kind of official status, though I am not quite
sure what, and was even less sure then. I had no idea what a
hospital was really like; I doubt if I had ever been inside one.
Our friends and relations would never find themselves in a hospital;
they went to nursing homes, especially the Acland at Oxford,
though there might well be arrangements there for almost free
treatment in certain cases. Some nursing homes or small, special
hospitals were quite well endowed. So St Thomas's was something
of a shock; the size, the long, clattering corridors and staircases
and the huge, undivided wards. Everything was, no doubt, sanitary,
but there were no frills.

We were worked very hard and it was a relief to come back to Wimpole Street in the evening. The Hale Whites' son, Leonard, had been in love with me; I can see this now from his letters. I had been very fond of him but had never thought of the possibility of his being hurt when I got engaged to Dick. And that again is now clear from the letters. No doubt he would have got over it. But his letters stop. As Tom Gillespie's stop. As Bey Gillespie's stop. As Geoff Wardley's stop. And as my brother-in-law Willie's stop.

So let me get away from the letters, back to St Thomas's: May and I, arriving on the early bus across Westminster Bridge, changing our shoes, hurrying off to our wards. It was difficult to learn that a nurse must hurry but never run. It was difficult to keep one's Sister Dora cap on straight. It was difficult to have to stand, even during sheet hemming (we were cheaper than sewing machines), when a doctor came into the ward, or for that matter a medical student one's own age or not much more.

I had brought the most interesting of the guinea pigs up with me and by special arrangement kept them in the animal house at the far end of the terrace along the river. They were, I think, an F2 generation and it was essential for our work on genetics to see how the offspring turned out. But visiting them was something else again, even though I did it in our nurses' dinner time, dashing away before the pudding, which was no great loss. But nurses were not allowed on the terrace, and once I was caught and severely reprimanded, though I tried to explain that this was part of a research project and might even have been approved by Florence Nightingale.

Unhappily one of the guinea pigs died. What was I to do? The Hale Whites' unperturbed parlour-maid told me: 'After dark, Miss, you take it out and put it into the middle of the street.' So I did and the Wimpole Street traffic disposed of the small body.

Of course May and I dodged the authorities if we possibly could. For years afterwards I thought of the boss class in the image of a hospital matron. However hard one had polished the brasses and the lockers it was never enough; we were always scolded, or at the very best ignored. We changed wards every week or fortnight but the routine was always the same: lavatories, bed pans, bottles, varied by floors and lockers. As we got more experienced there were temperatures and washing the patients. Once I was given some red paint for marking some bottles: I was even allowed to sit down for this. The beds had to be made exactly, the sheets squared and tucked in hard at the bottom with no regard for the patient's comfort. There was a great deal of sterilising to do; we were not immediately trusted with this. The wards were all the same, long rows of beds, perhaps thirty a side, each with a locker; a few patients could be out on the balconies with a view over the Thames, and the tiny figures on the terrace of the House of Commons, but most had nothing to distract them. No radio yet. Possibly a gramophone for an hour or two, when someone had time to wind it up. In the middle of the wards were, I think, the heating stoves and tables with sterilisers, heaps of sheets to be mended as well as any flowers which might be brought in; no room for them by the beds. Also in the medical wards there were usually one or two cots with small children. I cannot remember these children ever being visited by their parents. Probably at that time it was completely discouraged.

Of course I made awful mistakes. I had never done real manual household work; I had never used mops and polishes and disinfectants. I was very willing but clumsy. I was told to make tea but hadn't realised that tea must be made with boiling water. All that had been left to the servants.

Once when lifting a heavy patient my collar stud flew out and my stiff collar opened. Oh, dear! At that time we all wore stiff white cuffs, collar and belt into which we stuck our scissors, so much needed for bandages, dressings and sewing. One's blue skirt was ankle length with a long white apron over it. I ought to have had a proper uniform coat to go out in, but my mother had economised on that, thinking my own old one would do as well, but again I got an official scolding. We VADs waited in a crowd at the bus stop before Westminster Bridge; once a man spoke to me, but I turned away quickly and angrily and he saw his mistake.

Some of the wards were standard civilian patients, men or women, and often I couldn't understand their London accents, though I rather liked being called luv and ducks. There were always nephritis cases in great pain, usually terminal, with no treatment possible. I think the main pain-killer was still laudanum in some form. To combat sleeplessness, worry and any mental trouble or distress there were bromides and paraldehyde; I got to know the latter with its remarkably nasty and clinging smell only too well at the base hospital at Le Tréport where Dick, in the throes of hallucinations and some violence after his fractured skull in 1916, was regularly sedated with the nasty stuff. There were some effective purges and diuretics and of course bottles full of nicely coloured placebos. Anaesthetic techniques had made some advance, and surgery had gone a long way since the time of my broken leg seven years before.

The surgical wards with the real soldiers in their blue hospital coats, who had so lately come from the real trenches and the real war, were the most interesting for us. I write to Aunt Bay: 'They are much better fed than the civilian wards and there is scarcely any discipline; they sit on their beds and sing and smoke as much as they like.' Most had been treated first at dressing stations or base hospitals, then been sent on more or less cleaned up, but bad wounds had gone gangrenous and smelt awful. We VADs were put to help by holding dishes and so on during the hideously painful dressings, often with strong stinging antiseptics, when strong men whimpered or cried out: 'Hard,' as I wrote to Aunt Bay, 'to hold one's basin steady when a man is writhing about in his bed, white with pain and begging the nurse not to go on.' Here I disgraced myself once and once only by fainting. I was so scolded by Sister that I have never in my life done it again. However, as soon as I was allowed to help actively with the dressings I did all right. But becoming acquainted with all that pain did something so drastic that I had to write about it, to externalise it on to paper, in order to get it out of my mind:

hence the blood and pain in *The Conquered* and my earlier stories.

Probably by the summer of 1915 many of the best sisters and nurses from St Thomas's had been drafted off to base hospitals and ambulances; we VADs were the lowest of the low in the pecking order, and those who had been trodden on were happy to tread on us. We were seldom told what was wrong with the patients and the one and only Sister who did tell us and took some trouble to explain the treatment got increased loyalty and intelligent service. I was somewhat upset at being put into a VD ward and experienced a kind of moralising dislike for the patients, as well as being extra careful over sterilising basins and thermometers.

The other thing which I found upsetting was to see a patient with his eyes closed and throat heavily bandaged, with a policeman in full uniform sitting next to him. The patient was of course a suicide attempt and this was a crime. Was he arrested as soon as he was conscious? I never knew. Both disappeared from the ward. One thing missing was the blood transfusion apparatus which is now so common in an accident ward that one takes it for granted.

For many of the girls it was something of a shock to have so close an experience of naked male bodies, seldom beautiful. I had seen my brother more or less naked and handsome enough sufficiently often, though probably he had not seen as much of me under the usual family decency code. But whether I really ever had a full frontal view is something else again. A slight turning away or dropping of the eyes would have been the acceptable thing. But I don't remember being shocked by the soldiers I had to wash, only pitying, sometimes disgusted, usually matter of fact.

One of the servicemen with a leg wound had been a professional pickpocket. Even from his wheelchair he did marvellously, though we always got our scissors or hankies back from his locker. We dared him to get our wrist watches, and somehow he always managed it. One couldn't have advised him to take up any other profession. If by any chance he ever reads this, I would love to know how he got on.

There were a few air raids on or around London at this time, but so small by later standards that they seem irrelevant. We looked for Zeppelins on moonlit nights and once I thought I saw one. What I did see was the burst of flame when a gas main on the South Bank was hit, reflected splendidly in the river, and I remember the shaking of the heavy curtains in the drawing-room window at the Mitchisons' Chelsea Embankment house. But it was possible for some people to go on living quite an agreeable and often profitable life in many parts of Great Britain during World War One. That at least was barely so the next time.

The food at St Thomas's was awful, though I suppose better than hospital food a generation earlier. I thanked Aunt Bay wholeheartedly for her offer of cakes and chocolate: 'Most people do bring something extra for tea.' I still remember the dinner-time chunks of aged fish in batter. Finally there was milk from an infected farm and a number of us, myself included, went down with scarlet fever. This was then more serious than it is now; I was taken back to Oxford in an ambulance and put behind disinfectant-soaked sheets. A letter from Aldous in August 1915, thinking he had better not come to stay until my quarantine was over, dates this.

With even my short St Thomas's training I was snapped up to help with outpatients at the Radcliffe, which was very short staffed. These of course were the usual civilian patients, many children among them, often with small burns, cuts and so on. I would take off the dressings, clean up and then the Sister would inspect and probably tell me to get on with the same treatment. I think I did this reasonably well and became quick and expert at bandaging.

Meanwhile I started up my academic work again, rather half-heartedly, but I suppose I was persuaded into it, especially as I was too young to do VAD nursing in France. Frances was taking a degree, and I went to the same physiology lectures. I remember Professor Sherrington with his arm round the neck of a skeleton shark, looking affectionately at its rows of teeth.

There was also the soldiers' club in the High where I used to help, taking round tea, cutting sandwiches and so on. Heavy chaff went on, but always very decent by today's standards, no four-letter words, though I had heard a few in St Thomas's, usually from patients recovering after an anaesthetic. There was still a rather clear distinction between officers and men in general treatment, especially in convalescence. There were a number of small private hospitals in large houses given by individuals and with the running expenses partly at least paid by them, but mainly staffed by RAMC and other professionals. My parents-in-law offered Clock House on Chelsea Embankment as an officers' hospital which it duly became. They themselves were in the house next door. I expect treatment was as good as it was in the big hospitals; the consultants were much the same. Perhaps the young assistant nurses were rather prettier and more numerous, if sometimes less efficient. Cross-infection might have been less. But it was part of an amateur effort which did at least make people suppose they were all in it together and in so doing knocked some of the sharp edges off the class stratifications. One must also, I think, remember that some at least of those who made big amateur contributions, which really ate into their capital—and this certainly happened—in so doing helped on a bit of equalisation. For others it made absolutely no difference.

XIV

I would be different

It was not until three years after my marriage, when I was twenty-one, with a baby, that my mother took me to Coutts' to be introduced to the firm and open an account, with £250 a year, paid quarterly, half by the Trotter firm of Writers to the Signet, half by the Haldane firm. This was quite a lot of money in those days, though I spent it unwisely, in the excitement of having real money of my own. For instance, I got a beautiful white embroidered Chinese silk coat for evenings, out of which I must have shone. But at the time of my marriage I was still on pocket money, though it must have been quite generous, as I don't remember not buying books I wanted. And I expect I was taken to Coutts' in the Strand when we were in London and realised how different it was from the ordinary bank in Oxford. All Trotter lineage females, but not males, ought to bank at Coutts, thus commemorating an early nineteenth-century feud between the Coutts and Trotter families, which stipulated that no male Trotter should ever hold any position in the Bank! There was also, I think, some kind of marriage settlement drawn up by the family lawyers on both sides.

I did not indulge in the extravagance of a trousseau, but my mother insisted on supervising certain articles of lingerie. I had always worn flannel pyjamas, but it was explained that now I would need night-gowns and they must open in front. I knew why, but did not want to think about it, especially with her and the shop assistants looking at me. Also, because it was an early February wedding, these night-gowns must be wool. This wasn't easy; I felt the shop assistants being amused, and I got so upset by my mother's over-emotional approach to all this, that I burst into tears and rushed out of Debenham & Freebody.

From the old letters, it seems that there was some disapproval of the marriage taking place in 1916 from my in-laws, who perhaps felt that they might be left with this rather difficult young woman on their hands, possibly with a baby, should their son be killed. There was a distinct rift between the two mothers, with me, having decided that the marriage was going to happen, putting my not inconsiderable persuasive weight, both on the grown-ups and on Dick who, I think, found it all very embarrassing. I might so easily have been nicer to his parents. But I wasn't.

Nor did it help that I refused to be married in church or even to get a new dress. I wore the one Dick liked, black skirt—wool of course!—and a sleeveless black waistcoat top over a green silk shirt, and a felt hat kept on by hat pins with his regimental buttons as heads. That really upset Dick's mother who would probably have given me a gorgeous wedding dress with all the trimmings, if she'd had the least encouragement. By that time the war had gone into an austerity phase, especially for my mother and other sacrificers, so in the end there was no party, only a few close friends, including Aldous, asked to the registry office, and only a small wedding cake which we took to the soldiers' club where I had been working, and which was cut by me with Dick's cavalry sabre, the only use it was ever put to.

I had rather few wedding presents; my own young impecunious friends tended to give me books, though Rob Cross gave me a lovely Copenhagen china guinea pig, which I still cherish. The families produced some bits of silver and we put it all out in the school-room. I have many affectionate letters from this time and there were many, too, which my mother kept. Her dearest friend, Christian Fraser Tytler of Aldourie writes: '. . . It is everything that you should know Mr Mitchison as you do and that you can confide her life and happiness to his keeping with such absolute knowledge that he is worthy of such a trust.' Professor Alexander writes lovingly though a little teasingly. And there is a long and serious letter from Granniema at Cloan: 'Marriage is a momentous step, but the happiest when two hearts are joined in one and in determination to reach the fulfilment of the highest aims in life.' She goes on: 'My father proposed to my mother when she was sixteen and she was married at eighteen by her mother's wish for postponement, and certainly the fifty years (within a few months) they spent together were all that could be wished in happiness and perfect accord.' Being a true believer in freedom of conscience, she did not mind that I was not married in church.

As soon as the marriage was announced in the papers, a shower of advertisements came, including some for quite attractive clothes, including tea gowns, perhaps just too daring and immoral, in chiffon, brocade and lace, but also some remarkably ugly china, plate and so on. One was asked to favour firms with a visit to inspect their silver and gold fitted cases. I did in fact have a blue leather case with silk pockets and silver-mounted flasks, brush and comb with my initials, I expect from my nice, quiet father-in-law, but gradually everything got lost.

One could find suitable wedding presents, like a solid silver gadroon two-bottle ink-stand costing five pounds upwards, or a dinner service of Old Lavender pattern, 101 pieces for £8/7/6, or a toilet service including one chamber for as little as a guinea. There was little sign that we were in the middle of a war, except for one advertisement of military badge brooches, diamonds and enamel from seventeen pounds upwards, as well as wrist watches with luminous dials and hands, so that 'they can be seen on The Darkest Night'. And here are all these advertisements still, in one of the envelopes, as well as dozens of invitations from Court (and other) photographers to take my portrait with no obligation to buy, and others from florists wanting to do the church and reception and enclosing testimonials from the aristocracy.

None of this found its way to me during those few weeks in January, when I was thinking with increasing uneasiness and even alarm about the coming event, and the awful winter trench warfare went on, the duck boards over the sucking, stinking mud, the bodies of friends frozen onto the wire, tatters of uniform and human flesh. More of our twenty-year-old friends killed. I had a look at the Oxford registry office in the High, paid for the licence and a char to sweep down the stairs and passage, a total cost of fifteen shillings. So this was happening to me. I would be married and really grown-up. Everything would be different.

XV

The Pencil Diary

Well, there I was, a married woman, but still tied up with a host of attitudes, some of which I accepted, while others I questioned, but not enough to take really abrasive action. I was still treated as a young thing in need of protection. I was going on desultorily with bits of university education. Nothing to do with that, but I was also beginning to think on and off for myself. And our friends went on getting killed and I saw my father and mother both weeping for them. What was it all for? The younger people at least had begun to discount the patriotic rubbish which we had fed on at the beginning. I heard about the League of Nations Society. Surely that was an idea that made sense?

After our marriage leave we had another small one, which we spent at the Dalmally Hotel, where Dick went out fly-fishing, a highly skilled occupation with which I had little sympathy, though I tried to disguise this, always hoping that at some point he would catch a fish. I botanised happily, or drew bad plans of houses. Soon after this came the loss of the *Hampshire*; I was not at all unhappy that Kitchener was gone, considering how disastrously he had dealt with the gas mask situation the year before.

Some of the young men were now back at Oxford. Lewis Gielgud had been badly wounded and I felt a certain guilt at having egged him on into the army in the days of our early patriotic fervour. It did mean one saw something of them and got back for a short time into one's old world.

Lewis asked me to come to the May Day carols at Magdalen and then have breakfast. I looked forward to it tremendously; I would go down in my canoe, starting before dawn, crossing the rollers and paddling with the current and under the sweep of the young tender green. But then it appeared that this was unsuitable; I must have a chaperone; my mother would come with me. How could I say that this spoilt it all? Yet she must have known. I paddled from the stern of the canoe; she sat in the bows facing me in a thick grey coat; she looked pained and sad and perhaps she was. We had little conversation. And the young May leaves had lost their beauty and become flat paper. Lewis of course welcomed her with his usual excellent Etonian manners; nobody at that breakfast table was going to make a pass at me; we only wanted to be young together. The carols and the Morris dancing were as expected; I was aware that Magdalen on May morning was beautiful. But resentment came between all that and me. A nasty destructive emotion, as bad really as jealousy and as difficult, but equally important to get rid of.

My poor mother, who for so many people was a marvellous hostess, comforter, knowledgeable adviser, shoulder to cry on, in fact substitute parent, why had all this gone wrong between her and me? Are substitutes better than real parents? For some people and some purposes no doubt. My brother and I were perhaps the wrong children for her to have.

Meanwhile Dick had transferred to Signals. It was clear that there would be no more cavalry charges for the Queen's Bays. Instead he now had a motor-bike. They were just behind the lines in northern France. He was going to get three days leave and I was to join him in Paris; one went straight to Paris with no bother by train and boat. What fun it was going to be! My brother was around on leave or transfer and he and I went to a matinée in London; it was the Bing Boys and we enjoyed every moment; Gaby Deslys was dancing and Jack clearly found her luscious— as so many others did. Or was this another time? And someone sang *Another little drink* with the titillating lines about Asquith. I quote from memory:

In Parliament today when they get into a stew,
When they're all keyed up and don't know what to do,

Mr Asquith says in a manner sweet and calm
'Another little drink won't do us any harm.'

We went back in high spirits to the Mitchison house on the Embankment and there was a telegram. Dick had gone on his motor-bike on some errand for the Signals mess. At Gamache crossroads a French army car ran into him and left him for dead with the motor-bike on top and burning him. A British car which was following them picked him up unconscious and took him to the base hospital at Le Tréport. Here they found he had a fractured skull. The administrative wheels began to turn. I as next-of-kin was sent for; this was done in that war when possible for seriously wounded cases. His father came with me; it should have been a chance for him and me to get to know one another, but it didn't work out that way, which was a pity and mostly my fault. I kept a diary for this period which somewhat shows me up. It is written in pencil on a flimsy block of paper which I must have bought at Le Tréport, but is quite legible.

When I started it I was already extremely impatient with Dick's parents and yet felt guilty about my feelings towards them. The diary is very competently written with sharp and intelligent descriptions of people and places, and knowledge of myself trying to keep calm by thinking that now I knew how the heroine of a novel, which I was already trying to write, was going to feel. This habit of taking notes on one's own behaviour in periods of emotional stress is rather dangerous if people catch you at it.

At the beginning I was getting my main support from Jack (still called 'Boy' throughout). Here it starts, as we came back from the theatre to the house on the Embankment. When I was going back upstairs, my father-in-law

' . . . caught me by the wrist and half dragging me up to the stairs, said in a harsh and painful whisper "We've had a telegram. Dick is hurt." Then I, "How badly, my God, how badly?" "Very dangerous." I thought suddenly that he was breaking it to me that Dick was killed. "Give me the telegram. Where is he hurt?" "The head. Dangerously." I was in the dining-room by this time; Mrs M was sitting on a chair; she got up and kissed me and I thought to myself—the skull; probably he's dead now. And tried to remember about the respiratory centre and the vagus—suddenly all reality was sucked away from things and there was no way of telling whether I was dreaming or not. "Let me tell Boy," I said, but Mr M went to tell him leaving me and Mrs M in the dining-room: I still had the tune of one of the songs tinkling somewhere back in my mind; but the rest was completely a dream. I wanted Boy very badly. Mrs M was crying; she was all shrunk up and her emotion was catching at mine and breaking down my self-control. I looked at the telegram—dangerously ill—they wouldn't say that unless it was very bad indeed . . . Mr M came in, he was looking very old and both of them almost hopeless . . . I thought I should never see Dick again . . . Boy came in, and he was very calm and strong, but a little white and already thinking what to do . . . I felt very sick and clutched at the edge of the table and choked . . . I was being shaken by the certainty that Dick was dead; every few minutes I felt that suddenly and bit my hand but couldn't stop myself crying . . . the day went by and I can't remember exactly, only some things isolated . . . Boy alone with me in the dining-room when the crest of one of these waves of fear and longing for Dick caught me and I clutched at his arm with both hands and he was so perfectly and splendidly sane and spoke fairly sharply like cold water . . . and the queer feeling that I was acting and must do the thing expected of me in my part . . .'

Then there were all the arrangements to make and clearly I became reasonably calm and efficient and annoyed at the general assumption that I must be looked after. The night before we left, 'I dreamt that it would be all right and woke wondering whether that would be a good sign.' Goodbye to Jack and would I see him again before the end of the War—or then? We went down to Folkestone in a Pullman car—I for the first time—then embarkation, 'beautifully smoothly worked'. I looked about me.

'The lower deck of the boat was thick with soldiers, sitting or standing about, with their equipment and a haversack full of things. On the upper deck were officers—a lot of red tabs, and some French, sitting on ship's chairs, and a few like us, civvies, anxious looking. Everyone wore life belts, uncomfortable as they could be, but looking less stupid over khaki than over mufti . . . We started in half an hour or so, with a faint and not inspiring burst of cheering. A little spray came onto the decks; below a few of the men were singing *Michigan* and *Tipperary* spasmodically and with no great heart . . . I had recovered my *aequanimitas*, saying to myself: we shall find Dick better; in a little I shall be laughing at my fear now and wishing I had known that it was going to be all right, so as to be able to enjoy this crossing; therefore let me enjoy it now. I was also saying: if Dick is dead, what shall I do? I must have some plan; I think I shall take Greats or be a doctor . . . But still I was a little stunned and the clock of reality seemed to have stopped twenty hours before.

At Boulogne Dick's poor father fussed and tried to hurry things 'which was of course no earthly use. There was a crowd of RAMC people, a sturdy little woman, a canteen worker, very much pleased with her khaki, a tall, gaunt lady in black, dishevelled from the voyage, also trying to hurry her papers through . . . It was all very simple though; our things were not even looked at in the *douane*; an officer herded us through; we went off to a hotel in a car, Mr M hurrying me on when I wanted to change my money and then being late himself.'

By that time I had made friends with Mrs Johnstone, the dishevelled lady in black, whose boy was wounded in the leg and arm in hospital at Abbeville; she lent me a motor veil; one needed them in those days. Lunch was served by VADs in uniform—no doubt older than me, as one wasn't allowed out of the country until at least over twenty. The RAMC captain saw us into an official car and off we went through the cobbled streets of Boulogne, past a sentry onto a road with barley growing at each side, while the lady with the wounded son and I talked together, finding we were fellow Scots; the son was only twenty-one.

'I thought the harvest seemed very thin and poor; there were few boundaries and cattle grazed tethered . . . sometimes a girl, straight bodiced and barefoot, driving a cow; a few gleaners, old men and women, each with a ragged bundle of corn . . . villages with straggling houses, painted white or blue and usually an *estaminet* with the French soldiers in their pretty and unfamiliar horizon blue standing about. Along one stretch every village was full of zouaves, bronzed and handsome people with red fezes and baggy knickerbockers, who grinned at us as we went past bumping on the *pavé*, hooting wildly before corners . . .'

For we were driving at the unprecedented pace of fifty miles an hour with the wind beating and booming in our faces and ears.

After two tyre bursts, and my admiration for the RAMC chauffeur who changed wheels so quickly, we got to Abbeville and found the hospital where Mrs Johnstone's boy was, and waited.

'After a time the chauffeur came out saying, "That lady's had bad news; they say her son won't live." It depressed Mr M visibly but I thought it might be the natural delight in horrors —even after two years in France at war—of that class. And so it was, for after a long time she came out, more than ever dishevelled with her eyes bright, but saying he might have to have a leg off but would live. We left her things at the YMCA building in a little courtyard . . . It came on to rain, torrents all in a minute beating along the streets . . . we put up our canvas hood; I noticed how very many house pipes leaked.'

But by now I was worrying and wondering as we got nearer Le Tréport. I had

'. . . a picture in my mind: a long ward, just getting dark, a few yellowish lights along the walls, the evening grey outside; rows of white beds, a grave sister; red screens and two round one bed; inside a little light, on the pillow a head bandaged; eyes shut; perhaps a little muttering or a vague toss about of hands, not conscious life. I elaborate the picture; put in a basin or two on a locker by the bed—ice in a flannel bag—hear myself ask the sister how it goes—the watch through the night—'

About this time I began taking omens from the magpies in the fields. But Dick's father had no such irrational consolation. We got to Le Tréport and I put down every detail of the place. 'Suddenly I feel very queer.' We pulled up in front of the hospital, I jumped out and ran up the steps, asking the cheerful-looking RAMC sentry for Lieutenant Mitchison—Queen's Bays. 'Surely he would have known if there had been a death among the officers.' Then the doctor came, quite young, nice-looking, speaking to Mr Mitchison who seemed more upset than ever and couldn't speak. 'How is he?' I said. 'You are the wife, aren't you?' I nodded. He explained that Dick was slightly better, but the condition was still very dangerous. We went up three flights of white stone stairs, which I was to know very well. The hospital had been a grand hotel, as I write later 'the sort of hotel one has never been to oneself, bathrooms to every bedroom and landings one could dance on'.

'I wait outside, while Sister goes in, leaving the door ajar. Suddenly a voice, so strong and familiar I can hardly believe it. "What, my wife? Bring her in at once, Sister." I go in. It is a small white cheerful room, a bed with a silk quilt. Dick, looking very well and normal, but for a very unshaved chin: "Hullo Nou!" Sister leaves us for a few minutes. I try not to talk or let him, but he, talking rather too loud, asks questions, is very cheerful, moves his head about, is sorry he is such a wretched sight but he can't get his shaving things. There is a slight smell of paraldehyde . . .'

After that his father and I settled into the Hotel des Bains, 'a quaint place with a twisty stair . . . my room is small but has three windows that swing open like doors. One looks towards the *place* and the harbour with grey-sailed fishing boats, the other two onto a narrow street, very crowded in the evenings with poilus and their girls. I expect Mr M is writing letters in the salon or reading the Continental *Daily Mail*—a bad paper but with good news. His letters take three times as long to write as mine.'

At this point, we were going up to the hospital twice a day, though only I was allowed in.

'I see him every day for an hour or two . . . his head aches of course, very badly . . . I think it's a great pity they don't tell him more; as it is he is always trying to get up, even when I am there, and when I prevent him calls me all kinds of stupid fool, which I'm sure I am, but not for that. Mostly he is quite sensible, and even when delirious very rational, arranging a dinner party, talking about the Signal Troop or leave; he even wrote out a telegram to the Paris Hotel . . . The usual thing is five minutes normal though in pain, talking sensibly and not very restless; then a few minutes while the pain comes on, very restless, perhaps trying to get up, with his body and arms rigid, mouth open and eyes shut, cursing his headache or complaining of the pain, calling on himself to stop it, and then five minutes lying back, quite exhausted, often with one arm thrown over his forehead . . . His date memory has stopped the day of the accident; sometimes he asks how old I am . . . hearing all right, though eyes are not yet.'

I give a run-down on the doctors, who sound efficient and on the whole cheering, but my real praise is for Sister Holbeach, charming and sympathetic, 'not un-necessarily professional . . . as becomes a nurse, optimist'. I had told her about my nursing experience at St Thomas's and she said that she had spoken to Matron and I would be allowed to nurse Dick more of the time. What I don't say in the diary, and yet now I remember most vividly, is that, at the first interview, the doctor said he would probably not live, but conceded that he was in very good condition and might recover. I know I dug my toes in about this; it was just not going to happen; that is why I didn't put it into the diary. When it didn't happen I was told that he would probably never recover intellectually and might live in a somewhat crippled condition. I expect they were quite sorry for this eighteen-year-old, faced with a life sentence of this kind. But again, I refused to believe it and that is why it isn't in the diary. I was fighting to win, as Janet fought for Tam Lin.

Meanwhile I was taking in Le Tréport. By this time I was reasonably fluent in French, and, from looking at a notebook I kept for years with quotations in it, it is clear that I normally read quite a lot of French poetry. So now I looked about me:

'The blue French soldiers in the streets are slightly more untidy than their English *confrères*—a step nearer the battle-field—many of them wearing one or two medals. I never can tell the ranks apart. Some very fine horses . . . and there is khaki among the blue, officers mostly, either RAMC or from the regiments near here—come in mostly as far as I can see for a drink and a bath, possibly for a little distracting society . . . the ladies of the place are mostly bourgeoisie—a quantity of flappers, less obvious and more subtle than the same type at, say, Bournemouth . . . short skirts, bright coloured blouses and caps or veils tied over their hair.'

There were families staying at the hotel.

'A very nice French colonel with grey moustache and grey kind eyes; he has a boy of seventeen and one of about eight, delicate looking, both of them . . . a young mother and a charming little girl of five or six with masses of yellow hair, blue jersey and shorts and long bare legs . . . a good lady with hair in a tight knob who has a horrid snivelling son in a tight brown suit whom she is always looking after very carefully; I think French boys of that sort of age are particularly horrible. . . . at the *table d'hôte* a group of VADs in their blue caps, cheerful and English, sometimes a single lady in a velvet tamoshanter and a short coat edged with fur who looks incomplete without an officer . . . the hotel people are charming and friendly . . . but I find everybody's nice to me.'

We walked to the hospital every day through the middle of the market, and sometimes I bought a few flowers. There were 385 steps to the cliff top. 'We probably meet Mr and Mrs Sassoon, very Jewish, friendly and good folk, but somehow one cannot imagine her pearl necklace, which is probably extremely valuable, to be anything but rather a bad sham.' We filled in the day somehow; I still have two pottery animals I bought then. There was a shop which had about two dozen one-franc classics, which I bought; I read a lot of Guy de Maupassant at this time. But I daren't buy a copy of the *Vie Parisienne*, because Dick's father would be shocked. Clearly we get on dreadfully badly, and I realise that it is largely the generation gap, but that didn't help.

'He's very English (doesn't shake hands when I, as a Scot, would) and when some of Dick's superior officers came to find out how he was . . . he was very formal and a little nervous and, when one of Dick's Signal troop came to find out too, he tipped most adequately, but it was I who did the talking . . . I wonder how much I misjudge him and myself; it's partly shyness with him; I'm not shy in the same way.'

It was early September and sometimes there was a storm which made bathing more exciting. I bathed usually in the early mornings when there was no crowd and one could run down from the hotel.

'There are long flat shadows on sea and sand; the sun is bright but not hot and when one is knee-deep in the smooth grey water, rhythmically stirred by long slow ripples, it makes a pathway; but there is no-one to go with. I have a comic French bathing-dress with scarlet trimmings and two blue anchors on the collar.'

There was shopping, trying to get some silk to make silk

pyjamas for Dick. 'Sometime perhaps, I shall go into Eu, or walk along the beach to the rocks, but one wants someone to go with who will enjoy it in the same way.' But the days went by. Dick saw another specialist, Gordon Holmes, and was said to be out of danger. But the fight had to go on and was sometimes curious.

'Today for instance he didn't even know me. In the morning he had a long talk with me, calling me Lindsay—a Signalling Officer. I think he enjoyed it very much, for, by a curious coincidence, this Lindsay knew many people at Oxford, Willie for instance, and Joseph. He had known Heath [Heath had been killed earlier that year] and on his saying that he was the finest man he had known, he and Dick gripped hands. Dick also told him about his "missus" and her family and finally they shook hands and Lindsay went away promising to come back soon. A few minutes after, Dick called Sister to ask me to go to him, and when I was there told me what a nice man was this "Lindsay"—poor Lindsay who only existed for ten minutes. Then in the afternoon, after a sleep, Dick woke up to say that he was going off at once to East Hertford to contest the seat with Pemberton Billing. He sat up and was not put off long by my saying there was no need for him to go for a fortnight. Then, for I didn't want him to struggle to get up, I tried to make him remember where he was. "No," he said, "I'm in hospital at Bethnal Green; I must telephone to the other hospital; how did I get here? Please fetch my clothes, I must go to Hertford." I reminded him of who I was, but he was politely incredulous, a little surprised at my wearing his wife's rings. "Admit, nurse, that you have stolen them!" and utterly shocked—the picture of virtue!—at this strange nurse kissing him! "My good girl, I've never met you before; I quite like you, but I wish you'd go away." I couldn't stop him getting up, so I called the orderly and finally Sister who managed to quiet him, taking his orders about telephoning to Hertford with the greatest calm. Then, as she was going away, Dick remarked, "Oh Sister, will you please ask this nurse to go; I don't know her," implying that she wasn't a credit to any hospital. Exit me!'

Once we went up to the hospital and found a big convoy had come in and there was a correspondingly big evacuation of patients well enough to go back to Blighty.

'We found all the back part of the hall covered with stretchers, on each an officer in a brown blanket, a woolly cap, and labelled. Most of the MOs were there, giving orders, looking at the labels, bending over to talk to their patients. The Sassoon boy was there, also Major Cripps. A long string of ambulances, all driven by women, came up to the door, one by one. The first row were picked up one after another, two orderlies to a stretcher, with sometimes a man in front shifted so that they could get one out from behind, like a great game of patience. It all went wonderfully smoothly . . . The next day the Sassoons and Miss Cripps left, which I'm sorry for. We used to see the Sassoons every day up at the hospital . . . once I went in to see the boy—a typical young Eton Jew, who will probably get on in the world very well.'

But could this have been Siegfried?
I had gone swimming and walking with Miss Cripps; we said '*bon soir*' but disengaged ourselves from the poilus. Often there were a few officers in for two-day leave from the division near us.

'Two evenings ago, after dinner in the salon, Mr M was reading, I was playing patience. We heard three or four officers come in and begin talking to Madame . . . they wanted to know about bathing; then they began to talk to one another about some particular incident at Delville Wood. Finally I chucked my patience, got up and said I was going to give them chocolates; Mr M seemed somewhat surprised and said it would embarrass them. However I ran upstairs and came down with my chocolates and offered them; they were really pleased and began talking to me, all at once, and before Mr M came out of the salon—very shy—I knew their names and some of their histories, where they'd come from, what they'd been doing, and how very particularly pleased they were to get back to real dinners and beds and bathing . . . They were KSLI 5th Battalion . . . Last night about half a dozen came into the salon and started a conversation as soon as they possibly could. They were awful TGs* mostly, but they'd just come from fighting the Boche in Delville Wood . . . we had a long talk about Syndicalism . . .'

Another was an Australian ranker, who told me about holding a trench for thirty hours in an advanced position; he was recommended for the Military Cross.

I try to type them.

'They're all conscientious fatalists and they all try to talk about England or after the war, but always after a little you get back to shop. There was a Major and several others, also a nice little Canadian doctor up at the Hospital, whom we had seen several times before, and he was quite drunk; I think he often is: not a good thing for a doctor . . . Here am I, sitting on a table in the middle of the stuffy salon of a third-rate French hotel, being as charming as I can to an audience of TGs, all to give them the memory of a pleasant evening to take back to the trenches by Givenchy; that's why I wear pretty frocks and hats and do my hair just not anyhow, but to look nice; it's probably as much worth doing now as it ever will be again in my life. I would give a lot to be able to sing.'

At this time another specialist, Meyers, saw Dick, said he was to go to Netley Hospital, where most people with brain damage went, and apparently thought that ultimate mental recovery was only a matter of time. But, as I write, 'It's certainly rather disconcerting that he's still just as bad mentally.' I describe another incident:

* Temporary Gentlemen—who remembers that bit of class-slang?

'He gets violently angry with both me and the orderly when we stop him, calling us both dirty cads and damned liars; he also hits out like anything, and when the orderly has gone reproaches me bitterly for having called him, saying it's the sort of low thing I would do and often, which of course is the best thing, turning over and being offended till he falls asleep. But often I leave him to the orderly, particularly when he says "*Enlevez cette femme là, c'est la mienne, mais enlevez la.*" And then as a parting shot when I'm going out "I don't ever want to see you again." He forgets all about it by next time, but I'm so afraid it will stay in some sort of distorted image in his subconscious memory. Yesterday morning he told me how the doctors and orderlies had lured him to an opium den and nearly killed him, but how he had fought them all.'

Clearly this was fairly exhausting, especially as one could not be quite certain about ultimate recovery. But I had a last evening with two VAD nurses, Miss Duval and Miss Tozer.

'We went off in a car to the Forêt d'Eu . . . the most lovely evening . . . the Forêt still full of wild flowers and very green . . . long stretches of slim tall beech trees, sudden rises among birch and chestnut with a steep white bank at the roadside, trailed over with honeysuckle, small roads under an arch of beeches and a deer leaping across, a clearing with a reaped cornfield and back through high woods of straight thin trees and the pink sunset blinking behind the stems like jewels. I don't know whether they were lovelier when it was growing dark or before, when you get broken patches of sunlight lying across the road and clear, sudden greens, almost spring-like. We stopped at a little farm, in the middle of the wood like a fairy tale, a square court-yard, an orchard of apple trees covered with small red fruit and the forest closing in all round. In the quiet of the wood we heard twigs snapping, a bird, a dog far off, and then listening closer, every few seconds a thud, less sound than vibration, as if the earth were snoring a long way under, and that is the guns. When the wind is right they are quite loud and on dark nights they see from the hospital the horizon all lit with flashes.

'We had a perfect French dinner, omelette, chicken, haricot beans stewed in milk, cider, jelly and cream and bowls of thick soft coffee. And we all told one another our life histories and made friends and deplored the badness of a girl's schooling and how hard it is for her to make her way to any really educated work. Both the girls are scientists . . . it seems an awful waste that they should be VADs here in the position of privates under sisters who may or may not be nice, but anyhow discourage questioning and are very jealous. No chance of rising from the ranks or learning any more than they know now. They work for a twelve and a half hours' day, with three hours off and short meal times; once in two months they get a whole day off and once in eighteen months a week's leave. They're both going to chuck it when their terms are up and I think they'll be quite right.

'They were telling me one thing which must be particularly annoying to Miss Tozer, who was doing brain research before the war—that there are any amount of splendid head cases here which die, and it would be the chance of a century if there was anyone here to note symptoms and do a PM. Of course if she were to suggest such a thing—which she could probably do perfectly—the authorities would first faint and then kick her out. But it is stupid.'

So there was the magic again, but also the proper concern of the scientist. Miss Tozer, Miss Tozer, what happened to you? I looked you up in *Who's Who* just in case, but as we agreed, it is so hard for a girl to get up to the top—if that *is* the top.

We left the next day. There had been no more forty-eight hour leave people. But plenty of rumours. I add, 'Poor old Dick will be sick if the cavalry, as seems likely, get through in three weeks.' So, apparently, we thought!

There the pencil diary ends, with only a few more guilt feelings about my father-in-law. Typically, I never managed to arrive at what to call either him or Dick's mother. I couldn't think of them as parents and they were the wrong generation for first names.

So there we were, waiting very anxiously in London, where it had somehow been arranged that, before going to Netley, Dick should come to the Clock House hospital. It seems odd that these private arrangements could have been not only possible, but were not disapproved of. One only asks oneself whether the treatment of wounded officers was very different from that given to ordinary private soldiers. That wasn't a question I had asked, so far. One took certain things for granted. But Dick's parents and I were all in a rather agitated state, totally unsure of how he would be.

But something very odd had happened. For three weeks Dick had been in a strange country, usually in a hurry with something important he had to do. Sometimes he met people he knew, but often he was alone, or chased by non-human entities. Then he was on a boat in mid-channel and there were creatures crawling about the decks, sea snakes and whatnot. Then 'something clicked,' and he was back in the ordinary world, gradually realising where he was and why. And that was how he was when he came to us in London, very weak, but himself. He never quite recovered his sense of smell, though this is never strong with fairly heavy smokers as he was. But smell is supposed to come into taste, especially of wine, and this never left him. And quite soon he stopped being able to draw maps of the strange country.

XVI

War Marriage

Tough Dick got well quickly. The only sad thing was that he had forgotten that Geoff Wardley, his dearest friend, had been killed just before his accident. I had to tell him. He had a longish sick leave, during which he passed his Bar Finals exam; he had worried in case the exam-passing capacity had been damaged, but no. Once we were ragging around—it was at Aunt Kate's country house in Surrey—and he pretended to have gone mad; I was sitting on the back of a sofa and fell off, screaming with terror.

In late autumn we were up in Scotland in a huge house which couldn't let itself or its shooting during the war, so I suppose we got it very cheap. It was large and a little frightening. Dick gave me a gun and taught me to shoot, but I was never sure if I liked it, though I loved the dark woods and the crisp frost underfoot, and above all enjoyed my sporting costume—high boots and a short skirt. He tried to teach me proper games too, like chess, but I would always rather have been playing hide-and-seek or sardines, or some dressing-up game. But there weren't any other people to play with us. I made myself lists of improving books which I thought I ought to read, and stuck hopelessly in only too many classics. I went on writing verse.

At the end of his sick leave Dick applied for the Staff College and was accepted. He felt a bit guilty about this; it seemed like a way out of the real thing. There was always a certain amount of jeering at the red tabs. But I wanted him to be safe. How I wanted it! I loved and cherished him but there was an aspect that was not going well. We spent early 1917 in digs at Houghton Regis near Dunstable, where I was rather unhappy and not very well, for I was running a mild temperature every day. No doubt I was given tonics but they had no effect. This unhappiness would today have been rapidly sorted out and put right by any competent doctor or clinic. Or if I could have brought myself to talk straightforwardly to Dick he would surely have understood. But no, no, I couldn't. In some way it must, I felt, be my fault. I don't quite know what the Staff course was, but Dick was away all day. I used to go for walks, but chalk country always scares me and it was a long cold winter with few flowers. In the evenings the batman came and Dick and I had hot saucer baths in the bedroom which slightly brought up the temperature.

Food got gradually worse; by the beginning of 1918 we were on to ration cards, which was a good thing, as there had been, earlier, food shortages here or there, and quite a lot of food profiteering. My father was always upset if my mother managed to get him something a little special, especially for his midnight cake—though the milk went on. If there was anything, he always wanted me to have it. But I got a special ration card as a nursing mother as soon as my baby was born. At the same time we were put on to 'standard bread', though that was made very palatable later on in the year, because there was a splendid walnut crop at Oxford. But we had very little idea of how nearly successful the German blockade was being.

In March 1917 news of the Russian Revolution came through, but we thought of it mainly from the point of view of how it might affect us and whether it would help to bring the war to an end. Lewis, back in London at the War Office, with his wound still giving him trouble, wrote in considerable worry; on the Gielgud side, he had a good dose of Polish patriotism and he felt, not without reason, that Poland would suffer.

News still had to be dug out of newspapers. People did not normally communicate by telephone and a telegram still tended to be bad news. The telegraph boy with his orange envelope was the usual dark angel. Willie was killed on September 20th 1917; his father wrote me a very sweet letter, not mentioning his own pain.

It was perfectly possible for a letter to arrive at Oxford by the morning post. Read at the breakfast table and reasonably promptly answered, the reply would get to London by the last post. The penny post, of course, and very dependable it was.

Dick went back to France in summer 1917, to a Staff post. We wrote to one another every day and went on doing this during the whole of our marriage, unless at times when either of us was in a place without regular posts; for instance when I was in India or Botswana, letters might be spaced to two or three days. Even if the other one could be at their most maddening—as all husbands and wives are bound to be in a day-to-day, live situation—there was the feeling that the other one was there: a permanent area of trust and confidence. This kind of relationship has little to do with romantic love; it can develop just as strongly in an arranged marriage. I still find myself arranging the words to describe a view, a flower, a political situation, so as to put it into my next letter to Dick.

It was after Dick went back, but perhaps when I was staying with his parents, that I got in touch with the headquarters of the League of Nations Society. The then secretary, Margery Spring-Rice, remembers me coming with a silent duenna, perhaps my mother-in-law's personal maid. I don't remember her; such people were only a mild nuisance and didn't count, nor would they comment on what had been going on. But I know I came away convinced, and with masses of literature, and after that I had to do something about it. How and where? Not in undergraduate papers. Not the Home Student *Fritillary*, which was used to publishing my poems. No, I was intent on bigger game. The *Oxford Times*.

I had never written for a newspaper and my first letters on the need for a supernational authority took me hours to construct. I did not think it was sensible to sign my own name; everyone would know I was only a girl even if I was married. So I signed them 'Mother of Seven', 'Returned Serviceman' and so on. For two or three issues I argued with myself; the then Editor of the *Oxford Times* must have been very sympathetic. But then the big names came in, Gilbert Murray, Ernest Barker and so on.

The Oxford branch of the League of Nations Society got off to a splendid start. I gave up in December; I was expecting my first baby in February and it was being taken very seriously. Owing to my riding accident at nine I had a somewhat twisted pelvis which was liable to make birth more difficult. I had various measurements and tests done and at the end of December I suddenly had a slight haemorrhage. I was put to bed and fussed over and in fact I was rather frightened, though Dr Carew Hunt, the very nice woman doctor who was looking after me, was reassuring.

Meanwhile an enormous layette had been bought: binders, long clothes—that is to say long flannel robes bound with silk to tuck in over the baby's toes. There were long dresses to go with this, cotton or silk, as well as two nineteenth-century family robes for best. Nappies were soft with the towelling one to the outside. There were no waterproof pants for babies (or anyone else) as yet, but possibly this was better for the babies. I had a rocking cot trimmed with muslin and ribbons and a baby's basket with soft towel and powder and all manner of baby requisites. I am sure Dick's mother gave me many presents of this kind.

I regarded all this with some dubiety. Certainly it was all very right and proper that I was going to have a baby and the interest and excitement I was arousing seemed all right and indeed my due. It would be dangerous and painful but that made it all the more interesting. But would I like the baby or at any rate would I like it as much as I was supposed to?

Well, dangerous and painful it was. I had plenty of lovely chloroform but even so it was worse than I had imagined possible. I must have had some infection which would have been speedily dealt with at a later stage either by sulfonamides or antibiotics. But at this period all that could be used must have been antiseptic douches. I took against the monthly nurse who had appeared in some alarming form while I was mildly delirious. However, the good old *vis medicatrix naturae* worked and the baby was after all surprising and delightful.

Maya was in her glory. I suppose she would have liked a larger family herself—in some ways. But it was really, I think, that she was now in charge of an important event on the same status level as the doctor, considerably higher than the nurse. I was entirely a novice and could be made to do the right thing. At this period it meant a diet with no fruit as that would 'sour the milk' and this was a real hardship for me. In addition I had lost such freedom as I had; I was once more liable to do the wrong thing and incur displeasure or see it put right in such a way that I felt stupid and incompetent.

1918 was a bad year because events seemed to have stuck, at least those which got into the papers. There was a choking weight on everything. Dick's first Staff job was in France; later he was moved to Italy. He got leave in summer and came over in the same boat as the Spanish 'flu. He went down with it and so did I but the baby, Geoff, called for Geoff Wardley killed in 1916, whom I was nursing, was untouched. But we spent a few rather miserable days in bed with high temperatures while Dr Carew Hunt puzzled about what it could be and the sunshine and garden scents wheeled round outside. At least he had seen his son, though I don't think he quite knew what his attitude was or should be. But we were lucky to have had some immunisation, for by that winter the 'flu was a killer.

There was still plenty of household help so I was free of the ordinary baby chores and Maya was always bathing him and hanging over us supervising. In fact I was married, but I had scarcely begun to be free, and I was being somewhat conditioned into not wanting this. When I had a house of my own, I was told, I would have to engage (and dismiss) servants, order food, see that everything was just so. But somehow I did not at all like the idea of all that and the one person from whom I couldn't learn it was my mother—or, I suppose, my mother-in-law. Nor would I have accepted, say, a domestic science course if it had been suggested from above. How stupid can one be! And yet perhaps I was clinging on to some part of me that had to grow but only on its own.

Frances meanwhile had got away. She, like me, had wanted to do war work, so after getting through her Science degree she went off to a hospital and worked as an anaesthetist. She had managed to get to Garsington but found it too full of distinguished and much older people asking sudden embarrassing questions. But I never got to Garsington. Nor did I as yet have any kind of regular or adequate allowance though no doubt I could have the (first class) fare to London if I was taking my baby to see his other grandparents. Yet already I sensed a jealousy, which was to become more marked later, growing up between the two grandmothers.

The longing to get away which somehow I was too incompetent or inhibited to put into action came through in verse:

> Tonight, if I was free, I'd go
> Out of the house, into the rain,
> Because the clock ticks here so slow:
> Down to the station—to a train,
> And get somewhere, away, away,
> Oh anywhere, but not to stay
> In this same place, day after day,
> And from the school-room windows see
> The branches of the walnut sway
> Across the garden: oh dear me,
> If only I could get away.

What worried me, I remember about this, was that the trees which I saw swaying in the North Oxford wind were not walnuts but elms. Elm-tree would scan, but not so well, not right somehow. And there were walnuts, splendid big ones, at the far end of the garden, though not to be seen from the west-facing window. So I borrowed them.

I did at least manage one escape. It was right at the end of the war, though of course it didn't seem like that to most of us in October 1918. I felt as if everything was going to go on for ever. But Dick found he could get leave and arranged for me to come out. This seems an extraordinary thing to us now, with our experience of more total war, but nobody found it strange at that time, I was all the more anxious to come because I had just read Marie Stopes's *Married Love* which seemed to me to have the answers to some of my own troubles if Dick too would read it and put some of it into practice. This was the first serious sex-instruction book for my generation and must have made an immense difference to the happiness and well-being of thousands of couples.

Dick was acting as *Officier de Liaison* between the French and British armies in northern Italy. They had been for some time in rather a static position so that most of what he was doing was foraging for the ófficers' mess, shopping, and doing things like explaining to a senior French officer that the Order of the Bath (*'Un bain—vaut mieux qu'un saint, quoi?'*) was really quite important. He could get leave and we would spend it well behind the lines in Perugia. I could go via Paris. There were plenty of trains still running and no bother about getting tickets this end, nor did one even need a passport. But my parents and parents-in-law got together on the impossibility of my doing this journey alone, not so much for the physical danger which was not great in pre-air-warfare days, but for the moral dangers which they apparently could see all over the place.

I protested and sulked and tried to get round them in various ways. But they insisted on finding a chaperone who'd look after me on the journey to Paris, see me through that abode of wicked-ness and put me into the sleeper for Italy. We were introduced at Victoria Station; I said nothing but decided that this would not do. We were of course going first class; I suspect that they had paid for the good lady's ticket. On the boat crossing to Dieppe I seized my suitcase and plunged into the third class which struck me as much nicer as well as being so crowded that I could easily get lost. Luckily it was a very rough crossing. I take it that my chaperone was laid out; I never saw her again.

I enjoyed every moment. The train was so crowded that she couldn't have looked for me; in fact it was so crowded that, as I still remember vividly, I couldn't get along to the loo or rather I was too inhibited by some of this lady thing to push through with sufficient vigour. I took a taxi from one station to the other and duly got my sleeper. I felt suddenly and gorgeously free and grown-up. This time I'd really escaped and by my own wits. I had only twice before been 'abroad', once to Le Tréport and, earlier, once to Paris, always looked after. I talked to everyone I saw and told them all about going to see my husband. Later I recognised that there had been some slight attempt at getting off with me which I hadn't even understood. I would probably have been rather shocked if it had got through to me but I expect I looked very young.

It was terribly exciting going through the Simplon tunnel and coming out at the far end with Italy spread below one. This sense of a new country is something one misses entirely when one only arrives at another international airport. I leant against the window watching everything. I knew where I had to change and when I got out, perhaps at Milan, I simply used my main Italian phrase, *'Dove è il* R T O?' I was at once taken to the railway transport officer and carefully looked after as befitted the wife of a major. I got to Perugia ahead of Dick, found my way to the hotel but only just ventured out into the street, feeling that it was incredibly daring to be by oneself among a lot of Italians.

Then Dick turned up and we had a lovely time; I found to my delight that Italian pastry cooks were apparently not rationed on sugar; by that time I was really sugar-hungry and laid into cakes and biscuits. But on the last day or so a telegram came recalling Dick. It was the final push of October 1918. Following it came a telegram from his parents or mine—I can't remember which—telling me to return immediately. Dick saw me on to the train and rushed back to his division. We just didn't know what was going to happen.

But when I got as far as Paris I somehow met up with various old friends, including Lewis Gielgud and Gervas Huxley, who persuaded me not unwillingly to stay. I had enough money and they must have found me an hotel room. The three of us walked round the Place de la Concorde heaped with captured guns and cannon, a real old triumph, and the statues of Metz and Strasbourg garlanded with roses and chrysanthemums and the French crowds tossing with glory and excitement. But then I went down with the Spanish 'flu and spent two days in the hotel feeling rather ill. This was the 'flu which had killed or was going to kill many of my friends, but as I had managed to have it in the first wave this second attack was not too bad. There may have been another telegram and at any rate I felt I must go back.

I was in Oxford for the day of the Armistice. I remember buying a paper, jumping on to a bus in a state of almost hysterical excitement and half shouting at everyone else, 'The Armistice is signed!'

'Oh, indeed,' the lady on the opposite seat politely answered.

far as fungi or lichens. But plant cells are large and beautiful and convincing, stomata are easy to see; botanical drawing is a pleasure; and we could take our lunchtime sandwiches out into the gardens or down on the close-mown green grass by the river.

It was only when men came back on leave or wounded that we imagined at all accurately what the fighting was really like—so far from Oxford and ourselves. But could we really imagine it as it was? No. In the papers news was edited and censored; it always is in wartime but we were not yet used to automatic disbelief of the kind that is usual now. We kept on thinking that it must be over soon. Then came the first gas attacks, my father hurrying out to headquarters in France where Jack joined him, the post mortem on the Canadian officer, the certainty that it was chlorine, the experiments to get an efficient gas mask, then coming back across the Channel to find Kitchener appealing to the women of England to make a totally useless mask which would only betray the men it went to. My father describes this at length in his own papers and one gets a sense of his anger and frustration. But his own lab was mobilised; all the men who were still there were completely involved in the struggle to make a cheap and efficient gas mask. The house reeked of chlorine, the noise of coughing and retching was continuous from the study and beyond. Everything that would make into a mask was seized on—stockings, vests, Aldous' woolly scarf, my knitted cap. They got it right in the end and then there was violent telephoning to the War Office. Aldous did most of the necessary type-writing. I remember my father, cut off, shouting at the operator: 'Damn you, I'm the Lord Chancellor!'

More wrong gas masks, but at last the right ones getting made and going out, though exasperatingly slowly. The women of England ones never left London; that had simply been a ploy to ease civilian tension and fear. But I had been sent round to stop our neighbours making them, urging them to wait till the right design came out—every mother wanted to send a gas mask to her own boy. I felt even then that some of the neighbours were suspicious and probably felt that these Haldanes were promore, especially the elegant inside of a pithed frog. Worms were all right but the crayfish tended to disintegrate and the dogfish were foul. The rabbit was interesting but I didn't care for its dead face. Guessing slides was fun too and the lab technicians, I think, went out of their way to help Dr Haldane's young daughter. It was no part of that year's course, but I also went to some more advanced lectures on genetics. But I never got on well with physics and chemistry; one of the lecturers tried to kiss me, which I didn't like at all, yet probably giggled while dodging, which only led him on. One simply couldn't help this giggling and it often had quite unintended results.

I was what was then called a Home Student, though now we are St Anne's and have a very attractive College of our own and a high academic standard. But at that date there was a rather limited academic supervision. I remember nothing in the nature of a tutorial system. There was just tea with the Principal in one of those monumental houses in Parks Road. It was perhaps rather unfortunate that she was more interested in educating her girls than in getting them degrees. Perhaps those of us with academic homes were supposed to be looked after already. Women's higher education was still rather new and unorganised. I doubt whether Somerville, where I would have liked to go, would have taken a sixteen-year-old, as I was at the beginning of the academic year in autumn 1914. Somerville and Lady Margaret Hall were the only women's colleges which had really made strong and permanent growth by that time, though the others were beginning, sometimes in rather temporary buildings.

We did botany in spring in the old botany labs facing out across the botanical gardens, a lovely place. I learnt to cut sections of plant material with an old cut-throat razor that my father had given me; I learnt to stain and the elements of microscopy. It was more than half a century afterwards that I used again the techniques I learned then, at Mochudi with the microscope I brought to the school; they were still in my head and fingers. Professor Vines was our lecturer and I remember that the life cycle of ferns had just been discovered; I don't think we got as

XI

The Impact

Oxford in wartime still managed a certain amount of gaiety. But the colleges were emptying; Aldous Huxley came and stayed with us, which was nice. Now that Miss Blockey was away he played for my dancing and he asked me what being in love was like. But I, not being 'in love', did not answer satisfactorily. At first he was badly depressed though not speaking much about Trev, but gradually he began to unshell. There were things happening, a few poets left, the university co-op shop which we took turns to staff—this was great fun, almost like acting. I loved being behind the counter. That, rather than the political side of the co-operative movement, was the attraction. In the room above I experienced my first grown-up style committees. There was a co-operative dressmaker who made Earp, one of our poets, some pyjamas out of a piece of Liberty silk he had bought; they had the word 'Liberty' on the selvedge and this was incorporated in the trouser legs. How we laughed!

I was beginning cautiously to investigate politics, or rather to see the man who interested Agnes Murray so much, for I loved Agnes, Gilbert Murray's beautiful daughter—our families were by now on friendly terms—and she admired G. D. H. Cole, the dark and flashing Magdalen revolutionary. Or so he appeared to young sillies like me. I doubt if he ever spoke to me at this time, but that didn't matter. I was allowed to go, so long as the meetings did not go on too late. I went to several where guild socialism was discussed; I didn't understand, but liked the taste of it all.

Meanwhile I managed to absorb a fair amount of learning; for me lectures had a certain interest but dissection had much something else. It was an almost overwhelming present. My future mother-in-law wore coloured pearls, pink and grey, large, and I would think very valuable. But I never quite saw the point of them.

The only other one of the family whom I was really fond of was Dick's younger brother Willie. He had volunteered as a despatch rider; he was a dear, gay and affectionate, with a certain talent for drawing. He got a Blighty early on and a few months in hospital and on leave, but unfortunately it was too mild a wound. He was killed in 1916. I don't think his parents ever really recovered.